D1559377

Guantánamo Bay

THE PENTAGON'S ALCATRAZ OF THE CARIBBEAN

Mango Publishing Group
in collaboration with
the Miami Herald

HERALD
BOOKS

Herald Books

Copyright © 2016 Miami Herald and el Nuevo Herald. All rights reserved. This material may not be published, broadcast, rewritten or redistributed.

Published by Mango Media, Inc.
www.mango.bz

This is a work of nonfiction adapted from articles and content by journalists of the Miami Herald and el Nuevo Herald published with permission.

Front Cover Image: April 3, 2002 (Patrick Farrell/Miami Herald)

Guantánamo Bay: The Pentagon's Alcatraz of the Caribbean
ISBN: 978-1-63353-365-3

Guantánamo: "A beat like no other"

— Award-winning journalist Carol Rosenberg, describing her
Miami Herald assignment at the Columbia Journalism School

Table of Contents

INTRODUCTION

Carol Rosenberg in Iraq, 2004. (Courtesy of Carol Rosenberg/Miami Herald)

COVERING GUANTÁNAMO, A BEAT LIKE NO OTHER

Each year faculty members at the Columbia School of Journalism choose a leading American journalist to deliver the Pringle Lecture to the graduating class. Past lecturers have included Daniel Schorr, Maureen Dowd and Doris Kearns Goodwin. Here was Carol Rosenberg's 2014 talk:

Before I ever set foot in Guantánamo I was a reporter in the Middle East.

I had a house in Jerusalem and an apartment in Cairo and I traveled the region, Sudan, Syria, Baghdad, Beirut. It was before the web, so I wrote for tomorrow morning's readers. And often I was struck by how very tribal life and my work were there. Jews and Palestinians. Sunni and Shiite. The George Bushes and the Saddam Husseins.

And journalists were a tribe, too. Sometimes we traveled in packs and sometimes we tried to outrace each other to a scoop, an interview, to tell a story better. But we hung together in bars, raced together to invasions. We watched each other's backs at bombings, door-stepped peace talks, were fiercely loyal when someone got in trouble — got hurt, or kidnapped. And when one of us got killed (this does happen) we mourned together.

And I came to see the world through that prism.

So in the dozen years I've been reporting about the prison camps at the U.S. Navy base in Cuba called Guantánamo, the place America set up after the September 11 attacks to lock up suspected terrorists, I see tribes, too.

There, the detainees belong to one, in a system that lumps them together — al-Qaida, Taliban and men long ago cleared to go. There are the sailors assigned to the base, like "townies" who come with their kids and cars and settle in for three or more years. Most prison camp guards go for a year or less — "unaccompanied," live in temporary housing and are in a sense untethered. Some eat too much. Others drink too much. And another group spends their time obsessively getting fit, running, gym, spinning — prompting a clever Colorado National Guard soldier to observe that after a year at the detention center troops leave three ways: Hunks. Chunks. Drunks.

There are other tribes: The 9/11 families picked by Pentagon lottery to watch at the war court. Jamaicans and Filipinos who do the scut work. Defense lawyers who come and go and mostly have common interests.

Sometimes there are the journalists, too. But at times, I'm the only reporter down there — alone in media Tent City, where scoops are rare but possible, you can't get hurt, you won't get kidnapped but you do get sneered at by American soldiers for asking questions, for asking to see something at the prison whose military mission statement includes the word transparency. It's an assignment that frankly, when I'm not with my tribe, can be a bit lonely.

I'm not saying this in some bid for sympathy. Not at all. This is my long way of saying how grateful I am for this opportunity to talk to my tribe, you journalists, about what I do, how I do it and why.

My Beat

And that is ...

For the last 12 years I have had one of the most challenging, at times frustrating, rarely boring, and bedrock fundamentally important beats in American journalism. One I could never have imagined, and wasn't designed by editors or at a news lab. It grew organically out of an assignment that became an obligation and morphed into a beat like no other.

I cover the detention center at Guantánamo Bay, Cuba, for the Miami Herald — the paper that hired me to report in the Middle East, and considers Cuba a local story.

Most news organizations don't care about Guantánamo. But the Miami Herald and McClatchy believe in this story.

I write about a place. I write about people. I write about policy and politics in what seems to me to be the first no-exit-strategy, U.S. military enterprise since the Vietnam War.

I deal with a military that at times doesn't like to answer my questions, won't talk to me, censors my photos, restricts my movements, routinely threatens to ban me from further visits in a system of military intimidation — and decides at times on a whim that I should sleep in a tent rather than pay like anyone else for a hotel available to civilian guests.

From that tent, I write about an evolving system of justice, at times alone because no other news organization will make the trek. Or in the company of reporters who show up for a ticket-punch, a been-there, done-that dateline and a swipe at this historic system, the military commissions.

Make no mistake, this is a court like no other. Not because the United States seeks to execute six men there, five for the 9/11 attacks and one for the USS Cole bombing. And not because a soldier sits in the room behind me as I write, even when I'm the only one there. But because we're years into trial preparations for men who were long denied lawyers or Red Cross visits — and attorneys at the war court still argue about what parts of the Constitution apply.

I don't write about what happened to 3,000 people on September 11 or why 17 sailors had to die in al-Qaida's suicide bombing of the USS Cole off Yemen in 2000. I am certain that my fellow tribe members, other journalists, will show up for that part.

I write about whether the CIA will ever allow the accused — and the world — to learn how agents interrogated suspects in nations they won't name using now forbidden interrogation techniques we glimpse only through leaks and misconduct reports. I write about the FBI trying to turn a member of a 9/11 defense team into an informant, a snitch. This is a system that American lawyers in American military uniforms call un-American.

This American court has a motto: "fairness, transparency, justice."

As they close hearings and seal up the filings and soldiers sit behind me watching me work the motto comes to mock me.

I didn't understand why exactly. Then Eugene Fidell, who teaches law at Yale, explained it: If you're really fair, really transparent, really just, you wouldn't need a motto.

It would be, as the founders said, self-evident.

But it didn't start that way. It started with a phone call from the Pentagon's subsidiary in Miami, the Southern Command, notifying me that it was about to get into the prison business — and asking would I like to come along.

It was months after the September 11 attacks. America was scared. Our troops in Afghanistan were overwhelmed with foreign men dropped off and dragged into our outposts by Pakistanis and the Northern Alliance, by tribesmen looking for a CIA bounty, and, occasionally, by American troops who encountered suspected foreign fighters in their patrols.

These captives were cold; it was freezing in Afghanistan. Some were angry; they'd been treated brutally. And they were rather a mystery to us, mostly because we really hadn't much practiced the art of military intelligence in a foreign environment since Vietnam, not interrogated in any meaningful way.

And somebody had the bright idea to pick them up and fly them 8,000 miles to a U.S. occupation zone in southeast Cuba. Where it was hot, sunny, stuck behind a minefield and, the Bush administration thought, against all reason, out of reach of American law, out of reach of the Geneva Conventions.

I didn't know that it was going to be a place where we'd carry out tribunals whose endgame is meant to execute people. I didn't imagine that it would go on for a decade-plus, two U.S. presidents, four secretaries of defense, 13 prison camp commanders.

The Pentagon was setting up a prison: Donald Rumsfeld's "least worst place" in my paper's backyard. It was a story that hadn't been written.

My boss told me to go down there and not come back until it was over.

I watched the first 20 men come off a U.S. Air Force cargo plane like a poor man's Hannibal Lecter — in orange jumpsuits and shackles and surgical masks and blackout goggles.

And 759 more prisoners would follow, 625 would get to go — nine of them dead — and it's still not over.

Tradecraft

So what do I do?

Sometimes I'm a court reporter.

Sometimes I'm a cop reporter.

Sometimes I'm a feature writer.

People think I'm a human rights reporter.

My title is military affairs correspondent.

More often than not I feel like a foreign correspondent down there.

In the '90s I'd go to places like Iraq under Saddam Hussein to write about sanctions, Kuwait to report on life after Iraq's invasion. I got a visa to Khartoum while it was the haven for the outcasts of radical Islam the way I'd go to many, many countries — by landing a visa, an entry permit.

I'd get in by government invitation. If they wanted to show the press something, you'd hear from the embassy or Information Ministry. Or I'd pitch a story idea and hope to cover more than that one theme. They would let me in when confidence was high in their ability to control the narrative, or they were so embattled they were desperate to tell their version of the story. (And when they found the scrutiny stressful they could kick me out.)

Guess what it takes to get to Guantánamo to report at the prison? An "area clearance." It's like a Pentagon visa to their own private country with town and school and court and detention center, and when confidence is high in their ability to control the narrative or they feel they have a story to tell, getting in is easy.

For instance, after three detainees were found hanging one June weekend in 2006, the prison commander allowed me onto the base. With tremendous limitations, but on the ground. I wasn't allowed to see where they were found dead, or speak with the guards who discovered them. Investigators were at the base but I didn't even get a glimpse of them, or the nooses the prisoners were supposedly found hanging in. I did get to speak with the imam who was brought in to prepare their burial —but that's because I recognized him and he knew me from when he was posted there before. Mostly I asked questions, and more than a few by phone from one side of the bay to the other.

After a couple of days someone in Donald Rumsfeld's office sent in a plane to fetch me and three other journalists. Narrative control up at the Pentagon smeared me, said I'd slipped without permission onto base. It is surrounded by the sea and minefields — and guarded by the U.S. Marines. And you need an area clearance, permission to enter the base.

So often I treat the assignment like a foreign correspondent. Observation and explanation of something you can't see is a key ingredient. But you can only do so much Kilroy-was-here, peek over the wall with funny observation style reporting.

Going back again and again means going deeper.

That means I start reading and questioning and thinking and planning long before I get on the airplane to go there. And in that regard it's a virtual beat. I report from my desk in Miami, on the phone with people who frankly don't want to be seen with me. Or at the airport in Fort Lauderdale, where a small charter plane comes from Guantánamo. I get emails but not as many as you'd think. People are afraid — and after what happened to Private Chelsea Manning they have reason to be.

I report in Washington, where the coverage is political.

I go to people who want to keep Guantánamo forever if they're likely to give me the information I seek. Or advocates of closure if they might disclose.

I search the web for documents and news tips — contracts, PowerPoints, Facebook, Twitter by thinking like a member of the military.

I've gotten anonymous stuff in the mail — and been worried someone was trying to set me up.

Sometimes I start a story with an interview at Gitmo, we used to call this gathering string, and then I pull that thread as I go from place to place — Andrews Air Force Base, the McClatchy bureau, a conference.

Increasingly calling me the military affairs correspondent seems wrong. Yeah, it's a military base and these are military hearings. But it's more like I cover a small town that has a prison, a court, and McDonald's. And also the worst internet access you can imagine (for which I pay $150 a week) all controlled by the U.S. military.

That means, I write in a notepad. I go on foot or on the bus to ask people questions when military minders don't restrict my movement. And that's not the journalism most people practice these days. I describe places because the military won't let us show it on film. And I cover jury selection of unnamed U.S. military officers at the tribunals because it gives you a window into the soldiers who sit in judgment on the enemy.

I use just about every trick in a 21st century journalist's toolbox. I have Google Glass, when they let me turn it on. I tweet a live stream of court proceedings, bulletin-style, to show people who can't be there what's going on moment to moment. I write for tomorrow's paper and this afternoon's online reader — and I take terrible photos.

Sometimes, I use the Freedom of Information Act — if I can't persuade someone that the information is releasable. But I use it sparingly because you have to be willing to sue the government — something I did last year with a clinic from Yale Law School to shake loose a list of the prisoners the United States wants to hold forever. Now I have another suit for how much We the People spent building a secret prison down there. I hope to get a court hearing.

I don't blog because frankly I'm an old school reporter. And to me blogging is loaded with opinion. Plus, I don't know about other places but at mine we don't edit our blogs. It's self-publishing. And I am either dumb enough or smart enough to know I need an editor. Particularly when I'm writing in the press room at Gitmo, where everyone's talking, there's a soldier watching, and I haven't had enough sleep last night. In my tent.

I've been doing this since Day One, I've probably slept around a thousand nights there, and the military has never let me (or any reporter, any member of our tribe) talk to a detainee. It's one of those lifetime banning offenses. Even when they've wanted to talk to me. Even when I've arranged a waiver through an attorney. A few have called and emailed after they got out. You know what they say? Thank you for writing about me, thank you for telling my story.

Sometimes I follow the money. I spent 2011 ferreting out the costs of the place. I started by asking to meet with the money crunchers, do an interview. The military stalled for a while, then refused.

So I dug through contracts, worked through Congress, talked repeatedly to the Bureau of Prisons and consulted correctional experts, all to develop a theory of what I would need.

I never did get anything directly from that year's prison's public affairs officer, a Navy commander whose job was to provide information to the public.

But I asked microscopic expense questions in every prison camp interview, saved documents, pulled the string on searches, found friendly sources up at the Pentagon — and concluded it conservatively cost $380,000 a year per prisoner. Or liberally $800,000 a year per prisoner. That's about 30 times the cost of keeping someone in a federal prison.

We called it "The Most Expensive Prison on Earth" first. Lots of folks followed us — including members of Congress who want to close the prison and who last year did a soup-to-nuts estimate — $2.7 million per prisoner a year. They uncovered costs I couldn't — and included some I wouldn't consider directly related to the prison operations.

Why Do It

Sometimes when I get a bit lost or wonder why I write about these 154 men who nobody really cares about (except hopefully their families and their lawyers) I remember that the United States government built it to be out of reach of the American people, out of reach of American courts, to make it hard and remote, so we won't think about that fact that it is ours.

You know, the military calls Guantánamo the most transparent detention center on earth. Hundreds of reporters have visited there, they say, since the first al-Qaida suspects arrived in 2002. They skip the part about how few go back more than once — frustrated by the hoops, the time, and the costs of doing basic journalism. Being a court reporter. Writing a feature story. Conducting an interview. Sometimes I go back, honestly, because they don't want me to.

Recently, the military decided after eight months of releasing hunger strike figures that its transparency wasn't working for them. So now new troops down there call the daily hunger strike count classified. A state secret.

But part of it is the fault of American journalism, too. It's hard to be a reporter at Guantánamo. It takes days to travel there; the military can be abusive, or infantilizing.

The military supports big-sweep features that generalize to the point of being dismissible or dumb down the details. Newsroom money crunchers want crisp beginning-and-end budget travel. Editors want front-page stories that are candidates for prizes. Thank you for this invitation, really, because the incremental isn't much honored.

My stories can't be wrapped up with a ribbon, and declared done. Guantánamo? Didn't President Obama sign an order to close it during his first year in office? There are 154 men held captive at Guantánamo by a military operation staffed by 2,200 federal employees, mostly soldiers. The death penalty trials are just beginning. Next month an admiral will arrive at the base as the 14th prison camps commander. Sometimes I tell a story a day at a time.

And I know that's an unpopular thing.

Conclusion

Plus, I like the incremental. Important stories do unfold a day at a time. Process is part of reporting, the effort to distinguish in the cellblocks between prisoners so angry, who hate America so much or how they've been treated so much that they might do harm — from those who are just disappointed. Or beaten down. Or so ready to leave this life behind for the next one that they won't be a threat to anyone.

Court reporting is incremental. Police reporting is incremental. Political and policy reporting is incremental, too. The story's not going away. President Obama's pledge to empty the detention center? Totally incremental. And the clock is running against his administration. The last detainee to go was an Algerian who went home in March. Ahmed Belbacha. There are 77 other captives like him — on a list somewhere that says he can go if the administration sets up a sound plan for resettling him or repatriating him safely. Sometimes that means getting a country to agree to continue to lock him up.

So one message I have because this is the Columbia Journalism School and I've been reporting for 35 years is think about reporting in the traditional way: courts, cops, color stories, celebrities, corruption, and use the old tools as well as the new ones.

Beat reporting is its own virtue.

Getting up off your butt, stepping away from your computer, leaving those 99 Google searches to other reporters may be risky in some respects. But showing up has meaning. You can't see the progress on what you report without going again and again to watch, ask questions.

You have to take time out to read. If it's a court story, you have to read the briefs, footnotes, transcripts.

Keep your eyes open: Think about the logic of what you're being told and not told, shown or not shown.

Sure, call yourself an investigative reporter, but the same disciplines apply: Anonymous sources can weaken your point; errors can hurt your credibility. If someone doesn't want to put his or her name behind it, ask yourself what else that source is doing or protecting? Is there a better way to report it?

Having editors who support you is one part luck and one part tending to the relationship as much as you would a source.

And sometimes the best stories, the stories that may be the salvation of American journalism, unfold a day at a time.

But for now:

Use all the tools. Hone your craft. Care for your tribe.

Carol Rosenberg
New York City
May 20, 2014

Chapter 1

NEW ALCATRAZ

A Military Policeman and his guard dog stand ready at Camp X-Ray for prisoners, January 9, 2002. (Tim Chapman/Miami Herald)

Wednesday, January 9, 2002

'HUMANE BUT NOT COMFORTABLE'

When al-Qaida and Taliban prisoners arrive from Afghanistan this week, they'll hardly be trading their cave life for the creature comforts of the Caribbean.

Rather, this is what the Military Police have in store for them until they build a permanent prison facility:

Eight-by-eight-foot cells made of chain-link fencing that resemble open-air cages. Concrete slab floors with mats for beds and wooden roofs to keep out the rain. Guard dogs and MPs – both men and women – monitoring the every move of members of a movement that once hid their women from public view. Halogen lights by night, no running water but a container for a toilet, a "culturally neutral diet" without meat – all out of view of the sparkling waters of the Caribbean Sea.

And, just in case the al-Qaida and Taliban prisoners have visions of staging an uprising inside the compound called Camp X-Ray, Marines will patrol beyond several fences – armed to the teeth in the high grass beyond razor-sharp concertina wire, beneath a brand-new American flag that was flapping in the breeze Wednesday.

"It will be humane. But we have no intention of making it comfortable," declared Marine Brigadier General Michael R. Lehnert, commander of the prison project who arrived over the weekend from Camp Lejeune, North Carolina.

"I wouldn't call it a dog kennel. I call it a cell ... an outdoor cell," added Army Colonel Terry Carrico, commander of the MP contingent out of Fort Hood, Texas, who is in effect the prison camp warden.

Lehnert and Carrico spoke to U.S. media inspecting the facility for the first time. It is still under construction. The base receives its first detainees, fewer than two dozen, "by the end of the week," according to Bob Nelson, civilian spokesman for the prison project.

Lehnert, meanwhile, declared his prison camp prepared to accommodate 100 "al-Qaida, Taliban and other terrorist personnel that have come under U.S. control as a result of the ongoing global war on terrorism."

The chain-link-style cages are upgraded detention cells that were built during the 1994-95 *balsero* crisis that saw about 50,000 people housed at Guantánamo. The cells were used for holding Haitian and Cuban migrants who were accused of crimes, got into fights or broke camp rules. Lehnert likewise ran security for that operation but said the mission was much different.

"Our job is to take these terrorists out of the fight by locking them up," he said. "We will treat them humanely in accordance with international law – under strictest security for as long as necessary."

The assignment issued by Secretary of Defense Donald Rumsfeld two weeks ago has begun transforming this once-sleepy base known as "Gitmo" into the Alcatraz of the Caribbean.

It is rimmed on one side by land – nearly all of it mined by the Cubans – where Marines face off night and day along 17 miles of fence line with Fidel Castro's Frontier Brigade. On the other side is the sea, with U.S. patrol vessels.

"It is remote and isolated. It does make it convenient," said base commander Navy Captain Robert Buehn Jr. He said the prison project could nearly double the base population, which had dwindled from 8,000 military and civilians a decade ago to 2,700 before the newest assignment.

Like everyone else associated with it, the skipper cited security reasons in declining to describe how the prisoners would be transported – specifically when they would arrive or their exact identities.

But there are only two ways they could arrive: By a *Con-Air* style flight onto the lone working landing strip or by military vessel into the port. These are features that no doubt led Rumsfeld to declare it "the least worst" option for planners seeking a detention center outside of Afghanistan.

Moreover, Lehnert said there had been no formal protest from Cuba over the plan, and used the media opportunity to send a clear message to the Castro government.

"This force here that we brought does not pose any threat whatsoever to Cuba, the government of Cuba or the people of Cuba," he said, reading from carefully crafted language to reply to a reporter's question.

This base, sprawling across 45 square miles on Cuba's southeastern tip, has for years been a sore spot between the United States and the Castro regime, which declared null and void a series of earlier leases and agreements dating back to Teddy Roosevelt's time. Castro has consistently called the U.S. presence an illegal occupation and refused to cash the checks the United States cut annually to make good on a lease agreement.

Cuban concerns aside, the command staff at Guantánamo is pursuing a three-stage blueprint for detention of the new prisoners. The first stage is complete: the cage-like cells that could accommodate up to 100 prisoners, according to the general, with short-term plans to expand the compound to 220 cells.

It is on a remote section of the U.S.-controlled territory, less than a half-mile from suburban-style family housing for base officers along Nob Hill Road.

Soon, a Navy engineering unit of Seabees will start construction on a more permanent facility on a section of Gitmo called Radio Range. Working with civilian contractors, they will complete 400 to 500 indoor cells for the prisoners within 60 days, Lehnert said.

Then later, the Joint Task Force will add more buildings to accommodate up to 2,000 high-security prisoners – an inexplicably large number, considering that reports from the region showed only 364 Afghan, Taliban and al-Qaida prisoners held by U.S. forces.

Friday, January 11, 2002

FIRST PRISONERS ARRIVE

One by one, manacled and masked, the first 20 of up to perhaps 2,000 Taliban and al-Qaida prisoners arrived in this sweltering U.S. military outpost four months to the day after the September 11 attacks.

Some apparently struggled, and Marines appeared to push them to their knees. Most, however, seemed to offer little resistance as they hobbled from the huge Air Force cargo plane that ferried them halfway across the world to a jail for terrorism suspects on the edge of the Caribbean.

They wore fluorescent orange jumpsuits, and those whose legs were shackled walked with baby steps. Apparently, when a few resisted, one of two Marine MPs at each arm deftly dropped them to their knees, then quickly pulled them up, to show who was in charge.

On their heads were matching orange ski caps, guarding against the cargo plane's cold, topped by earmuff-style noise protectors against the engines' roar.

On their mouths were turquoise surgical masks, supposedly to protect troops against tuberculosis. And some had blackout goggles over their eyes.

The first Taliban and al-Qaida detainees kneeling in a holding area at Camp X-Ray, January 11, 2002. (Petty Officer Shane T. McCoy/U.S. Navy)

"These represent the worst elements of al-Qaida and the Taliban. We asked for the bad guys first," declared General Lehnert just hours before their huge C-141 Starlifter set down from a 27-hour journey from Kandahar, Afghanistan.

The military left nothing to chance in the first arrival of captives from Operation Enduring Freedom.

They ringed the aircraft on the leeward side of this sprawling base with Marines in Humvees, some armed with rocket launchers, others with heavy machine guns. A Navy Huey helicopter hovered overhead, a gunner hanging off the side.

And television and newspaper photographers who formed part of a Pentagon news pool were forbidden to document the first arrival and transfer of prisoners at Camp X-Ray, a rugged prison camp with eight-by-eight-foot open-air cells.

The operation was shrouded in secrecy and high security.

Then, suddenly Friday afternoon, reporters were led to a hill and allowed to watch the delicate transfer of the 20 from the aircraft to two white school buses. They were taken on a ferry boat to cells on the base's windward side.

Neither Lehnert nor any other military official involved in the camp would provide the prisoners' names, affiliations, or even their ages. Nor would they say whether the American Taliban, John Walker Lindh, was among them.

About an hour after landing, the first appeared, surrounded by a knot of Marines. In all, the unloading part of the mission lasted 31 minutes, time enough to lead the prisoners off one by one, frisk them and in some instances take off their shoes.

"It looked like a well-rehearsed operation, a very thorough operation," said Army Lieutenant Colonel Bill Costello, spokesman for the Joint Task Force that in less than a week set up the prison camp.

Marine Lance Corporal John Poma on guard with his 40mm heavy machine gun at Camp X-Ray, January 9, 2002. (Tim Chapman/Miami Herald)

Later, a spokesman for the operation commander, Marine Major Steve Cox, disputed that Marine MPs had struggled with some prisoners coming off the plane. "No, quite to the contrary. They were wobbly and disoriented."

It all took place on a sultry afternoon in Cuba, along the single working runway at this naval station that until it got its latest detention assignment was in virtual caretaker mode.

Friday it bustled with purpose.

A small U.S. Navy boat patrolled offshore, within view of the huge aircraft while the Huey made passes between the airport and the sea.

Cox said the prisoners' goggles were blacked out for security reasons. Had they not been led blind from the airplane, they would have seen a cactus-studded landscape of heavy brush with vultures soaring overhead – far different from that in Afghanistan.

Their face masks, he said, were to protect the U.S. troops escorting them, because some prisoners had previously tested positive for tuberculosis.

But the biggest impression was that of force. In addition to an ambulance, three fire trucks and some sort of command post, the military rolled out a heavy presence of Marines in Kevlar vests, helmets and face shields – plus heavily armed Humvees.

Mindful of earlier Taliban rebellions, in Northern Alliance-run prisons, the Army MPs and Marines worked deliberately throughout the evening to process the prisoners into their cells.

By 9 p.m., Cox said, only 13 had received physicals, showers and fresh jumpsuits and were already in their cells.

The last seven were expected to be incarcerated by 11 p.m.

"It was calm," he reported. "There was no particular resistance put up. There was not struggling. There was not wrestling. There was none of that type of thing taking place."

Lehnert, who arrived to run the operation that will eventually move the prisoners to permanent cells, said that "their existence will be humane but not comfortable. They will be practicing the free expression of their religion."

To that end, the general said, they will be provided with halal diets, a reference to the Muslim proscription against eating pork. Cox displayed an example: a vacuum-packed vegetable-and-pasta dish, plus an accessory pack that included peanuts, a granola bar and a box of Fruit Loops.

To drink, they will be given water, Cox said.

It was 88 degrees at noon Friday, and soggy, something likely unfamiliar to fighters from Afghanistan. By night, mosquitoes swarm and bite.

Each man is confined to one cell, a mat on a concrete block floor, and gets a bucket in which to relieve himself. The camp warden said MPs would lead them, one by one, to latrines as need be, and conceded that when it rains, some will get wet.

Other supplies they will receive, described by Cox as "comfort items," include two bath towels, one to use for bathing, the other to serve as a prayer mat; toothpaste and brush; soap and shampoo, plus flip-flops for footwear.

"They get the two towels but no blanket," the major said.

The captives' status and their future are unclear. Military spokesmen went out of their way to describe them as "detainees," not prisoners of war, although Lehnert described them at a news conference as "EPWs" – enemy prisoners of war.

There are no provisions for lawyers, arraignments or tribunals, although the Department of Defense has said the prisoners' detention will be consistent with the Geneva Conventions.

U.S. Army Military Police escort a detainee to his cell at Camp X-Ray, January 11, 2002. (Petty Officer Shane T. McCoy/U.S. Navy)

Meantime, President George W. Bush is deciding whether the prisoners will be brought before military tribunals, and U.S. government lawyers are writing proposals for how such trials might take place.

So the prisoners' fate is uncertain, and so is how long they will stay.

Officials repeatedly declined to say whether representatives of the International Red Cross and Red Crescent were on the base. Nor would they say how many interpreters they had managed to fly in.

Military spokesmen did, however, confirm that military investigators, both of the Navy and a joint command, were on hand eventually to interrogate the prisoners.

Lehnert said Friday's was just the first of what was expected to be periodic prisoner shipments. He would not provide a timetable.

Sunday, January 20, 2002

A LEADER EMERGES AT CAMP X-RAY

As 34 new detainees arrived from Afghanistan, guards at Camp X-Ray said Sunday that a beefy one-legged inmate tried to use Muslim prayer time to unite his fellow al-Qaida and Taliban prisoners.

"We put a stop to that. They told him to pray," said Army Private Jeremiah Rose, an MP who observed the prisoner facing the wrong way during Muslim prayer and chanting in Arabic what a linguist translated as, "Be strong. Allah will save us."

Several guards noted that the amputee, who uses a prosthetic device from the knee down, is emerging as a leader among the collection of 144 detainees whose international population expanded with the arrival of six Algerians captured in Bosnia – the first from outside the Afghan theater of war.

Army Captain Luis Hernandez, 31, a Gulf War veteran from Bayamón, Puerto Rico, described the one-legged prisoner as "fat and strong" while "the little kids are coming very skinny." Several MPs have concluded that more chunky members, who appeared to range in age from their 20s to their 50s, were leaders, while the skinny ones were ordinary fighters.

No one could provide a name for the man. Reports indicate that the most prominent inmate is Mullah Mohammad Fazl, the former Taliban army chief of staff. But U.S. commanders consistently refuse to name any of the inmates or give their countries of origin. The prison camp warden said the camp now held prisoners from more than 10 countries.

The new arrivals emerged from a C-141 Starlifter flight from Kandahar, stepping out of the cargo bay in arm and leg shackles. Like four earlier batches of arrivals, they were wearing orange jumpsuits and had their eyes covered by taped-over goggles, hearing muted by headsets and mouths covered with turquoise surgical masks.

A few appeared to limp during the high-security unloading operation, in which Marine infantrymen surrounded the detainees, frisked them, and hustled them to a waiting bus. After one man stumbled, two Marines grabbed him under the arms and carried him.

A U.S. Air Force C-141 at Guantánamo after bringing 20 detainees from Afghanistan, January 11, 2002. (Tim Chapman/Miami Herald)

Army Lieutenant Colonel Bill Costello said about a third of the arrivals had "sustained battle wounds, gunshot wounds to the arm or leg. I'm told there are no life-threatening injuries in this group."

The latest arrivals also marked a watershed for America's growing offshore pen for international terror suspects as six of the new arrivals were identified in Kandahar as Algerians arrested in Bosnia, not related to the war on Osama Bin Laden's al-Qaida network and Afghanistan's now vanquished Taliban regime.

Also for the first time Sunday, two delegates of the International Committee of the Red Cross watched the unloading operation from about 60 feet away. They left the airfield without comment.

Earlier, reporters were permitted to interview several MPs who work 12-hour shifts in the cellblock of eight-foot-by-eight-foot open-air cells called Camp X-Ray one day after commanders revealed that an upset detainee had bitten a guard who had been trying to subdue him.

Overall, however, the guards described the prisoners as compliant. "It doesn't feel like they're the worst of the worst. I thought they'd try to attack us. They could all be waiting right now for the moment to do it," said Rose, of Atlanta.

Mostly, they come off as "pathetic," Rose said. "They ask where they're at, 'Why am I here?' One guy said, 'I want to talk to my dad. I'm supposed to get married next week.'"

Several guards confirmed that an Australian and at least two Britons were in the camp, and Rose said the Australian appeared fluent in Arabic and at times relayed guards' English instructions to fellow inmates.

The Australian has been identified as David Hicks, 26, of Adelaide. Rose said two British captives he met appeared to be natives of Britain — one white, the other black.

Private Jodi Smith of San Antonio, Texas, said that regardless of their places of birth, the British, Australian and Arab prisoners were behaving alike — sleeping, eating, praying. During breaks from their cells, two MPs lead each, arms and feet shackled, to other cells that contain showers and latrines that have no doors.

She added that some prisoners looked to be about 17 or 18 years old but solved the mystery of an exceptionally short inmate who arrived in leg shackles and handcuffs. He's 23 years old, she said, but does indeed have the height of a child.

Others, though, "look young and you wonder: Did they make a choice?"

Besides English and Arabic, other languages spoken in the camp include Farsi, which is spoken in Iran, and Urdu, a language of Pakistan.

Reporters have been allowed only to view the camp on four occasions, and from afar, since the prisoners arrived, to avoid speaking with them or identifying them further. A new feature could be seen atop a post: a huge "Qiblah," a sign in Islamic green and white that points in the direction of Mecca.

U.S. Army Private Jodi Smith watches from the
outer perimeter as the first detainees to arrive sit in
a holding area at Camp X-Ray, January 11, 2002.
(Petty Officer Shane T. McCoy/U.S. Navy)

Thursday, January 24, 2002

INTERROGATIONS BEGIN AT 'HOLIDAY INN'

Military investigators began interrogating the first batch of
suspected al-Qaida and Taliban terrorists at Camp X-Ray, hours
after prison guards gave each prisoner a pocket-sized copy of the
Quran, Islam's holy book.

Meantime, the military suspended the 8,000-mile Afghani-
stan-to-Caribbean air bridge that in six shuttles has so far brought
158 prisoners to this southeastern corner of Cuba.

General Lehnert, the prison commander, said the suspension was more about security than an international controversy that has swirled around camp conditions and the United States' refusal so far to grant POW status to captives of Operation Enduring Freedom.

Camp X-Ray had only 160 cells on Wednesday morning, meaning any new arrivals would have to be placed two to a cell, a scenario that concerned both commanders and the MPs in the razor-wire topped prison compound. Wednesday night, the number of cells rose to 220 as 60 more came on line. Another 60 are expected in coming days.

"This is a Holiday Inn," said Army Colonel Terry Carrico, warden of the two-week-old encampment, when asked by British journalists to compare the camp to the so-called "Hanoi Hilton" where American POWs were held in the Vietnam War.

Lehnert, likewise, defended conditions in the camp but said commanders were reviewing all the security procedures for improvement. He was asked specifically about the sensory deprivation treatment captives have received during full-day journeys from Afghanistan.

Military commanders also confirmed for the first time that interrogations — Lehnert chose to use the word "interviews" — had begun. They refused to say whether the FBI or other civilian agencies were involved. Marines, sailors and civilians of the Naval Criminal Investigative Service arrived earlier this month to take part in interrogations.

No lawyers were present to assist the captives.

"At this time of interrogations of individuals that are suspected of having committed terrorist acts, our view is that legal counsel is not appropriate at this time," Lehnert said. "We're looking for information, not necessarily for prosecution purposes, but for sorting out the al-Qaida and where they are and what their connections are."

At Camp X-Ray, Navy construction workers in yellow hard hats were still working on the interrogation center — five windowless wooden buildings outside the prison camp's perimeter, which will eventually get air conditioning.

Meantime, Carrico said, the questioning was taking place inside a special section of the camp. Prisoners were being shuffled around the compound, changing cells, he said, to keep the detainees from knowing who took part in interrogations "so there's no reprisal from fellow detainees for doing that."

Morning began for the prisoners with a 5:20 a.m. wake-up call for the first of five-times-a-day Muslim prayers, guards said. Breakfast was hot, and included oatmeal. At about 7 a.m. a Muslim Marine who serves as a linguist went through the camp handing out some of the first 400 copies of the Quran to reach this base on the Caribbean's edge.

They arrived overnight and were published by Amana Publications of Beltsville, Maryland.

"Some of them smiled. Some of them said, 'Thank you,' " said Army Specialist Kristy Martin, 25, of Alabama, an MP who does overnight duty and assisted in the distribution. The few who came with a Quran did not take a second one, she said.

An abandoned interrogation room at the then defunct Camp X-Ray, April 1, 2009. (John Van Beekum/Miami Herald)

"Some grabbed them and kissed them. It was good, a good morale booster basically," reported Army Captain Luis Hernandez, a Gulf War veteran.

At the base hospital, Navy Captain Al Shimkus confirmed that doctors successfully conducted surgery on two prisoners who arrived Monday from Kandahar on stretchers, with four- to six-week-old bullet wounds.

MPs in surgical scrubs were in the operating room, even though the prisoners were unconscious from sedation, he said. The prisoners were shackled, unless that interfered with the medical care. More operations were expected.

Sunday, January 27, 2002

NO POW STATUS FOR PRISONERS

Brushing aside suggestions that terror suspects in U.S. custody are entitled to POW status, Secretary of Defense Donald Rumsfeld toured Camp X-Ray and declared conditions sound for the 158 captives at the open-air compound.

"I have absolutely full confidence in the way the detainees are being handled and treated. It's a tough job," Rumsfeld said, tieless in shirt sleeves after an hour-long tour of the prison's razor-wire enclosed compound.

Rumsfeld's emphatic description of the prisoners' status underscored a division among members of President Bush's Cabinet. Secretary of State Colin Powell has urged Bush to declare these captives subject to the protections of the 1949 Geneva Conventions, even if they are not classified as POWs.

Rumsfeld said that as terrorists and fighters for an illegitimate Taliban regime, the captives are "unlawful combatants" who don't qualify for Geneva Conventions status, even if their treatment meets the conditions of the international treaty.

Powell has argued that the Bush administration should change its stance to bolster international support for the war on terrorism and to protect Americans who may be detained abroad.

Reporters watched from about 200 yards away as Rumsfeld, the chairman of the Joint Chiefs of Staff, Air Force General Richard Myers, and four senators wound their way around the cells. They stopped in just-built plywood buildings used for interrogations as a U.S. Navy cleric broadcast the midday Muslim call to prayer over a compound speaker.

"I would rather be here in an eight-by-eight with a breeze rather than locked down in Folsom," said Senator Dianne Feinstein, a Democrat, referring to the prison in her home state of California.

Workers build new cells at Camp X-Ray as Navy Captain Al Shimkus, commander of the base hospital, briefs Secretary of Defense Donald Rumsfeld, January 27, 2002. (Helene C. Stikkel/Department of Defense)

Following reports of a rift in the Bush administration over the detainees' status, Rumsfeld and senators Daniel Inouye, a Democrat, and Ted Stevens, a Republican, said they weren't POWs under the Geneva Conventions because they neither wore uniforms nor followed a traditional rank structure. Both senators are World War II veterans.

"They are not POWs. They will not be determined to be POWs," Rumsfeld said. "They are among the most dangerous, best trained, vicious killers on the face of the earth."

Monday, March 25, 2002

CELLS HOLD MOSTLY YOUNG FOOT SOLDIERS

As guards shuffle them in chains to showers and interrogation, most look no older than the Marines with M-16s who stand watch in the towers above. Some ran away from home to study Islam and were swept up in Osama Bin Laden's shadowy war. Others claim their capture is accidental.

One is Ugandan-born Feroz Abassi, 22, who declared while growing up in South London that he wanted to become Britain's first black astronaut. But in 1999, the British press reports, he quit computer college, embraced radical Islam and ran off to Pakistan. He was captured this year as an alleged al-Qaida member in Kunduz, Afghanistan.

Today, two months after the Pentagon first brought prisoners to Guantánamo, the 300 men interned at Camp X-Ray are a mostly mysterious collection of nameless, faceless terrorism suspects. In a bid to spare their home countries embarrassment, or perhaps to avoid stirring up unrest, U.S. commanders flatly refuse to name what they say are the 33 nationalities among the prisoners. News people cannot get close enough to talk to them.

But the overall picture that emerges from reports from abroad, information from diplomatic sources and two months of observation is that "the worst of the worst" of Afghanistan's Taliban militia or the masterminds of Bin Laden's al-Qaida movement are not at Guantánamo.

There are at least a couple of exceptions:

Reports have said the most important captive is Mullah Mohammad Fazl, the former Taliban chief of staff. In his orange jumpsuit, he is indistinguishable from the other 300 prisoners, similarly attired, who can be seen from afar shuffling twice a week to take showers.

NBC has identified Abd al Hadi al Iraqi, one of the 25 top al-Qaida military commanders, as a Guantánamo inmate. But Marine officials won't comment on the report.

By and large, however, the captives of Camp X-Ray are at best foot soldiers — people like Abassi.

Many of those whose names and faces have emerged are citizens of countries that are U.S. allies, not U.S. enemies.

An example: Six or seven of the inmates are Kuwaitis, such as Fawzi al Odah, 24, whose father said he went to Pakistan to take part in a Muslim humanitarian aid effort. He disappeared from sight only to turn up in Guantánamo after his capture in Afghanistan.

In fact, a third of the prisoners are Gulf Arabs, including at least 50 citizens of Saudi Arabia, the country from which the United States staged the 1990-91 Gulf War liberating Kuwait from Iraq. At least 25 are citizens of NATO countries, including Denmark, Belgium, France, Great Britain and Turkey.

By far, they are mostly Muslim. But commanders say there are also a few Christians. Some have received higher education in the United States; others are so illiterate that U.S. soldiers take dictation from them when they want to write home.

Snippets of information are scarce, however, as the military refuses to say much about the inmates. What emerges is a group of young men who got carried away with a cause fueled by Islamic fervor.

One Washington-based diplomat from a U.S.-friendly Muslim nation, who did not want to be named, said he was no fan of Bin Laden's, but he sympathized with the more youthful residents of Camp X-Ray.

"I can understand when the hormones are surging and you need some sort of cause célèbre in your life," he said, choosing his words carefully. "People do it all the time. Some ran away to the Spanish civil war, some ran to the Sandinistas. Some were misguided. But in no way do we support terrorism."

Commanders say the population ranges from men in their late teens to 50-somethings. But the few that reporters can see the closest, in a huge Navy hospital tent, appear to be no older than their 20s.

Pakistani officials will not confirm reports that 25 to 30 Pakistani citizens are in Camp X-Ray — among them Essa Khan, 23, a homeopathic doctor, whose family says he wrote recently that he was picked up by mistake while running a clinic in the Afghan city of Mazar-i-Sharif.

Afghanistan so far will not say how many of its citizens are held, and neither will Egypt. A diplomat at the Chinese Embassy said officials are still checking. Russia says the United States has informed Moscow that it has citizens in Camp X-Ray and will send investigators to question them.

Meantime, European countries such as Sweden, Denmark and Belgium acknowledge that some of their citizens are imprisoned, while Iran, which the United States accuses of sponsoring terrorism, says there is no one from the Islamic Republic in the camp, contrary to a finding by Amnesty International.

Other so-called terror list countries such as Syria, Iraq and Somalia won't comment.

A detainee is being taken by golf cart from interrogations back to his cell, April 3, 2002. (Patrick Farrell/Miami Herald)

The International Red Cross may know. It has observers in the camp every day, interviewing the inmates and meeting with commanders. But to preserve the organization's independence, Red Cross officials won't comment on the names, ages or home countries of the captives either.

Perhaps the best-known al-Qaida captive is Australian David Hicks, 26, a high school dropout from Adelaide who ran away from home to join the Kosovo Liberation Army and ended up a continent away, where he was turned over to U.S. troops in Afghanistan.

He made an early impression on Camp X-Ray guards by vowing to kill at least one American before departing from Guantánamo Bay. Australian press reports say he wrote to his parents recently, via the Red Cross, saying how sorry he was for the trouble he'd caused. But whether he will face a military tribunal or be sent home to Australia is still to be determined.

Australian Attorney General Daryl Williams is reported to be studying the case, and Australian law, to see whether there is a crime for which Hicks can be charged. It is a precondition, the sources say, set by Secretary of Defense Rumsfeld on whether to release him.

Less is known about the 37 Yemenis held at Guantánamo, aside from the fact that they carry passports issued by Bin Laden's ancestral homeland, whose government is a U.S. ally in the war on terrorism. The charge d'affaires at Yemen's embassy in Washington, Yahwa el-Shawkani, said he did not know the identities of his fellow citizens held as prisoners but characterized them as "usually young, around 17," who probably ran off to study in Afghan schools and perhaps came from the Hadhramawt region, the rugged ancestral home of Bin Laden.

There are Turkish citizens too, brought on the last flight on February 15.

One is reportedly Murat Kurnaz, 19. In Bremen, Germany, his mother told reporters that her son as a youth loved weight lifting and wanted to learn shipbuilding, but then he started shunning discos, growing a beard and going to a mosque at age 17. On October 3, he left for Pakistan, she said, to study the Quran. Next thing she knew, he was captured in Kunduz, she said.

She has written to President Bush seeking her son's release, noting that he was at home on September 11.

Spain, too, has an inmate at Camp X-Ray. Diplomats from Washington visited him recently and identified him as Hamed Abdelrahmam Ahmed, 27, of Ceuta. He is one of at least three Europeans of Moroccan ancestry in the camp. Ceuta is a Spanish enclave on the north coast of Morocco.

Algeria says it is unable to acknowledge officially that there are at least six of its citizens present, captured in Bosnia for plotting attacks on the U.S. Embassy in Sarajevo, because the U.S. government has not formally told Algerian officials.

Positive identification of the prisoners has been slow. General Lehnert announced that the number of nations represented by inmates in the camp stood at 33.

And after nearly 10 weeks of Caribbean confinement, some prisoners are protesting that they were improperly captured.

Army Private Cortney Gletten, 21, of Waconia, Minnesota, who is a guard with a Texas-based MP unit, gave examples of some of their protests:

"I was visiting my girlfriend," one said to Gletten. Another said, "I was just trying to get some drugs."

And more than a few have said plaintively: "I shouldn't be here."

Sunday, May 26, 2002

AN ESSAY: CAMP OF MYSTERIES

Carol Rosenberg

Sometimes we see them shuffling to a latrine, shackled hand and foot, a soldier on each side. Sometimes we see them on the back of golf carts, shackled hand and foot, being driven to wooden interrogation huts. Mostly they lie on mats in their eight-by-eight chain-link cells, napping or reading U.S. military issue copies of Islam's holy book, the Quran.

When the first 20 captives came on January 11, camp commanders told us they were "the worst of the worst" of captured al-Qaida and Taliban fighters — airlifted for 27 hours and 8,000 miles from Afghanistan. And they imposed a strict security doctrine that took no chances with the men they considered suicidal fanatics. Yet the most serious scuffle with a soldier had been when a captive lunged and bit a soldier on the sleeve. The prisoner was agitated, a general said, but didn't break the skin of the soldier.

Now it's three months later and in more candid moments officers connected to the prison camp's secretive intelligence section say they are not certain of some of the prisoners' true identities. Some were handed over to U.S. troops from the Northern Alliance, now our allies, after the prison uprising at Mazar-i-Sharif, with no evidence trail or helpful documentation. So, while the dozen or so who came with shrapnel and bullet wounds were surely taken from a battlefield, many are still mysteries as the MPs hand out their meals or escort them to showers.

Mostly they are a mystery to me, too. When the first batch arrived, you practically felt the soldiers' fear of them as they emerged from a huge C-141 cargo plane looking like a surreal group of Hannibal Lecters. To make sure they didn't resist in

flight, soldiers shackled them hand and foot and pulled bright orange ski caps on their heads, against the cold. They also put
blacked-out goggles over their eyes, headsets over their ears and
turquoise surgical masks over their mouths, in case they were carrying tuberculosis.

A detainee being moved from one part of Camp X-Ray to another, April 3,
2002. (Patrick Farrell/Miami Herald)

They were quiet at first, stunned by their new sultry Caribbean surroundings. But these days you can hear them chant of
"*Allahu Akbar, Allahu Akbar*," God is Great, the Muslim call to
prayer that is also sometimes used as a punctuation mark or
phrase of protest. It rattles the guards. They've told me so. But I
worked in the Middle East for years and have heard the chant before. I've heard it used in anger. I've heard it used in violence. I've
heard it uttered in absolute pleasurable astonishment. But at
America's extraterritorial offshore detention center it mostly
sounds like frustration — echoing from the prison camp where
unknown men face an uncertain future that could end in death
sentences from military tribunals.

Sunday, September 15, 2002

WALKING A LEGAL TIGHTROPE

Captives penned up in steel cells have been allowed to grow back their beards. They can keep their Pentagon-provided Qurans. They have flush toilets and wash basins and, since moving to the sprawling $30 million detention center called Camp Delta, no longer get splashed by Caribbean rain.

Despite those amenities, a key circumstance has not changed: The United States still refuses to consider POW status for the 598 suspected terrorists being held without charge or trial.

U.S. officials argue that the men are treated humanely and with sensitivity to their religious practices, but that the nature of al-Qaida disqualifies them from treatment as POWs under the Geneva Conventions. For the Army, safety for the soldiers who guard them comes first.

The U.S. selective-enforcement policy toward the Geneva Conventions still stirs criticism among international and American human-rights advocates. Without case-by-case consideration of whether each prisoner is a POW, the critics say, the Pentagon is simply paying lip service to the Geneva Conventions.

Further, they argue, as Washington edges toward war on Saddam Hussein, the United States has lost a measure of moral authority to argue for POW privileges if an American soldier is captured in an invasion of Iraq.

Amnesty International, Human Rights Watch and the International Red Cross, as well as Mary Robinson, the just-departed U.N. high commissioner for human rights, have all urged the United States to lift what they call a state of "legal limbo" from the captives from 43 countries.

An initial step even now, eight months after the first prisoners arrived masked and manacled from Afghanistan, would be hearings to determine whether each captive deserves POW status, said Eugene Fidell, president of the nonprofit National Institute of Military Justice.

Not making individual determinations "may be an error," he said. "It denies us a certain amount of legitimacy in the eyes of the world, including the Red Cross."

Red Cross delegates have been allowed to meet with prisoners — the only outsiders allowed on this base to press U.S. commanders on conditions.

Antonella Notari, a spokeswoman for the International Red Cross, said: "We say any and all combatants captured in the framework of an international conflict such as took place in Afghanistan are entitled to be POWs, unless a competent tribunal rules otherwise. These people have rights. Any person detained needs to know why they're detained and where this is going to go."

Construction of the new Camp Delta, a more permanent facility for housing detainees, April 4, 2002. (Patrick Farrell/Miami Herald)

U.S. forces got most of the suspects in Afghanistan and Pakistan late last year. They got some from the Northern Alliance, which helped topple the Taliban for giving sanctuary to Osama Bin Laden and his al-Qaida organization. What has emerged is an evolving internment center — part detention complex, part interrogation compound — while Pentagon policymakers have drawn up rules for military tribunals. But no one in this U.S.-controlled corner of Cuba has been charged.

Two separate federal court rulings this year supported Pentagon and Justice Department arguments that foreigners held at Guantánamo Bay get no constitutional protections.

Yet advocates such as the Red Cross' Notari say the Pentagon has failed to meet worldwide human-rights standards by refusing to adopt any internationally recognized rule book to govern their incarceration.

POW status would mean that prisoners could someday be set free, if the United States declared an end to its war on terrorism. Criminal trials could end in confinement for life, but a prisoner would be able to hear charges, mount a defense and know his sentence.

In August, Baltasar Garzón, the Spanish judge who ordered the arrest of former Chilean dictator Augusto Pinochet, used a peace conference in Puerto Rico to reprimand the United States for lacking a legal process at Guantánamo Bay.

"It's completely unacceptable that to date the charges against the prisoners in Guantánamo remain unknown," Garzón said. "Where is their right to a defense?"

Meantime, desperation may be mounting among the captives. Guards have stopped four prisoners from hanging themselves in their cells with a "comfort item," probably a sheet or towel. Some of the presumed Islamic radicals have asked a Christian cleric about conversion — suggesting a loss of faith or a bid to curry favor with their captors.

The prison operation's commander, Brigadier General Rick Baccus of the Rhode Island National Guard, calls conditions humane.

The Bush White House notes that al-Qaida members are not covered by the Geneva Conventions because the Bin Laden network neither hails from a single nation that is a signatory to the treaty nor has a command structure of a modern military.

"This is not going to be the Hogan's Heroes kind of stalag where they can run around," said a Department of Defense official who was involved in choosing which of the 143 articles of the Third Geneva Conventions would apply.

And so, most prisoners get an identical eight-by-eight cell, separated by steel and metal mesh. About 80 are in steel-walled isolation cells with a single window. All get identical 2,000-calorie-a-day rations, sensitive to Islamic dietary restrictions, that have added pounds to the once malnourished captives.

But captives cannot prepare their own meals, one provision of the Geneva Conventions, for fear that the utensils could be turned into weapons. Military Police have not permitted the men to pick a representative or have a prison shop, other provisions of the Geneva Conventions, for fear that they might plot against the United States or compare interrogation experiences.

Each has been issued a personal copy of the Quran, a prayer cap and beads and can hear the five-times-a-day call to prayer in his steel cell. A Navy cleric is on duty to hear their religious concerns.

Notari, the Red Cross spokeswoman, does not agree that it is a U.S. prerogative to apply the Geneva Conventions selectively. They were written, she said, "to try to make sure that people don't act on emotions or resentment or revenge."

Amnesty International went further in a recent angry report. In the absence of POW status or recognizable criminal charges against the men, it said, they should be set free.

Brigadier General Rick Baccus, commander of Joint Task Force 160, April 3, 2002. (Patrick Farrell/Miami Herald)

Baccus has characterized his "detainees" as war-tested "killers" captured on the battlefield, denying them any presumption of innocence.

Asked whether the selective enforcement of the Geneva Conventions could come back to haunt American forces, he pointed to Iraqi abuse of U.S. POWs during the 1991 Gulf War.

In essence, his analysis was this: The Iraqis don't respect the rules of war, anyway. Still, some U.S. officers are sensitive to the Geneva Conventions question. The Pentagon denied a Herald request that lawyers tally up how many of the 143 articles are now being applied at Camp Delta.

Fidell, of the National Institute of Military Justice, warned that the present limbo-like situation could limit U.S. options "in the future when our GIs are seized, kidnapped, captured by the bad guys of one kind or another around the world."

Monday, October 20, 2003

INMATE'S TRUE NAME OFTEN STILL A MYSTERY

Nearly two years after this terror prison was established, U.S. interrogators are still searching for the real names of some of the inmates, commanders say, as they extract intelligence and shun rehabilitation of their al-Qaida and Taliban suspects.

Interrogations continue around the clock, and just the other day military intelligence ordered a name change for a prisoner's official record, said Army Colonel Nelson Cannon, currently chief warden of Camp Delta. "We thought it was so-and-so. New information has been developed, and it's not him, it's him. Holy smokes!" said Cannon, the Kalkaska County, Michigan, sheriff with a 60-bed jail in civilian life.

These and other details emerged during a four-day media visit meant to illustrate humane conditions and business-as-usual at the U.S. prison for terror suspects.

Cannon said it can be stressful securing prisoners once considered fanatics and "the worst of the worst." But the work at the isolated Caribbean outpost is much like being a prison guard at home — with one key exception.

"Our philosophy in the States is some kind of rehab, turn them around," he said. "That's not our mission here. The big thing is intelligence."

His guards therefore take their cue from the Army's secret 219-member interrogation and analysis team — dispensing privileges such as an extra shower or permission to keep more mail from home in a cell, depending on how much a captive reveals.

"Everybody's not initially honest and truthful," overall prison commander Major General Geoffrey Miller said. "But our Tiger Teams, our interrogation teams, they spend months going through with the same people. They will know more about you than you know about yourself, and your family and events that not only let you into terrorism and the how of terrorism but part of the why of terrorism that helps us.

"The names may change but we know what they have done and we have lots of information and intelligence that validates that," Miller added.

Prisoners started coming in January 2002 from Afghanistan, ballooning to a population today of 660 men and boys from 32 different nationalities who have been denied POW status and instead have been declared enemy combatants.

Chapter 2

INSIDE THE PRISON

Outside Camp 1, at that time an unused portion of Camp Delta, February 6, 2008. (Carol Rosenberg/Miami Herald)

Tuesday, February 10, 2004

BIN LADEN'S DRIVER IN GUANTÁNAMO CELL

A Yemeni captive at the Guantánamo Bay prison admits he was Osama Bin Laden's $200-a-month driver in Afghanistan but says he was neither a member of al-Qaida nor a terrorist.

Salim Ahmed Salim Hamdan, 34, is now held at the terrorism prison in Cuba in segregated accommodations for prisoners facing possible military tribunals, said his lawyer, Navy Lieutenant Commander Charles Swift.

"He fully admits that he was an employee of Osama Bin Laden" from 1997 until the U.S. attack on Afghanistan in 2001, Swift said. "But he adamantly denies that he was ever a member of al-Qaida or engaged in any terrorist attack. He worked for Osama Bin Laden solely for the purpose of supporting himself and his family."

Swift spoke about Hamdan for the first time in an exclusive interview with the Herald. Pentagon policy has prohibited troops and civilians at the Guantánamo prison from disclosing specifics about prisoners.

He obtained special Pentagon clearances to discuss his client, whom he has met with for about 25 hours using an Arabic translator — making him the first detainee at the terrorism prison publicly identified as having a link to Bin Laden.

Starting in 1997, Hamdan worked for Bin Laden on his farm in the southern Afghan city of Kandahar, Swift said, and drove a Toyota pickup truck. He sometimes ferried farm workers to the fields and sometimes transported the al-Qaida mastermind of the 9/11 attacks.

Hamdan first went to Afghanistan in 1996, the lawyer said, intending to travel to Tajikistan to join Muslims there fighting former Soviet communists. He never made the trip but found the job with Bin Laden that paid $200 a month, a huge sum for a poor Yemeni in impoverished Afghanistan.

"He is a civilian worker who was caught up in the war," Swift said.

If his lawyer doesn't get a plea agreement with the U.S. government, Hamdan is likely to be among the first Guantánamo captives to face a military trial. Air Force Colonel Will Gunn, chief of the tribunal defense team, said this week that he assigned Swift to represent the Yemeni after prosecutors named Hamdan in a "target letter" as a candidate for "plea negotiations."

Not one of the four terrorism suspects who now have lawyers at Guantánamo has been charged with any crime. Gunn said no charges have been identified but would likely involve "conspiracy."

Hamdan, who is married and has two daughters, ages 2 and 4, was captured by Afghan forces during the U.S. attacks, Swift said, and turned over to the Americans about two years ago.

At the time of his capture, he was alone and driving a borrowed car in a mountainous portion of Afghanistan near Pakistan.

He had just evacuated his pregnant wife and daughter to the safety of Pakistan, the lawyer said, and was returning the car.

Swift said Pentagon rules prevented him from describing his client physically, saying how long Hamdan had been held in Cuba or saying whether the Yemeni had cooperated with his interrogators.

An early goal of the terrorism prison was gathering intelligence in the hunt for Bin Laden. Commanders now say interrogations are more concerned with understanding the inner workings, appeal and training of al-Qaida.

Since Hamdan was given counsel December 18, 2003, Swift said, he has been held in solitary confinement, segregated from the other Camp Delta prisoners in a windowless air-conditioned cell and permitted exercise only at night, "so he never sees the sun."

He suffers from arthritis, Swift said, which is aggravated by the prison's air conditioning. "He gets cold, ironic in Cuba."

"I find him to be engaging and pleasant and upbeat at times," he said. "His conditions make him despair at times."

Hamdan has a fourth-grade education but a sophisticated understanding of the difference between a military and a civilian court proceeding, Swift said. And he wants a civilian trial.

"He has asked me to implore the president to allow him a civilian trial in which he may demonstrate his innocence," the lawyer said. "He's adamant that he is a civilian and belongs in a civilian court."

The Pentagon has created a military defense team for the Guantánamo tribunals even before a decision on whether to charge any of the 650 prisoners there. The team includes career Army, Navy, Air Force and Marine lawyers who usually defend U.S. servicemen.

Sunday, March 6, 2005

CAPTIVES ALLEGE RELIGIOUS ABUSE

Captives at the Guantánamo Bay prison are alleging that guards kicked and stomped on Qurans and cursed Allah, and that interrogators punished them by taking away their pants, knowing that would prevent them from praying.

Guards also mocked captives at prayer and censored Islamic books, the captives allege. And in one incident, they say, a prison barber cut a cross-shaped patch of hair on an inmate's head.

Most of the complaints come from the recently declassified notes of defense lawyers' interviews with prisoners, which Guantánamo officials initially stamped "secret." Under a federal court procedure for due-process appeals by about 100 inmates, portions are now being declassified.

The allegations of religious abuses contradict Pentagon portrayals of the Guantánamo prison for Taliban and al-Qaida suspects as respectful of Islam. Commanders at the base in Cuba have showcased the presence of Muslim chaplains and the issuance of Qurans, prayer rugs, caps and beads and religiously correct meals.

Army Colonel David McWilliams, the spokesman for the U.S. Southern Command, which supervises the prison, said he could not confirm or deny the specific complaints. They could not be independently investigated because the U.S. military bans reporters from interviewing detainees.

But McWilliams denied any policy of religious abuse.

"There's certainly no planned approach from guards to interrogators that pits Christianity against Islam," he told the Herald. "The policy has been to show respect for the Islamic religion — and that runs the gamut from providing the items they need for prayer to making sure their diets are appropriate."

The accounts of religious indignities and abuses come from at least two dozen captives and a range of attorneys — from U.S. military lawyers assigned to defend prisoners to activist law professors and private corporate lawyers who have sued since the Supreme Court ruled in June that the captives can contest their detention in U.S. courts.

"On or about Christmas 2002, the head of shift banged on detainees' cells, yelling Merry Christmas and cursing Allah," said New York attorney Joshua Colangelo-Bryan's notes from his interview with Jumah al Dossari, 31, of Bahrain. "Subsequently, a lieutenant arrived and ... he hit Mr. al Dossari and insulted the Quran."

After Dossari asked an MP identified only as Smith why Smith had beaten him unconscious in one episode, according to the lawyer's notes, "Smith replied, 'because I'm Christian.'"

New York lawyer Adrian Stewart said one of his 14 Yemeni clients, a man in his 20s, had his eyebrows and head shaved three times as punishment — and one time the Army barber left what his client described as a cross-shaped patch of hair on his head.

Military spokesmen would not say whether they believed that the incident was the same one for which a prison barber was reprimanded for giving a detainee a haircut described as a Mohawk in February 2003.

The latest allegations of abuses at the prison in southeastern Cuba come as a three-star Air Force general is investigating FBI accounts of harsh interrogation tactics — and subsequent reports that women soldiers used sexual taunts during interrogations. Some devout Muslim men believe they must not touch women other than their wives.

New York attorney Marc Falkoff said his 13 Yemeni clients, men in their 20s and 30s, were also victims of religious humiliation.

"The things they always complain about is their trousers are routinely taken away from them for a variety of disciplinary actions, including not talking during interrogations," Falkoff said. "Now, the reason this is a punishment ... is that these guys can't pray without being covered head to foot ... and they see this as a religious insult."

The military says soldiers take pants from prisoners who might try to hang themselves; captives call it calculated punishment because Islam requires that they be covered as they pray.

Boston attorney Rob Kirsch said detainee Mustafa Ait Idir, 34, an Algerian-born Bosnian detained on suspicion of links to a plot to blow up a U.S. embassy, told of being transferred to a no-trousers cell section known as Romeo block.

When he refused to give up his pants, he was tackled, punched and pepper-sprayed, and had a testicle squeezed and a finger broken by soldiers of a quick-reaction force, Kirsch's notes said.

"Mr. Ait Idir desperately tried to reason ... and again explained that he could not give up his pants for religious reasons since, without pants, he could not pray," the notes said. "He asked if it would be possible for him to wear his pants only during prayer. The IRF [Immediate Reaction Force] began to spray tear gas again."

German-born Turkish citizen Murat Kurnaz, 23, said he headbutted a woman soldier who rubbed her breasts against his back and stuck her hand down his shirt during an interrogation, said his lawyer, Seton Hall University law professor Baher Azmy.

Kurnaz claimed that in reprisal, the soldiers beat him and left him hogtied for about 20 hours, put him in isolation and denied him food for six days, Azmy's notes said. He drank water from his cell sink.

Defense lawyers were unwilling to speculate on which alleged religious abuses involved approved U.S. interrogation techniques and which were committed by soldiers acting on their own.

Friday, May 13, 2005

LETTERS ARRIVE AT FEDERAL COURT

In the latest twist in the Guantánamo Bay legal struggle, 16 prisoners ranging from a self-described nomadic shepherd to a disabled 78-year-old Afghan man are suing the U.S. government — acting as their own attorneys from behind the razor wire at Camp Delta in Cuba.

The U.S. District Court in Washington docketed the cases on May 3 after a series of single-paragraph pleas from captives arrived in the court's mail.

The latest suits are extraordinary because the 16 captives wrote to the court directly, without benefit of a lawyer, from their prison camp 1,300 miles away. Further, some of the prisoners suing on their own are illiterate.

"My wish from you is please inquire about my sad story. I've been detained here unlawfully and sinlessly," writes Sharbat Khan, age unknown, the self-described shepherd who said he lost 300 sheep and 10 camels when he was captured in Afghanistan and sent to the base in Cuba.

The military is holding about 500 men and teens from at least 42 nations as "enemy combatants" at the Navy base in Cuba, alleging they are al-Qaida or Taliban members or sympathizers. About 150 already have filed suit, through lawyers lined up by family members from the Persian Gulf to Europe.

The 16 captives dictated their pleas to military payroll linguists at Guantánamo, according to military sources, who translated them and submitted them to military censorship.

Officers then sent them to the court by certified U.S. mail, along with 16 others, still unfiled, that arrived this week.

The U.S. Supreme Court ruled in June that detainees can sue for their freedom. The Defense Department began giving captives the court's mailing address in December.

U.S. District Judge Paul Friedman ordered that the first 16 letters be filed as habeas corpus petitions, or writs, and waived the routine $5 filing fee. The petitions name President Bush, Secretary of Defense and two Army officers as defendants.

"My imprisonment is unjustified," self-described blacksmith Alif Mohammed says in a 61-word statement. "I'm a poor person and am feeding 10 children of my own. Now I want justice and freedom to return to my country and ... be reunited with my family."

Each statement bears a stamp "APPROVED BY U.S. FORCES" from the prison camp's intelligence unit, showing each was cleared by military censors before being sent to the court on Constitution Avenue. They are dated in late February and early March, and arrived the last week of April.

Attorney Eugene R. Fidell of the National Institute for Military Justice predicted that federal judges would appoint lawyers to help the 16 captives, rather than leave them to manage their cases by mail from Camp Delta.

State and federal prosecutors often file informal, sometimes handwritten, legal papers on their own. But Fidell said the latest development showed the strength of the U.S. legal system: A single paragraph from a prisoner in Cuba, translated and subjected to military censorship there, emerged as a writ of habeas corpus in a federal court.

"What you're seeing is the first turning of the wheels of justice on their cases," he said, "against considerable odds." Fidell, who has chaired the Advisory Committee on Pro Se Litigation at the U.S. District Court for the District of Columbia, said the judges can assign the captives lawyers from a pro bono list maintained by the court.

Or, he said, the court could seek lawyers with expertise on the Guantánamo cases, for example from the Center for Constitutional Rights, which is coordinating a habeas corpus project.

Attorney Barbara Olshansky of the New York Center for Constitutional Rights cast the suits as tragic because the captives are likely incapable of representing themselves in the courts.

"It breaks your heart," she said, because the Pentagon has spurned defense lawyers' requests to offer their services in the cellblocks to prisoners who may not know how to acquire an attorney.

Moreover, she said, it is unclear how prisoners who speak little or no English and likely don't know about U.S. law can represent themselves in the court.

She said she was troubled that the military transmitted the documents to the court without an affidavit explaining who helped the captives create them, or who translated them.

The single-paragraph pleas give little information about the 16 men, some of whom have been held at the U.S. detention and interrogation camp for more than three years.

But they arrive as the Bush administration argues before a federal appeals court that the military's review processes at Guantánamo should be sufficient to derail any civilian intervention authorized by the Supreme Court.

A court spokesman said that more prisoner letters arrived this week from Guantánamo and were being reviewed.

Twenty-four of the 32 prisoners who wrote to the court are illiterate, said Air Force Major Michael Shavers, a Pentagon spokesman. They dictated their statements to U.S. military linguists, who then translated and submitted them to a security review.

From some of Guantánamo captives' letters to the federal court in Washington:

• I have been here over two years for no reason. ... I did not hurt any Americans and I did not have any weapons with me. ... If the United States is accusing me of something they should prove it. ... I was walking to the market and the Americans arrested me for no reason. I am innocent. Abdul Wahab, prison translation.

• I have done no crimes against the U.S., nor did the U.S. charge me with any crimes, thus I am filing for my immediate release. For further details about my case, I'll be happy for any future hearing. Best regards, Mohamedou Ould Slahi, in English.

Monday, July 4, 2005

CALL IT ENEMY COMBATANT ELEMENTARY SCHOOL

It's 8:30 on a Tuesday night, President Bush is addressing the nation on Iraq and two Afghan prisoners are sitting side by side at a picnic table, learning simple math and how to write in their native Pashto.

Afghan detainees receive basic math instruction during an intermediate-level Pashto reading class in Camp Delta, July 1, 2005. (Petty Officer Christopher Mobley/U.S. Navy)

U.S. troops may deem these two bearded men too dangerous to go home, for now. But behind the razor wire at Camp Delta a U.S. contract linguist draws a compass on an easel — and teaches his Pashto-speaking pupils north from south, east from west.

Call it Enemy Combatant Elementary School. And it takes place six nights a week under the stars, a fledgling effort to bring

U.S.-style rehabilitation training to the Pentagon's premier prison camp for suspected terrorists.

The controversial prison is at a crossroads again: Some members of Congress want it shut down. Others want swifter adjudication of detainees' cases. The Bush administration counters that the 500-plus captives from 42 or so nations are well-treated enemies of the United States whose interrogations aid the war on terrorism.

Meantime, with no exit strategy in sight, several dozen detainees have taken part in the pilot course. Its goal: to give captives something to absorb them beyond five-times-a-day prayer, plus some skills in case they ever return home.

"A lot of the detainees arrived illiterate," explains Army Colonel Brad Blackner, a prison spokesman. "The graduation exercise is writing a postcard home."

No one knows how long the prisoners will be at Guantánamo, says Army Colonel Mike Bumgarner, who took charge of the prison guard force about two months ago.

So his boss, Army Brigadier General Jay Hood, asked him to come up with ideas for some safe, culturally sensitive programs along the lines of, "What if it's another year? What if it's two? Or three? Or more?"

And they don't mean setting up a license-plate factory, either. These captives are assumed to hate America, considered so dangerous that they eat with a plastic spork, a combination spoon and fork.

Now, Bumgarner says, officers are looking at perhaps creating a "horticulture" program for rural villagers among the more cooperative captives in the desert-like landscape overlooking the Caribbean.

So the reading course is the model. It is held in a portion of the sprawling prison camp called Camp 4, home to about 160 prisoners considered "the most compliant." In Guantánamo-speak that means they don't spit on their guards.

The two Afghan men studying at the picnic table this night wear baggy white trousers and blousy tops with black flip-flops, the uniform of the least-worst captives. They sleep eight to a room in barracks-style housing, under lockdown at night and monitored by guards.

They dine together communally, can pray in small groups, hip-to-hip facing Mecca, and can even organize small pickup soccer games in a brown field below a watchtower.

But, even as the two students practice writing in Pashto, using flexible rubber pens considered safer than a sharpened pencil, five Navy guards in desert battle dress stand nearby, swatting mosquitoes buzzing around their necks.

General Hood boasted in an interview earlier this year that a reading program graduate, a tribal leader, returned home to Afghanistan so grateful for his newfound literacy that he was collaborating with coalition forces.

U.S. military officials won't provide the man's name, or village, citing his right to privacy. But the general has agreed to a Herald request to watch the class, from a distance, a first for a civilian news organization.

The military also doesn't say how many of the captives speak Pashto, and how many are illiterate. Neither will they identify the prisoners by name or permit them to be interviewed by the news media, although about 200 are trying to tell their stories through habeas corpus petitions in Washington federal court.

But commanders have described Guantánamo detainees as ranging from those with advanced, Western educations to simple, uneducated foot soldiers.

An example: Self-described nomadic shepherd Sharbat Khan, age unknown, sent a message to the federal court in Washington this spring with the help of a Department of Defense contract linguist. Now he is one of about 30 illiterate Afghans with habeas suits against the Bush administration.

Meantime, Camp 4 is not only the prison camp's most permissive environment but a prisoner's likely last stop before he is paroled home or sent to jail in his native country.

While the two men were studying with their tutor the other night, a few detainees were watching a sports video on a portable TV at a corner of the compound.

Other prisoners, separated by a chain-link fence, were eating dinner, having served themselves from collective containers. And others were jogging back and forth in an enclosed area.

The other 360 or so prisoners are kept in solitary cells, and get about an hour a day of exercise and shower in enclosures that look like oversized kennel cages.

Commanders are now exploring ways to expand Camp 4's living arrangements to make it even more self-sufficient, along the lines of Geneva Conventions POW-style compounds, says Bumgarner.

The idea is to let them increasingly care for and organize themselves, giving them more responsibility. They're even considering installing washers and dryers in a shower room, a modern convenience for captives now washing their clothes in a bucket and hanging them out to dry on a fence.

Bumgarner outlined the idea in a recent media tour, which included Fox News and Al Jazeera television news crews, and emphasized Islamic sensitivity after revelations that some soldiers had perhaps inadvertently mistreated the Quran.

The colonel said he doesn't characterize his charges as "the worst of the worst," an expression coined earlier in the Bush administration.

"We don't describe the detainees that way," he said. Instead, he said he urges guards to see them as "human beings that we must treat with dignity and respect."

Soon after he spoke, the media tour drove past Camp 4, where some prisoners were playing pickup soccer. The TV cameramen tried to capture the moment, which under media ground rules means photographing them from the neck down. But the prisoners spotted them — and sullenly walked off the field.

Tuesday, June 27, 2006

COMMANDER: SUICIDE PLOTS CONTINUING

War-on-terrorism captives continue to plot suicide attempts in what the prison's commander cast as jihad warfare Tuesday, the same day a senior medical officer said three Arab captives were found mentally fit just days before they hanged themselves.

Navy Rear Admiral Harry Harris Jr. said that since the June 10 suicides of the three men, guards have confiscated hoarded drugs and hidden nooses in the cells housing about 450 captives with alleged links to al-Qaida and the Taliban.

He and medical staff provided very few details but said increased searches had uncovered captives with drugs hidden in their waistbands — and one enemy combatant with 15 pain pills concealed inside his prosthetic leg.

Medical personnel are giving prisoners 200 to 400 fewer pills a day (notably fewer sleeping pills) from the estimated 1,000 distributed daily in mid-May, said the Navy doctor in charge of the prison hospital, who declined to be identified by name.

Medical teams are now crushing detainee medications, delivering them as powder that presumably can't be hoarded, and have switched some pill prescriptions to liquid medicine.

"It's not possible to make a detention facility or prison suicide proof," said Harris. "We do the best we can."

Harris also staunchly defended his characterization of the suicides of two Saudis and a Yemeni as a well-planned, choreographed act of "asymmetrical warfare" — remarks that had drawn criticism by defense lawyers, who argued that the deaths were a result of widespread despair.

The deaths were the first at the prison, where some captives have been held for four-plus years.

"Detainees view this as a struggle, they view this as a jihad," Harris said. "They are trying to figure out ways that they can continue the fight. One of the ways is hunger strike. Then they tried to kill themselves by overdosing. And now they succeeded in killing themselves by hanging."

The Navy doctor said all three men found separately hanging in their cells June 10 had just weeks before abandoned hunger strikes — one of them after shunning food for 180 days and getting nourishment through a tube.

By prison camp protocols, he said, each former hunger striker was visited at his Camp 1 cell by a mental health specialist for a routine exam that disclosed no signs of depression less than two weeks before the suicides. "They were sleeping well, eating well — no problems," the doctor said.

Wednesday, May 23, 2007

REPORTER'S NOTEBOOK: A GARDEN AT GITMO

Escorts recently allowed visiting reporters to inspect a 10-week-old detainee pastime inside a prison camp for more cooperative captives in barracks-style housing: two concrete planters of gardening beds where seedlings were sprouting but had yet to yield fruit beneath the searing Caribbean sun.

Carol Rosenberg

"This is part of the intellectual stimulation program," said Army Lieutenant Colonel Todd Melton, deputy commander of the Joint Detention Group. "It just gives them something else to think about. They enjoy doing the plants. They have tomatoes, and I believe the other ones are some type of melon."

On May 8, 2007, the prison showed reporters a garden kept by about 40 captives living in barracks style housing in Camp 4, a 10-week old project. (Carol Rosenberg/Miami Herald)

The camp was the scene a year ago of what commanders called a detainee uprising, captives battling guards with metal parts ripped from a bunkhouse.

It has downsized from up to 175 minimum-security enemy combatants. Present population, including the gardeners, is fewer than 40 Arabs and Afghanis.

Said Melton: "The younger ones like the sports. But the older guys like to come in here and fool with the garden rather than playing soccer or basketball."

Notebook free zone: It may be the military's sixth year of detention operations here, but returning journalists are finding new rules in the Detention Center Zone.

After years of carrying reporters' notebooks through the various prison buildings, an Army escort officer ending a one-year tour declared Camps 5 and 6 a notebook-free zone.

He said he feared someone, somewhere, during the media tour might "weaponize" the tiny spiral springs holding the pad together.

So a reporter scratched out her notes on the back of a Public Affairs handout entitled Mishandling of the Quran. The first item on it: "The United States takes credible allegations of misconduct seriously."

Souvenir shop: There's a smaller selection of T-shirts at the base souvenir shop, which also offers refrigerator magnets and shot glasses with three sets of blood-red lips and the logo "Kisses from Guantánamo Bay."

Gone are the $9.99 T-shirts showing two Camp X-Ray watchtowers boasting "Taliban Towers — the Caribbean's newest five-star resort."

Also no longer for sale are the mock guard undershirts imprinted with "Behavior Modification Instructor." A store clerk said those shirts disappeared from the racks in late 2006. "I guess someone thought they were too funny."

Instead, there's a spoof on the popular milk slogan. "Got Freedom?" it says.

A Quran, prayer beads and skullcap on a prayer rug in a display of religious items the Pentagon provides detainees, April 2, 2009. (John Van Beekum/Miami Herald)

Monday, November 5, 2007

BEARDS ARE SAFE FOR NOW

Guards earlier this year stopped cutting the beards off unruly war-on-terror detainees, according to the military, confirming for the first time a practice that enraged Muslim captives and their American advocates.

Prison commanders withdrew the policy of "beard trimming" in May, said Army Colonel Bill Costello, a spokesman for the U.S. Southern Command in Miami.

From 2005, he said, it had been an approved "disciplinary action for severe physical assaults against the guard force, to include the throwing of feces, urine, semen, vomit, blood and/or saliva."

But, he said, beard trimming "was not designed as a religious punitive measure, nor was it ever carried out by interrogation personnel."

The issue cast a spotlight on religious tensions behind the razor wire at the Pentagon's showcase detention and interrogation center: Detainees and attorneys have long protested policies they said were designed to humiliate Muslim captives. The U.S. says it respects Islam while providing safe and humane detention to allegedly dangerous al-Qaida members and sympathizers.

"Some of the beards are long — you can hide a bazooka in there," Navy Captain Patrick McCarthy said during an October visit by reporters in which he defended what he called an earlier policy of "beard shortening."

Countered New York attorney Martha Rayner, who represents a Yemeni client named Sanad al Kazimi, 37, whose beard was cut in October 2006, allegedly for throwing urine and feces at the guards: "They do it to humiliate. As punishment. It is how they truly can humiliate a Muslim man: shave his beard."

Beard cutting has long been controversial at the Guantánamo prison camps. Captives arrived at Camp X-Ray clean-shaven and with their hair shorn from their heads for health reasons, according to commanders.

Later, tours for reporters and visiting business leaders pointed to captives' long, flowing beards as proof of respect for their religious identities. The tours also showcased a range of Muslim amenities including halal food, prayer beads, rugs and Qurans in a variety of languages.

The military denies that the guards ever shaved off a captive's beard entirely as part of its disciplinary measures for "noncompliant detainees who assaulted the guard force" and "may have had their beards trimmed because it represented a threat to the operation of a safe and humane detention facility."

Added Costello: "Beards were trimmed to within inches, not clean-shaven."

But he said detainees can shave themselves entirely, if they want, during their shower periods.

Veteran Guantánamo attorney Clive Stafford Smith said one of his youngest clients, Mohammed Gharani, 18, a citizen of Chad, was punished by having his first beard completely shaved off in February.

Former CIA captive Majid Khan protested that Guantánamo guards shackled him and shaved off his beard for refusing to return his breakfast tray on November 15, 2006.

Khan is a 1999 suburban Baltimore high school graduate who was seized in Pakistan and held for years in secret CIA detention. Although the U.S. alleges he plotted unrealized attacks on U.S. gas stations and water reservoirs, he has not been charged with a crime.

He told a panel of military officers April 15 he was so upset by his treatment at Guantánamo that he twice tried to commit suicide by gnawing through arteries in his arm.

"They just came in with eight guards and took me to main rec and forcibly shaved my beard to humiliate me and offend my religion," he told the panel. "While they were shaving my beard, the female Navy head psychiatrist was watching the whole thing."

Navy Admiral James Stavridis, commander of the U.S. Southern Command, ended the policy in May in consultation with detention center commanders, Costello said.

He declined to say why, and whether the admiral received a specific protest.

Earlier this year, Washington attorney David Remes circulated a Holocaust-era photo of a Nazi cutting a Jew's beard, and likened it to the Guantánamo policy.

"I don't think that anyone who is doing this [at Guantánamo] understands the historical association," he said.

Captives claim the military magnified their humiliation by videotaping the beard cutting. The military declined a Herald request to view one.

Thursday, December 25, 2008

CAMP IGUANA SERVES AS 'UIGHURVILLE'

At Camp Iguana, 17 Muslims from China taken captive in Afghanistan seven years ago now get Pepsi, Ping-Pong and a 42-inch plasma screen for sports and religious videos.

They asked for a live sheep recently to celebrate Islam's holy Eid al-Adha, the Feast of the Sacrifice, and were rebuffed — even before commanders realized they would need a super-sharp knife to slaughter it. They asked to watch some soccer matches and got hours of World Cup and other highlights.

What they can't get is an answer to the question of when they might leave this place — a judge ordered their release in October — and what nation might grant them asylum.

A Uighur Muslim detainee hides in a plywood hut in a compound at Camp Iguana, June 1, 2009. (Carol Rosenberg/Miami Herald)

"They're very compliant with everything. Very understanding. And patient, actually," said a Navy chief petty officer who oversees guards at the barbed-wire-ringed camp.

While Defense Secretary Robert Gates has staffers in Washington writing plans to close the prison camps, the saga of these 17 men called Uighurs (pronounced *wee-ghurs*) shows what the architects of any new detention policy are up against.

Gates wants Congress to write legislation to block former terror suspects at Guantánamo from asylum on U.S. shores.

But that's precisely the remedy of lawyers who have for years helped these men sue for their freedom. Because they are from a Muslim minority in China, all sides agree that sending them back would doom them to religious persecution, perhaps torture, in their Communist homeland.

Uighurville, as it is known, is the latest Guantánamo lab in the U.S. experiment in offshore military detention.

On a recent Saturday, an older Uighur was sitting cross-legged in a corner of the compound reading a Quran, while another man squatted nearby, washing both his hands and feet for mid-day prayer.

Pentagon rules ban the media from talking to them.

So a Miami Herald reporter stood just outside a chain-link fence and watched while a Navy guard learned by walkie-talkie what DVDs the men borrowed from the detainee library: footage of the recent pilgrimage to Mecca, *A Decade of Great Goals*, *Matches* and *Good Morning Kuwait*, news from the oil-rich emir-ate.

For years, the men were kept like any other enemy combat-ants in austere, chilly steel-and-cement cells copied from a Michigan prison. Days revolved around one recreation period, three meals delivered to each man's solo cell, and the echo of oth-ers' prayers through the walls.

Now they pray together, eat together and kick a soccer ball around a dirt patch at Camp Iguana, a prime piece of prison real estate on a cliff overlooking the ocean.

Uighurville "is a significant improvement," said lawyer Seema Saifee, one of several attorneys who shuttle to meet the men and noted they have "greater mobility and access to fresh air and sun-light."

It is a space roughly the size of a McDonald's drive-thru and parking lot and the only place in the sprawling prison camp com-plex where sleeping captives aren't locked up at night.

Plywood huts provide shelter for sleeping, eating and prayer, and one holds the flat screen TV. Guards say the Uighurs put mops and brooms inside, and they divvy up the chores, like a platoon. There's no phone, and the mail is slow, screened by the military. Guards set up a washing machine inside, and the men now laun-der their underwear and dry it in the sun.

Saifee met her clients this month through a chain-link fence that encircles their encampment. She found them "tired, sullen and despondent."

"They are being confined like caged animals," she said. "They want to be released."

But no one knows when.

In October, guards say, the men celebrated like kids upon learning that U.S. District Court Judge Ricardo Urbina ordered them brought to his court in Washington, D.C., a move that edged them closer to U.S. asylum. They ran around the compound, their arms outstretched in imitation of the planes they can see come and go from Guantánamo.

A soccer ball sits in a corner of a recreation area at Camp Iguana, April 1, 2009. (John Van Beekum/Miami Herald)

The 1,000 or so Uighur-American community near Washington teamed with the Lutheran Refugee Service to offer to sponsor the men. Religious groups in Tallahassee, Florida, also volunteered to resettle three of them.

Instead, an order came from Washington to detain them as a population apart as though they are no longer enemy combatants. With the courts still studying detainee files and more release orders expected, Camp Iguana could be a model for a coming, more liberal phase of Guantánamo detainees.

But absent a diplomatic breakthrough or change of heart by the incoming Obama administration, says former U.S. State Department lawyer Vijay Padmanabhan, Camp Iguana could emerge as a symbol contrary to the one of closure the new government is courting.

"Building new structures and expanding the camp there cuts in the face of the image that the United States is trying to cultivate," he said.

Until recently, Padmanabhan's job was to seek third nation resettlement for the Uighurs and others on behalf of the Bush administration. He discovered "nobody wanted to displease the Chinese government."

Now he is a professor at Yeshiva University and urges the new administration to "think hard" about bringing the Uighurs to America, to encourage other nations to take in some detainees, too.

"People want Guantánamo closed, but they don't want Guantánamo detainees in their backyard," he said.

Camp Iguana is not waiting to see what becomes of the latest chapter of Guantánamo at the crossroads.

Prison camp contractors are adding a soccer yard, 40 feet by 60 feet. And the Uighurs have a little garden. They planted orange seeds and have inch-high seedlings they are cultivating.

Says Navy Rear Admiral Dave Thomas, the prison camps commander: "What that says about their thoughts on long-term detention, I leave it up to you."

Monday, January 11, 2010

AN INTIMATE LOOK BEHIND THE WIRE

For years, the Pentagon has shielded them from public scrutiny: Few people have seen Omar Khadr's shrapnel-clouded blind eye, Khalid Sheik Mohammed on his knees in prayer, or the shy grin of Yemeni Suleiman al Nadhi.

The Miami Herald has collected portraits that offer a rare glimpse at war-on-terror captives inside Guantánamo — a snapshot in time before some are moved to the United States for trial, and others are released.

"They just look like, you know, pious Muslims," marvels former CIA analyst Jarret Brachman, an expert on Islamic extremism who studied the collection. "You can't really distinguish between the mass-murder killers and the wrong-place, wrong-time guys. It's a microcosm for the complexity of the fight."

Taken in 2009 and scattered around the world, the photographs are among the most extensive public collection of detainee portraits anywhere. Only the closed files of the International Red

Cross, which took the photos, and U.S. Defense agencies have more.

While the White House will miss President Barack Obama's January 22, 2010, closure deadline, the prison camps enter their eighth year at a sensitive time and with no new closure date set.

Obama, who still vows to close the camps, stopped all transfers of cleared captives to Yemen, the nation of nearly half the prisoners today, after U.S. intelligence tied two former Saudi captives in the troubled Arabian Peninsula nation to the Christmas Day terror attempt on a Northwest airliner headed to Detroit.

Meantime, the collection of 15 portraits gives the most intimate look ever of the detainees, an unintended outcome of an agreement between the Red Cross and Department of Defense to let the men send photos home.

Brachman discovered two of the most controversial images in the collection on an Arabic language electronic message board.

One is the widely circulated image of a spiritual-looking Mohammed kneeling in prayer and gazing serenely at the camera at Guantánamo, where he once boasted he was responsible for 9/11 "from A to Z" and now awaits transfer to New York to a trial that could cost $200 million to secure.

The doe-eyed image is a startling contrast to the CIA's leaked 2003 "gotcha" photo of the disheveled kingpin at his capture in Pakistan before U.S. agents waterboarded him 183 times to get him to spill the terror group's secrets.

The other is of Mohammed's nephew, an accused accomplice, who sat for a portrait at the same time. The self-described Microsoft-certified software engineer is holding up a page of the Holy Quran.

"Most of the guys, our adversaries, are not these three-headed monsters. They are average human beings," says Brachman, who paraphrases the ancient Chinese military strategist, Sun Tsu, to explain the photos' value: "Know one's enemy as they are, not as we imagine they would be."

But the images also include men whom the Bush and Obama administrations decided to set free, an up-close look at those the world first saw as anonymous captives in orange jumpsuits, kneeling in submission when the prison camps opened, January 11, 2002.

Undated International Red Cross photo
of Khalid Sheik Mohammed obtained
by the Miami Herald.

Oybek Jabbarov, an Uzbek, clowned for the camera with his
foot on a soccer ball. He wore a black and white checked headdress
and the orange uniform of a detainee who defies the guards. He's
also a Guantánamo success story at a time the Pentagon says it
suspects that up to one in five men freed from the prison camps by
the Bush administration have re-emerged as militants.

In September, Ireland gave asylum to Jabbarov, who was captured as a foreigner in Afghanistan but never accused of a crime,
to start a new life there because, as a devout Muslim, he feared
return to his homeland. His wife and two sons have joined him
there.

There's also a close-up of Khadr, acne and all, who is on track
to go to trial this summer. He allegedly throwing a grenade in a
July 2002 U.S. assault on a suspected al-Qaida safe house in
Khost, Afghanistan, that killed Sergeant First Class Christopher
Speer, 28, of Albuquerque, New Mexico, and cost the Toronto-
born man the sight in his left eye. He was 15 at the time.

"The smiling faces really feel incongruous with where they
are," says British documentary filmmaker Alex Cooke.

Cooke produced a one-hour program on Guantánamo that aired on the BBC and saw in the faces of the men a far different place than the one she'd visited four times.

"You don't have any sense of where they are or the conditions they're held under or the day-to-day life they have at all in those pictures," she said.

Journalists are forbidden to photograph the captives' faces, a Pentagon policy that cites the Geneva Conventions.

The captives smile in many of the photographs, said ICRC delegate Jens-Martin Mehler, to reassure family back home, "I am fine, safe and well."

That's also why they donned traditional head coverings, brought to the photo shoots by the Red Cross.

Sketch artist Janet Hamlin, a New Yorker who has drawn Guantánamo captives at the war court for years, was struck by how ordinary the men looked.

"I could easily see these guys walking on Fifth Avenue, not seen in the crowd."

September 11 victim Debra Burlingame sees the photos as "just propaganda" made public by their lawyers and families to portray Guantánamo detainees favorably.

"No one still at Gitmo is innocent. No one," says Burlingame, an attorney and former flight attendant whose brother was pilot of the hijacked American jetliner that slammed into the Pentagon on 9/11.

The International Committee of the Red Cross began taking the photos, by agreement with the Department of Defense, in February 2009.

Families of the nearly 800 captives held there across the years had sent the men photos from home and "from a humanitarian point of view, those families hadn't seen their relatives for quite a long time," Mehler said.

The Pentagon let the ICRC arrange telephone calls home in April 2008. With the introduction of the photos, "the voice became a face," he said.

In 2009, 119 sat for the photos, eight of whom were later transferred from the prison.

Undated International Committee of the
Red Cross photo of Suleiman al Nadhi
obtained by the Miami Herald.

Red Cross delegates brought a selection of head coverings, by permission of the military, to make them look more like family photos. And some of the men gave real thought to the image they wanted to send home.

"You take an hour out of the cell and you have the opportunity to dress up a bit, arrange your hair, and look into the mirror," Mehler explained. "The majority of them did not want their children to see them in a prison uniform."

Prisoner number 511 smiles as he stares into the Red Cross' lens. He's Yemeni Suleiman al Nadhi, 35, and a U.S. military panel approved his repatriation in February 2008, even though, like many at Guantánamo, he admitted to traveling to Afghanistan in 2001 for jihad-style training.

"I need to get married, I need to find a job," he told a military panel in November 2005, adding that he was "shocked" to learn of the attack on the World Trade Center.

He described himself as a cooperative captive with one exception: He threw a glass of juice at a soldier after learning that his mother had died. "Our religion teaches us to use good manners," he said.

The images also emerge as the White House heads into the second year of its initiative to find many of the men new homes in new lands, because they fear persecution as devout Muslims or being stigmatized by their stays at Guantánamo.

Of the 44 released in 2009, 19 went to Europe, the Bahamas and the Pacific nation of Palau for resettlement in deals struck by the State Department's Guantánamo closure czar, Ambassador at large Daniel Fried. The U.S. sent three to trials elsewhere, a Tanzanian to New York and two Tunisians to Italy, after their cases were examined by Justice Department lawyers working for Attorney General Eric Holder.

Gazan Walid Hijazi, 28, cleared for transfer, looks fit as he squats in flip-flops and tan uniform in a prison camp recreation yard, a traditional headdress draped around his neck.

"They are nice photos of him," says his Chicago attorney, Matthew O'Hara. "They made his family very happy."

Tuesday, March 1, 2011

DOING TIME ON THE CONVICTS' CELLBLOCK

One Sudanese prisoner is filling his hours until release reading *Decision Points*, George W. Bush's memoir on why he quit alcohol, ran for president and approved the waterboarding of war-on-terror captives.

Another is being home-schooled every other week inside a cell, learning the astronomy, math, grammar, Shakespeare, even elocution that he never got as a child of al-Qaida.

These are the war criminals of Guantánamo Bay. They are four convicts (captured as a cook, a kid, a small-arms trainer and a videographer) kept out of sight of visitors in a segregated cellblock of a Supermax-style 100-cell $17 million penitentiary.

Because each man was sentenced for war crimes by a U.S. military jury, three after guilty pleas in exchange for short sentences, theirs is what the Pentagon calls "punitive confinement."

They are "prisoners" set apart from the other 168 captives at what former Defense Secretary Donald Rumsfeld calls "one of the finest prison systems in the world."

Yet, military defense lawyers say that the convict cellblock at Camp 5 is especially austere and that their clients are doing hard time reminiscent of Guantánamo's early years when interrogators isolated captives of interest.

A detainee reaches from inside his cell for lunch as guards deliver meals at Camp 5, March 31, 2009. (John Van Beekum/Miami Herald)

Each man spends 12 or more hours a day locked behind a steel door inside a 12-foot-by-8-foot cell equipped with a bed, a sink and a toilet.

They get up to eight hours off the cellblock in an open-air recreation yard, a huge cage surrounded by chain-link fencing. If recreation time coincides with one of Islam's five times daily calls to prayer, the convicts can pray together. If it coincides with meal time, they can eat together.

Once locked in their cells, they can shout to each other through the slots in their steel prison doors that troops use to deliver meals and library books.

TV time is spent alone, each man shackled by an ankle to the floor of an interrogation room, always under the watch of a special guard force implementing a Pentagon policy for "punitive post-conviction confinement." That policy is still in flux, says a spokeswoman, Army Lieutenant Colonel Tanya Bradsher, so the Department of Defense won't let the public see it.

At 50, Ibrahim al Qosi of Sudan is the eldest. Early in his captivity, Bush-era prosecutors portrayed him as al-Qaida's payroll master. By the time he pleaded guilty to supporting terror in the summer of 2010, his crime was working as a cook for bachelor irregulars in Afghanistan and occasionally driving for Osama Bin Laden and others in al-Qaida.

Now up for release from the cellblock in July 2012, he's passing time with a copy of Bush's recently released best-selling memoir. His Navy defender couldn't find an Arabic translation. So Qosi's learning about the man who waged the global war on terror with the help of an Arabic-English dictionary.

In a failed bid for clemency, Qosi's attorney, Navy Commander Suzanne Lachelier, wrote in January that, after years in communal custody, living in a POW-style setting, his post-sentencing conditions are "grueling" and "reminiscent for him of the eight difficult months he spent in complete isolation when first arriving at Guantánamo."

But a senior guard who works at the prison said it's far from isolation. "They do get to commune together," said Army Command Sergeant Major Daniel Borrero, whose 525 MP Battalion pulled guards from the blocks interning U.S. criminal soldiers at Fort Leavenworth to work at Guantánamo.

"It's a prison, ma'am," said Borrero. "I make the assumption they don't want to be here."

The cellblock's youngest is confessed teen terrorist Omar Khadr, 24, and he's on the fast track to freedom.

He pleaded guilty to war crimes in exchange for a promise to repatriate him before his 26th birthday. A military jury sentenced him to 40 more years in prison for hurling a grenade that killed an American commando in a July 2002 gun battle in war-time Afghanistan. But once back in Canada, Khadr's parole is all but certain because he was captured as a juvenile, 15 at the time of the crime.

At his sentencing hearing, a government-paid psychiatrist said Khadr spent his years at Guantánamo "marinating in a radical Islamic community" — memorizing verses of the Quran in the company of captives who got to eat, pray, watch satellite TV and shoot hoops in groups as a reward for good behavior.

Now Khadr is cut off from that group, as a war criminal segregated in circumstances his Army lawyer, Lieutenant Colonel Jon Jackson, calls "horrific and stupid and don't make any sense." Khadr's father, a since slain al-Qaida insider, moved the family from Toronto to Afghanistan when the boy was in elementary school. So to prepare him for life back in Canada, Khadr's Pentagon defense team is visiting with him twice a month in a compound, Camp Echo.

There, for four days out of five military lawyers and paralegals are drilling Khadr from a home-school-style curriculum designed by a Canadian college professor — history, astronomy, math, grammar, elocution.

English is the emphasis, said Jackson, to help him achieve "mature student" status in Canada, a gateway to college admission.

Not so long ago, the al-Qaida convict played Romeo to the Army officer's Juliet.

"He's very serious about his education," said Jackson. "His attitude is positive. There's been a real change in him now that he has the legal matters behind him."

Also on the cellblock are Guantánamo's lone lifer, al-Qaida filmmaker Ali Hamza al Bahlul, and former weapons instructor, Noor Uthman Mohammed. Bahlul keeps to himself, according to military sources, and Noor is just settling in. On February 2, he traded 34 months imprisonment on the cellblock for testimony at future trials about terrorists he knew in Afghanistan.

Theirs is a prison within the sprawling prison system, cut off from the other captives regardless of how good their behavior.

Elsewhere on the base, the military has built a secret lockup for men interrogated by the CIA and suspected in some of the most heinous attacks against America — 9/11, the 2000 suicide bombing of the USS Cole off Yemen, the beheading of Wall Street Journal correspondent Daniel Pearl. There are five Uighurs, ethnic Muslims fearing religious persecution in their native China, likewise segregated from the other captives because a federal judge found them unjustly imprisoned.

But Bahlul and Qosi, Khadr and Noor are segregated because they are "serving punitive sentences," says Navy Commander Reese, a Guantánamo spokeswoman.

Under the 1949 Third Geneva Conventions, she said, the other captives are "detained under the Law of War only as a security measure" and "should not be subjected to a penal environment or comingled with prisoners punitively incarcerated as a consequence of a criminal conviction."

Once their sentences are over, under Pentagon doctrine, they become ordinary detainees again. They can be put back in with the others in Camp 6, the closest thing at Guantánamo today to POW-style barracks housing.

Or they may leave Guantánamo if the Obama administration chooses to negotiate their release, and congressional restrictions don't hamstring them.

Sunday, April 26, 2015

DIARY CHRONICLES FEAR AND FORGIVENESS

There's a moment early in the memoirs of Mohamedou Ould Slahi, the Guantánamo prisoner whose account of prison camp brutality has partially emerged from U.S. government censorship, when he's immobilized in shackles and blindfolded in a cargo plane en route to what is now his 14th year of detention and struck by a chilling thought:

Perhaps, he thinks, the Americans are about to extra judicially execute him by blowing up their U.S. plane over the Atlantic Ocean — and declaring it an accident.

It's a brief scene, mostly describing how a guard fastened Slahi's seat belt so tight that he labored to breathe in the August 2002 flight to Cuba. But it symbolizes the *Through the Looking-Glass* quality of the 372-page book by the Mauritanian captive once considered such a prized Pentagon catch that Secretary of Defense Rumsfeld personally approved a special interrogation package that descended into torture.

Slahi's fleeting suspicion that he is a pawn in an American suicide mission seems to answer the chairman of the Joint Chiefs of
Staff, Air Force General Richard B. Myers, who months before
gave this explanation for why war-on-terror captives were trussed
up and hooded to the point of sensory deprivation.

"These are people that would gnaw hydraulic lines in the back
of a C-17 to bring it down," he said. "These are very, very dangerous people, and that's how they're being treated."

Empty Camp Echo cell with a separate room for interrogations, April 2,
2009. (John Van Beekum/Miami Herald)

And therein lies the import of *Guantánamo Diary* — an account of his fear, loathing and occasional sympathy for the mostly
anonymous Americans who have passed through Guantánamo. It
is written by Detainee No. 760, a now 44-year-old German-
educated electrical engineer who joined the anti-Communist jihad
in Afghanistan in 1990, but claims he broke with the movement
years before the September 11, 2001, terror attacks.

Each side assumes the worst, as captive and captor occasionally try to convince the other of their humanity in a book that
made The New York Times nonfiction bestseller list. It has been
released in 14 countries with 12 more in the pipeline, from Leba-
non to Brazil. Britain's spy novelist, John le Carré, calls the book

"a vision of hell, beyond Orwell, beyond Kafka," in a jacket endorsement.

As the only detainee memoir to emerge from inside the prison (others wrote after they left) it offers a near real-time account of early experimentation at Guantánamo. It is something exceptionally rare because the U.S. military has never allowed reporters to talk to its prisoners, neither those cleared to go nor those awaiting trial.

Slahi is neither. He's never been charged with a crime and he has no date for a hearing with the inter-agency parole board that decides which never-convicted captives can leave Guantánamo.

The book recounts beatings, sleep deprivation, sexual molestation, being driven mad through isolation, a threat of rectal refeeding. It is material that would frankly be unbearable if it weren't at times clever in Slahi's capacity to frame it with irony.

Of a particularly brutal period of U.S. forces trying to break him by leaving him shivering in freezing cold air-conditioning after drenching him in ice water, he observes: "It was so awful; I kept shaking like a Parkinson's patient."

In another passage, he pokes fun at his U.S. guards' preoccupation with video games as an addiction, "one of the punishments of their civilization."

He marvels in page after page at how ignorant U.S. soldiers are about what it means to be a Muslim even as he describes debating religion with them.

In one exchange, Slahi is trying to persuade a Catholic guard of the "logical necessity" of the existence of God.

"I don't believe in anything unless I see it," the American soldier says.

"After you've seen something," Slahi explains, "you don't need to believe it."

It's a curious juxtaposition to Slahi's quest throughout the book to rid himself of a U.S. intelligence profile as an al-Qaida captive of consequence. His interrogators want to tie him to the foiled Millennium Bombing plot, if not 9/11, which he confesses to after nearly going mad through isolation, only to retract it later, apparently convincingly through lie-detector questioning that is blacked out by censors.

Slahi's lawyer, Nancy Hollander, won't say how much money the book has made. Cash advances go into a trust; some of it, she says, has already been used to pay for the education of a nephew from the family's native Nouakchott, Mauritania.

"It's not going to be a book that makes Mohamedou rich," says Larry Siems, a writer and human rights activist whom Hollander entrusted to edit the book. "But it will stand as a real legitimate work of literature."

Siems was talking by phone from Perugia, Italy, recently while on a book tour in Europe. He says there are historical examples of editors like him, who couldn't speak or correspond with their writers: U.S. publishers of Soviet-era dissident *samizdat* literature, for example. But this is unusual, as he sees it, because he is an American editing a book based on a handwritten manuscript censored by Americans of a man in American custody.

Slahi wrote the book in English, his fourth language, Siems says, much of it learned in U.S. custody.

Overseas, Siems says, the conversation about the book centers on why the Guantánamo prison still exists so many years after President Obama vowed to close it. At home, he says, more ask, even if indefinite detention without charge is wrong, shouldn't people fear releasing somebody likely radicalized by years in U.S. military custody?

Slahi's is a complicated case. Members of Congress and reporters who tour the prison won't see him as they peer through one-way glass in the penitentiary-style buildings that contain most of Guantánamo's current 122 captives.

He's across the street in a compound of small wooden buildings called Camp Echo, where commanders once segregated certain captives for interrogation or trial. Now, those held there are described as having cooperated with their captors.

As a reward for providing "voluminous information," according to a Pentagon statement, Slahi has at times gotten special "comfort items" such as a non-networked computer, microwave, television and garden.

It was in Camp Echo where, in 2005, Slahi wrote the 466-page manuscript in installments, a running handwritten narrative for his eventual lawyers of what happened to him after he voluntarily turned himself in to his native Northwest African nation's security forces after September 11, 2001, and was moved around the globe in a series of secret and brutal interrogations.

Camp Echo cell with steel bunk and toilet separated by a mesh cage from a table for meetings, April 2, 2009. (John Van Beekum/Miami Herald)

Siems calls the fact that Slahi wrote it "an enormous feat of faith and courage." This was a man who'd not only been systematically denied lawyers and Red Cross visits but exposure to sunlight.

In his book, Slahi offers insight into how he was able to discern night from day in his windowless cell. He studied the drain in his crude toilet for light: "Very bright" versus "lightish dark."

It also serves as a study in U.S. censorship by anonymous intelligence contractors who in one instance deny release of a poem Slahi wrote. Sometimes they black out the gender of a female interrogator, and sometimes they don't.

The portion of the manuscript that would "not harm U.S. personnel or damage U.S. national security" was released, says Army Lieutenant Colonel Myles B. Caggins III, after "an extensive interagency classification review."

In the end, it's just one man's story. And he's a man who's been held apart from the others at Guantánamo for nearly all of his years there. At first, it was to isolate him. Later, perhaps, to rehabilitate him.

But in the regime of anonymity that only gives a detainee a voice if he can find a judge to hear his story, Slahi serves as an everyman for those both steeped in the history of Guantánamo prison, and for first-time readers.

DETAINEES SHUN WOMEN'S WORLD CUP

War-on-terror captives have long been portrayed as soccer fanatics. The sport was so popular that some years ago the military built a $744,000 soccer field outside Camp 6, the prison building for cooperative captives.

Library staff members report constant interest in the sport, from requests for old video recordings of big matches to near-real-time recordings of the 2014 World Cup to video games and magazines about the sport.

However, prison staff reported that the Muslim captives expressed no interest in the recent Women's World Cup tournament in Canada won by Team USA.

No detainee asked in advance to see the games, so nobody taped them, according to the Army lieutenant in charge of detainee diversionary programs, which just got PlayStation 3's *Pure Futbol* back from a cellblock. Nigeria, Cameroon and Côte d'Ivoire were the only Muslim-majority nations in the tournament.

It's Ramadan, when traditional Muslims fast from dawn to dusk and devote themselves to prayer and pure thoughts — pursuits that apparently left no room or interest in women athletes wearing shorts.

This is, after all, the place where censors for a time blacked out immodestly clad photos from magazines before later leaving it to the captives to decide whether to look at women in Western films and books. It is the place where, at the library, troops display a National Geographic cover with a woman's face scribbled out, and blame a detainee for the damage.

"Typical Middle East mentality, thinking soccer is not for the women," explained Zaki, an Arab-American cultural advisor employed by the Pentagon to counsel prison commanders. He's been at Guantánamo for a decade, slightly less than the majority of captives who arrived in 2002, and wasn't a bit nonplussed by the non-interest. "Nothing surprises me," he said.

U.S. troops on the base, however, caught the fever. Several soldiers said they followed the games on cable TV in their town houses, while dozens of other base residents cheered on Team America's victory at the base's Irish pub, O'Kelly's, on the night of the Cup Final.

Sunday, September 20, 2015

YEMEN'S WAR COMPOUNDS CAPTIVES' DESPAIR

For years, Guantánamo prison has portrayed the lives of the Army guards on mostly nine-month duty as a lonely, isolated business. Disconnected from family, they peer through cells at angry and resentful enemy prisoners. Only after hours do they phone home, check email or manage a Skype chat at internet cafes or in the solitude of their quarters.

In stark contrast, for the captives who've spent more than a decade in detention, the disconnect from home and family is much greater and getting worse. Sixty percent of the prisoners are Yemeni, from the Red Sea nation shattered by civil war and airstrikes. Their country is imploding, and so is their precious link with family.

"It's the biggest issue that everyone's talking about, and it's been this way for months," said attorney Pardiss Kebriaei of the Center for Constitutional Rights, who recently visited with two Yemenis at Guantánamo. "It's not helping an already desperate situation."

Spiraling violence in the ancestral homeland of Osama Bin Laden has partially paralyzed the work of the International Red Cross (the U.S. military's partner in connecting captives and their families) cutting detainees' contact with wives and children and stirring anxiety in the cellblocks.

On the prison's free satellite TV, they see their country in chaos from car bombs, airstrikes and homelessness. It magnifies their sense of helplessness in a place where early interrogation techniques were designed to do just that — make them feel helpless.

The Soufan Group, a think tank with expertise in Yemen, estimated recently that more than 2,000 civilians there "have been killed through inaccurate coalition bombing and indiscriminate Houthi shelling." Aid workers are not immune. Two Red Cross workers were shot dead earlier this month.

So Red Cross communications between Yemen and the U.S. Navy base in Cuba have suffered with the growing warfare. Sometimes it's too perilous for family members to reach Red Cross offices in Sana'a, Aden and Taiz. At other times, it's too risky for the aid agency to go to the Guantánamo detainee's relatives to arrange the phone call, something the U.S. military requires for a captive to get a call from home.

"There are currently areas in Yemen where we don't have access because of the immense security risks involved," said Nourane Houas, the Red Cross protection coordinator for Yemen, in an email from Sana'a. "It's frustrating that the fighting prevents us from doing more. And we know it's frustrating for the detainees, as well as their families."

Twice since late March, the Red Cross had its Washington office notify the military at Guantánamo that a captive's family member had died. The prison, in turn, had to notify the prisoner. The agency wouldn't elaborate on whether the kin had died of natural causes or in the war. Nor would it say what prevented the prisoner from hearing directly from home.

The lost links are "a huge issue" for Yemeni captive Sanad al Kazimi, 45, who hasn't heard from his wife and four kids since February, according to his lawyer Martha Rayner. They apparently fled Aden and are OK, according to a message he got at the prison via the Red Cross.

But "he's extremely stressed about it. I saw him in early August, and he's struggling to cope with this on top of all the other stress of being indefinitely detained," Rayner said. Kazimi has been a prisoner of the U.S. military or CIA since his 2002 capture in Dubai and wants to talk with his family to ask directly if they are OK.

Part of the problem is that, just like for the hundreds of guards who do temporary duty at Guantánamo, phone and video calls are emotional lifelines for the prisoners — those approved to go and those who aren't. Red Cross links have brought prisoners photos of babies born during their time in captivity, word of the deaths of parents and, since 2008, phone calls from home as a perk for cooperative captives.

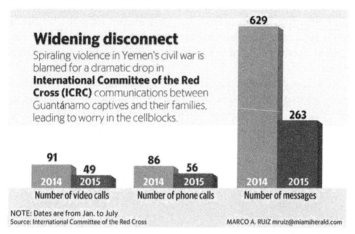

Widening disconnect
Spiraling violence in Yemen's civil war is blamed for a dramatic drop in **International Committee of the Red Cross (ICRC)** communications between Guantánamo captives and their families, leading to worry in the cellblocks.

629

263

91

49

2014   2015
Number of video calls

86

56

2014   2015
Number of phone calls

2014   2015
Number of messages

NOTE: Dates are from Jan. to July
Source: International Committee of the Red Cross   MARCO A. RUIZ mruiz@miamiherald.com

For the prison's first six years at Guantánamo, the Pentagon only permitted the Red Cross to carry messages between the captives and their kin. Then, as now, U.S. military staffers read the mail and censored information they didn't think the prisoners or their families should know.

Then, with the blessing of Admiral James Stavridis at the U.S. Southern Command, the Red Cross started family phone calls in April 2008. Video calls for some came later.

Prisoners who spent years in CIA "black sites" were excluded. For the rest, calls worked like this: A captive was taken to a special cell and shackled to the floor at a prearranged time for the call from home. Prison staffers listened in and could cut the line if conversation strayed into forbidden topics. On the other end, Red Cross delegates verified that family was on the call, either from an ICRC office or from a relative's home. No recording was allowed.

Then this summer, a U.S. Navy medical officer at the prison's psychiatric ward offered that instability in Yemen had become a key source of stress for the prisoners. Military mental health professionals were devoting "a lot of counseling time dealing with that." Now detainee lawyers, in a rare example of harmony, echo that prison doctor on the No. 1 source of anxiety.

Into this vacuum, some of the detainees' lawyers now call their clients' families, using Arabic translators to help track them down before each visit. For years, lawyers brought treats to the meetings, like Big Macs from the base McDonald's or traditional foods for a taste from home. Since May, the military has forbidden food at meetings. So now all the attorneys can offer is word from home.

"I always do that before a visit to Guantánamo because the guys are really, really worried," said David Remes, who represents 18 Yemenis. "The detainees don't know if their families are alive or dead. This problem compounds misery upon misery."

Chapter 3

POPULAR CULTURE

Kristen Stewart as Army Private Amy Cole in *Camp X-Ray*, directed by Peter Sattler. (Beth Dubber, Courtesy IFC Films)

Sunday, September 9, 2007

GUANTÁNAMO IN COMEDY, MUSIC, MOVIES

In Boston this summer, an Irish comedian staged a one-hour show in an orange jumpsuit and a crown of thorns. He played Jesus Christ at Guantánamo Bay.

As the son of God, he has returned to Earth and rattled nerves at New York's Kennedy Airport by making the mistake of saying, yes, he's willing to die for his ideals.

"Let's be fair," the comedian said, delivering his shtick from a stool, in a black-lit theater. "The guy works for U.S. Immigration, and he's just seen a single male Palestinian traveling alone with suspiciously little hand luggage. Not very reassuring in the present climate."

In the five years since the Pentagon started holding war captives in southeast Cuba, the policy and the place called Guantánamo have seeped into popular culture in America and beyond.

Fed by the internet, the phenomenon has spread across the planet with blinding speed, transforming a place into an icon, perhaps like never before. Not Nuremberg. Not Pearl Harbor. Not the Watergate.

Post-9/11 Guantánamo has inspired a book of poetry, several stage productions, a punk-rock songstress, a country song, a movie, two novels, more than a half-dozen memoirs and a hip-hop concert in Washington, D.C. It even made a cameo in Michael Moore's latest shock documentary, *Sicko*, as a metaphor for American health inequities.

Collectively, they convey antipathy for the policy, a political theater of sorts, far removed from the base whose message is of humane custody of would-be anti-U.S. fanatical terrorists.

An example: singer-songwriter Patti Smith's dirge *Without Chains*, about life after years at Guantánamo for the German-born Muslim ex-detainee Murat Kurnaz, whose tale captured the New York artist's imagination.

"I wrote as a citizen," Smith said while on summer tour in Boulder, Colorado. "I don't have any political rhetoric, or deep knowledge about these things. But just as a human being, and a mother, I found it horrifying.

"I think that the idea of some kind of political prison where people can just be put there because there might be some suspicious activity and just be left there, to me is horrifying."

Kurnaz's homeland has in fact been fertile ground. He has already published his memoirs, in German, with an English translation due out early next year. Meantime, a 2004 novel by the German literary critic Dorothea Dieckmann, about life behind the razor wire as seen by a fictional prisoner, Rashid, is due out in English this year.

Australia, the homeland of former captive David Hicks, has also been a lab for artistic enterprise — sculpture, dance, music.

And, as with most political popular culture, the message is overwhelmingly dominated by opponents of the policy, from the left.

When country legend Charlie Daniels entertained at the Navy base in 2002, signaling his support for the prison camps, he improvised new lyrics to an old hit and came up with this:

The devil went down to Gitmo,

just looking for a Taliban....

The troops roared with delight. But Daniels said that he performed the song only twice, both times at Guantánamo as "a spur-of-the-moment thing."

It never occurred to him to record it, he said, calling entertainment as opposition "just a Hollywood thing. I ain't afraid of no kind of backlash, I ain't afraid of anybody. I'm not a politically correct person. I'm 70 years old and I've been pilloried by the best."

On another track, historical accounts are still coming off the presses even as America debates the wisdom and benefit of continuing to keep captives in legal limbo there.

In Illinois, law professor Marc Falkoff has published *Poems from Guantánamo*, crude English translations of flowery Arabic and Pashto verse written by 17 captives from behind the razor wire.

The former U.S. poet laureate, Robert Pinsky, wrote in a blurb that the poems deserve "not admiration or belief or sympathy — but attention."

Gore Vidal declared: "At last Guantánamo has found a voice."

The poems speak of desperation and humiliation, telling a story starkly different from the package tours for press and distinguished visitors that the Pentagon has staged weekly since bringing in the first captives in January 2002.

Navy Commander Rick Haupt, the prison spokesman, said the command staff at Guantánamo hasn't "reviewed" the poetry yet. But he said by email that the title suggests that lawyers "exceeded the limitations" on their access to the captives arranged with the courts.

His Pentagon counterpart, Commander Jeffrey Gordon, told reporters on their publication in June that the poems were "another tool in their battle of ideas against Western democracies against whom they are at war."

The anthology's editor, Falkoff, said the Pentagon has not filed a protest over the poems with any of the U.S. lawyers whose detainee clients contributed to the book, which is on track to be the bestselling U.S. poetry anthology this year.

Five thousand copies were sold in the first six weeks, prompting the publisher to print 5,000 more in a market where most poetry anthologies have an initial 2,500-book run.

Collectively, the ubiquity of the name Guantánamo in 21st-century popular culture (coupled with its international controversy) is evolving into a linguistic shorthand.

From the 20th century, Watergate has emerged as a code word for scandal, Munich for appeasement and Auschwitz for the death camps.

But there is still an emerging consensus on the meaning of Guantánamo.

"Obviously, 'Ground Zero' is the central spot in the spiritual geography of our time," said the cultural commentator Todd Gitlin, a Berkeley-trained sociologist who now teaches at New York's Columbia University. "Guantánamo is now a reference point however you code it."

"If you're a civil libertarian, it symbolizes executive abuse of power," Gitlin said.

"If you're a true believer in the administration approach, I suppose it symbolizes the special recourse you claim to deal with this sort-of warrish non-war.

"If this administration or the next actually shuts it down, I suppose it might fade as a place name, as the placeholder. But I think the name Guantánamo will have staying power."

Google "Guantánamo" (with no accent over the "a") and you get 11.5 million hits in 13 seconds. Do the same for "Watergate" and you get a little more than half as many hits, 6.2 million.

You get 1.8 million for "Nuremberg," the German city where the Nazis stripped the Jews of citizenship in 1935 and where the post-World War II war powers staged the infamous war crimes trials.

Performance art, meantime, has appeared in pockets of outspoken opposition to Guantánamo — notably in Australia and

Britain. It was no coincidence that Abie Philbin Bowman chose to do his Jesus shtick in Boston, an Irish Catholic stronghold, to be sure, but also a stronghold of liberal politics.

By telephone from Boston this summer, Bowman said he took the show to America after sellout performances in Dublin, Belfast, Galway and Edinburgh. It blends his opposition to U.S. detention policy with an emerging career as a stand-up comic.

"I do think that Guantánamo is un-Christian," he said. "Jesus said, 'What you do to the least of these you do also to me.' So, if you believe that, in a sense he is in Guantánamo."

Bowman, 26, comes from the Irish Catholic side of the great divide in his homeland. His grandparents, he said, were practicing Catholics. His parents chose agnosticism. And he declares himself an atheist.

The thesis is, as a Palestinian willing to die for his cause, he winds up in indefinite detention in southeastern Cuba and ruminates on U.S. policy.

But dressing up as Christ himself and quoting God?

"People say it's blasphemous. But I say it's not as blasphemous as torturing people."

For the record, the Pentagon and prison camps spokesmen describe the treatment of captives as humane. Vice President Dick Cheney point-blank told *Larry King Live* recently, "We don't do torture." All "enhanced techniques for interrogation," he added, are carried out with permission of Congress.

Still, the perception of mistreatment has become synonymous with the place and the practice of indefinite detention at Guantánamo.

In mainstream movie houses, Michael Moore bobs just beyond the base in his latest leftist shock documentary, *Sicko*, making the military's offshore mission a metaphor for American health inequities.

Moore has set up the scene by reminding moviegoers that the Pentagon has long boasted that it provides top-notch, free universal healthcare to Guantánamo captives. It's a wily juxtaposition to his central theme of why the White House can't cure the national healthcare crisis.

"Permission to enter. I have three 9/11 rescue workers," Moore says. "They just want some medical attention — the same kind that the evildoers are getting."

He doesn't get inside.

And neither does the film. The prison camps spokesman, Haupt, said *Sicko* has not been shown among first-run movies screened nightly at two base cinemas.

"We've not yet seen the movie here, either in our theaters or on DVD," he said by email, "but have read the reviews."

Friday, January 11, 2008

PHOTOS ECHO YEARS LATER

The first surprise may be that the most damning, enduring images of the prison camps were taken by a U.S. sailor doing his job.

Second is that Navy Petty Officer Shane McCoy didn't look through a viewfinder to capture the panoramic of captives in shackles on their knees with Army guards hovering nearby.

He set a timer, hoisted his Pentagon-issue digital camera on a stick, a monopod, and it clicked.

"I've seen them in magazines, on television, on the internet," said McCoy, as he was ending a 14-year Navy career. "If I do a search for my name, there's like 16,000 hits on those photos. They're everywhere."

McCoy took those now-iconic images of the first detainees. Much to the Pentagon's chagrin, they won't go away.

They have been printed and reprinted across the globe, reenacted in protests from Europe to the steps of the U.S. Supreme Court, even on film, symbols of the United States' detention and interrogation policy.

"Iconic photos cut through ambiguity," says Michael L. Carlebach, professor emeritus of art history and photography at the University of Miami. "They resolve things. They explain things. And it cuts through a lot of rhetoric; you can see for yourself."

Other examples:

The naked girl fleeing napalm in Vietnam, debunking the Pentagon line that civilians weren't caught up in the war.

The Chinese protester stopping a tank's advance in Tiananmen Square.

"They can't spin it," Carlebach said. "Is it fair? Is it representative? All photographs take things out of context. They stop time, just one little split second, and you can get very philosophical and say they're not real. But that's irrelevant."

The date was January 11, 2002, and homemade snapshots of guards tormenting nude detainees in Abu Ghraib, Iraq, were two years away. News photographers in Baghdad had yet to swarm around toppling Saddam Hussein statues.

In Guantánamo, Marine Brigadier General Michael Lehnert told a handful of reporters that the nascent prison was getting "the worst of the worst" from Afghanistan, 8,000 miles away.

McCoy was assigned to Combat Camera, an elite unit that took secret pictures not for the public but for the Pentagon brass. He was outside a makeshift open-air holding compound where the captives were kept on their way to registration. The sailor said it was just another job: Take pictures. Choose some. Write captions. Send them to Washington.

A week later they were on CNN.

At the Pentagon, the Bush administration was debating how to reassure the world that its evolving detention strategy was humane, if not exactly in keeping with the Geneva Conventions, in what commanders would come to call "its spirit."

So, as then Pentagon spokeswoman Torie Clarke wrote in her memoirs, *Lipstick on a Pig*, releasing pictures that didn't show detainees' faces seemed like a smart thing to do.

Pentagon policy to this day dictates that shielding a detainee's face from view (blurring it, chopping him off at his beard, or in that instance, hiding it beneath a cap, surgical mask and blindfold) spares a captive humiliation banned by the Geneva Conventions.

"Did I ever misread what was in those photos," Clarke wrote. "The problem wasn't that we released too much, it was that we explained too little ... which allowed other critics to say we were forcing the detainees into poses of subjugation."

The reaction was swift, and furious.

In England, The Mirror tabloid slapped the photo on its cover and questioned the post 9/11 alliance Prime Minister Tony Blair had forged with the United States with this screaming headline:

What the hell are you doing in our name, Mister Blair?

Recalls McCoy, sheepishly: "I actually called my mother right after it happened and told her that my photos had caused an international incident."

Lost in the furious response, the sailor said, was that detainees "simply weren't kept like that."

"They were wearing gloves because it was cold. I mean, they were flying at 30,000 feet in an unheated back part of the plane; they were wearing hats for the same reason. They did say the goggles were blacked out so they couldn't communicate and plan to attack a guard. It made sense to me."

Soon after their release, the Pentagon took the photos off its websites and labeled them "For Official Use Only," to prevent further distribution.

U.S. troops also tried to discourage news organizations from using the pictures. But Carlebach says the military's efforts overlook the point of why a photo becomes iconic. Time moves on, but the instance comes to tell a larger story.

"They're kneeling with that anti-personnel barbed wire in the foreground and it does not describe bloodthirsty jihadists. These guys are pathetic-looking in their bright orange pajamas."

For those who want to see a captive bowed, it provides a certain satisfaction. For those who believe the policy swept up innocents, it tells another story.

Just in case anyone is wondering, McCoy never got in trouble for making those pictures.

A few weeks after he took them, Secretary of Defense Donald Rumsfeld toured Camp X-Ray and McCoy spoke to him. "I told him, 'Hey, I'm sorry my photos caused all these problems.' He told me not to worry about it, I was doing my job. And that was about it."

Saturday, June 21, 2008

WHAT'S A BORED GUARD TO DO? GET A TATTOO

Tired of guarding terror suspects in the scorching Caribbean sun? Looking for a change from the routine of squiring dignitaries around the Navy base that's been in the news lately?

Get a tattoo.

Four tattoo artists opened a 10-day body art parlor above an Irish bar near the base bowling alley, open day and night to U.S. service members and Department of Defense contractors willing to pay on the spot.

"I'm kind of addicted to this right now," said Petty Officer Third Class Tameka Jones, 32, as she winced her way through inked "tribal lines" just above her tush.

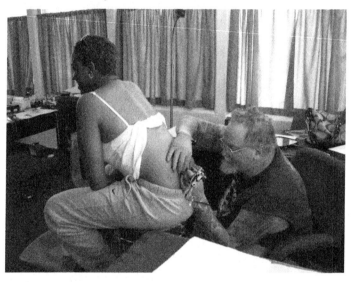

Petty Officer Third Class Tameka Jones gets a tattoo, June 18, 2008. (Carol Rosenberg/Miami Herald)

A Navy cop on the base, and mother of three from North Carolina, Jones said the latest was her seventh tattoo.

It was applied by Rich Green, 44, of Worcester, Massachusetts, who arrived a day earlier to set up shop with three fellow tattoo artists and sported his own advertisement, a blue inked GTMO INK, just above his elbow. GTMO is the military's acronym for this base that is home to 7,500 sailors, other U.S. forces, Department of Defense contractors, families and, of course, 270 suspected terrorists.

Green's kid brother Tyler, 38, got the contract to bring the staff of five aboard a military charter. It was his fourth trip to Guantánamo.

The off-duty distraction is the latest recreational offering brought to Guantánamo, whose prison camps website boasts, "Sun, sand and a close-knit community make the naval station one of the finest 'gated communities' in the Caribbean."

On Memorial Day weekend, the alternative rock band Everclear played a concert for the troops on the ferry landing near the desalination plant, then took a tour of the prison camps.

Next, the first-run movie *Harold and Kumar Escape from Guantánamo* is due to arrive for screening at The Lyceum, an outdoor cinema across the street from a scuba supply shop.

Tyler Green, owner of the Port of Worcester tattoo parlor, predicted his team would ink up to 300 paying customers.

"It seems like there's an almost endless supply of people who want to get tattoos," he said, reporting brisk business that in the past has stretched from 8:30 a.m. until past midnight.

Back in 2005, when he first came, "I really believed it was going to be anchors and bulldogs all day."

Instead, he said, there were similar requests to those back home, notably kids' names and tribal art. One trooper had a tattoo done of the prison staff motto "Honor Bound."

It is Navy policy "to try not to promote tattoos," said the base commander, Navy Captain Mark Leary, with a sigh of acknowledgement that he was bowing to popular demand in sanctioning the special visit.

Wednesday, August 8, 2012

'FRESH PRINCE' POPULAR ON SOME CELLBLOCKS

Harry Potter books are passé among the prisoners. The adventures of the boy wizard have been supplanted by early episodes of Will Smith's 1990s TV comedy *The Fresh Prince of Bel-Air* as a popular way to pass time among the 168 captives now in their second decade of U.S. detention.

"I just ordered all six seasons," says librarian Milton, a Department of Defense contractor who gives only his first name to visiting journalists.

He offered no explanation for the sudden popularity of the half-hour sitcom about an inner-city Philadelphia kid who moves in with his affluent cousins in California beyond the observation that comedy is widely popular among requested items from the detention center library's 28,000 books and videos.

Overall, he said, circulation has slowed as captives pass their 11th Ramadan in detention with other pursuits — praying, eating and talking together between dusk and dawn in their communal areas. But even before this holy month, demand for J.K. Rowling's *Harry Potter* series had dwindled.

An Arabic copy of *Harry Potter and the Goblet of Fire* is pulled from a shelf in the detainee library, March 31, 2009. (John Van Beekum/Miami Herald)

The stories about Harry Potter now sit unborrowed on the shelves of the library, an air-conditioned trailer where contractors examine and assemble material for distribution in the prison camps. "They're over that; it's been more than a year," the librarian said in an interview.

A civilian, Milton maintains the multilingual collection of books that mostly circulate in Arabic, Pashto, English and French that reach the four lockups. But the librarian leaves it to the members of the uniformed military to distribute the books, magazines and video material on the cellblocks.

Instead he detects trends by demand and noted that before surging interest in *Fresh Prince*, a show that first aired September 10, 1990, a Bill Cosby series had a period of popularity.

Cooperative captives, who make up the majority of the prisoners, can watch the show communally pretty much around the clock. They're in medium-security cellblocks of up to 20 men equipped with a flat-screen television bolted to the wall inside a Plexiglas box.

A maximum-security captive can watch the show alone for perhaps an hour or two a day. He gets a special solo cell, shown to journalists on a recent Ramadan visit, that lets him watch from a recliner, with one ankle shackled to a bolt on the floor.

Detainee attends a class with his ankles shackled to the floor of a common area at Camp 6, March 31, 2009. (John Van Beekum/Miami Herald)

Commanders consider activities like TV, reading, art classes and outdoor recreation like soccer to be key to keeping the captives distracted, and reducing friction with the guard force.

The detainees who were captured around the world in the years after the 9/11 attacks are apparently using the material to hone their English, favoring novels that feature side-by-side trans-lation. In addition, Milton said, he has ordered 10 copies of the *Oxford English Dictionary,* one each for nearly every cellblock.

Also, two hardcover sets of the popular, post-apocalyptic *Hunger Games* trilogy are in circulation this Ramadan, Army Cap-tain Jennifer Palmeri said in response to a query. All the versions are in English, she said.

In addition, one captive got an audio version. Palmeri, a pub-lic affairs officer, would not elaborate.

But an attorney at the New York Center for Constitutional Rights solved the puzzle. The law firm that defends Guantánamo detainees sent the audio trilogy to the library for Algerian captive Djamel Ameziane, 45, a long-held English-speaker, said attorney Wells Dixon.

Ameziane lived in Canada and Austria before his capture in Pakistan in 2001, and was long ago cleared for release. Lawyers have been seeking a third country to resettle him as a refugee. "He read *Twilight,* too," Dixon said, "but wasn't a huge fan."

Past librarians have reported interest in Barack Obama's *Au-dacity of Hope,* and an attorney advised that one convict served out his sentence reading George W. Bush's *Decision Points.*

Two books that have yet to make it to the collection tell the stories of the capture and interrogations of some of Guantánamo's best known prisoners: former FBI agent Ali Soufan's *Black Ban-ners* and former CIA agent Jose Rodriguez's defense of waterboarding and other controversial tactics, *Hard Measures.*

Monday, November 18, 2013

'LET 'EM OUT,' SINGS ESPERANZA SPALDING

Grammy-winning musician Esperanza Spalding has joined forces with human rights groups advocating closure of the Guan-tánamo prison camps in a new protest music video.

"What does in the name of freedom mean?" the artist sings as she alternately dons red, white and blue attire during the five-minute video that features cameos by Stevie Wonder and Harry Belafonte to the refrain of "Let 'em out."

Spalding, a bass player who straddles classical, jazz and pop, released the video as the Senate considers whether to continue restrictions on transfers from the prison camps.

The video *We are America* also features a shackled person in a trademark Guantánamo orange jumpsuit and black hood.

"In my America they don't stand for this," sings Spalding, who won a Grammy for Best New Artist in 2011. "We are America, in my America we take a stand for this."

Spalding is known in political circles. She performed at a 2009 White House ceremony that honored Wonder with the Library of Congress Gershwin Prize for popular song, and played at the Obamas' 2009 White House poetry jam as well as at the 2009 Nobel Peace Prize ceremony at Oslo City Hall when the president received his prize.

In comments released with the video, Spalding says she made the music video because she was moved by this year's hunger strike, which engulfed more than 100 of the 164 captives. "I was touring in Europe and I was appalled and embarrassed about what was happening," she said.

At the Department of Defense, spokesman Army Lieutenant Colonel Todd Breasseale panned the politics if not the performance.

"While certainly an evocative performance," he said, "the artists involved in this particular song and video leave out this crucially important piece of information: Until Congress changes the law regarding the transfer requirements for detainees held at Guantánamo Bay, the department will continue to humanely safeguard those in its charge there."

Friday, October 24, 2014

'CAMP X-RAY,' THE MOVIE

Earlier this year, the U.S. Marine general who opened Camp X-Ray in 2002 called guarding detainees there a "soul-numbing experience."

"I think that we need to be very careful that these young people, the guards themselves, don't become changed for the worst by just having to lock up other human beings and see what's going on," retired Marine Major General Michael Lehnert told the Miami Herald. *

Now, Hollywood captures the soul-numbing nature of the work with *Camp X-Ray*, a two-hour drama starring Kristen Stewart of *Twilight* fame as an American soldier guarding war-on-terror captives.

And despite the star power, the film has perhaps drawn more attention abroad than at home. Filmmaker Peter Sattler, passing through Miami on his way to the Abu Dhabi Film Festival, disclosed with a mixture of amusement and bewilderment that it opens this month in Beirut and Iraq.

"That's the interesting marketing challenge," said Sattler, a first-time director. "How do you get people to go see a movie about a topic they've run from for 13 years?"

Not since Harold and Kumar donned orange jumpsuits and escaped from a Hollywood version of the prison in 2008 has the big screen tackled the topic of detention without charge at the prison President Obama wants to close. Then, it was a comedic spoof that suggested abuse through rape of two Americans who were, oops, mistakenly profiled as terrorists.

This film is more subtle. It sweeps aside the "We're the good guys" narrative that the U.S. military promotes at the prison. Captive and captors come across as caught up in something larger than themselves.

Sattler said in an interview that he wrote the movie to get people "to look at your enemy as a human being" and make "some larger, archetypal philosophical statement about the core relationship you have with a stranger."

Stewart's character is not glamorous. She gets splattered with feces flung by a detainee from inside his cell. She's lonely, disconnected from family in this non-war zone where troops get danger pay. She dons white socks and Adidas flip-flops for a party, drinks too much, gets sloppy. She opines on why detainees don't get the Geneva Conventions.

The film itself pays meticulous detail to set design, right down to the library cart the private pushes around a replica of Guantánamo's maximum-security lockup for low-value detainees. Yet it diverges from detention center doctrine in ways that are sure to annoy members of the military.

Private Cole spends, it seems, her entire tour of duty on one cellblock, often alone, chatting with Detainee 471, played by the Iranian film star Payman Maadi. She calls him by his name, Ali, a breach of prison doctrine.

"Policy does not allow members of the guard force to engage in or hold conversations with the detainees beyond the mission at hand," Navy Captain Tom Gresback wrote by email from Guantánamo to a Herald query about whether guards and captives had long hours to "shoot the breeze."

Sattler says a 2002 Camp X-Ray guard, Brandon Neely, did befriend some detainees, and told him how realistic the film felt.

It was filmed in California across just 21 days, mostly at an abandoned correctional facility that the film industry can use. Nobody from the movie ever visited the real prison at Guantánamo Bay, Cuba.

Had they, perhaps they'd know that the guards Velcro numbers where their names go on their battle dress — a through-the-looking-glass version of the detainees, who are called by their internment serial number.

The filmmakers did, however, consult former members of the military and comb through prison materials and news reports on the internet to give a sense of realism, including an Iraqi actor shouting Arabic slurs in the soundtrack, a juxtaposition to the American soldiers' vulgar language.

In fact, it feels at times like it was copied off the imagery that emerges from the prison's censored package tour for visiting news reporters: Food preparation, cell checks every three minutes, Harry Potter books at the detainee library.

But it piles on with ripped-from-the-news improvisations — a restraint-chair force-feeding, sleep deprivation as punishment, a hunger strike.

There's plenty in the film that may annoy the succession of Army censors who double as docents delivering memorized talking points to reporters, starting with the movie title. It's a misnomer. The action takes place in prison buildings, not the 2002 outdoor cells that resembled dog kennels.

Another portion sure to annoy is the film's punitive, promiscuous use of "forced cell extractions."

No one knows what the tackle-and-shackle technique really looks like, yet, because the prison is resisting a court order to make public some video recordings of the real event. In Sattler's version, Private Cole volunteers during first-day orientation, suits up, is slugged by a detainee and gets a fat lip.

To write it, Sattler studied a leaked prison handbook and portrays his as a brawl undertaken by amateurs rather than the well-rehearsed, choreographed operation portrayed by Justice Department lawyers defending prison force-feeding practices in the federal courts.

It's a device, says Sattler. "You have to show this place being hostile and intense before you get into how boring it is."

And that's the point, as he sees it.

He had watched a National Geographic documentary exchange between a soldier and a captive over a library book at a cell door — and said he was lured to the topic by his imagined interactions between those two men.

"In the same way that the terrorists aren't monsters," he said, "these soldiers aren't some asshole guard who wants to kill people."

His film soldier became a woman, he said, long before Stewart agreed to take the part. His wife was pregnant with their first child, a girl, and Sattler said he started thinking about "what heroes am I going to show her?"

The film dispatches Guantánamo's good-guy, bad-guy narrative in a single lunch scene in the guards' cafeteria.

Private Rico Cruz, played by actor Joseph Julian Soria: "These motherfuckers did 9/11. And now they're in jail. End of story."

Private Cole, played by Stewart: "The motherfuckers that did 9/11 died there."

Book editor's note: In the period covered by this collection of stories, Michael Lehnert was promoted from brigadier to major general.

Chapter 4

CAMP JUSTICE WAR COURT

The flag at half-staff at the original military commissions court building at Camp Justice, September 11, 2008. (Carol Rosenberg/Miami Herald)

Friday, March 30, 2007

AUSTRALIAN CAPTIVE MAKES A DEAL

Confessed al-Qaida foot soldier David Hicks pleaded guilty to supporting terrorism in exchange for a nine-month prison sentence under a deal that forbids him from claiming he was abused in U.S. custody.

In return, Hicks, 31, will be allowed to leave Guantánamo to serve out the sentence in his native Australia within 60 days. And he will be free, at home, by New Year's Eve.

It was a startling conclusion to the first U.S. war crimes tribunal since World War II.

"They told us this was one of the world's worst terrorists, and he got the sentence of a drunken driver," said Ben Wizner, staff attorney for the American Civil Liberties Union.

The Bush administration had originally sought life in prison. A panel of senior U.S. military officers was told they could sentence him to seven years for providing material support to terrorism, which they did.

But moments after they were ushered out of the tribunal chambers at 8:15 p.m, the presiding officer, Marine Colonel Ralph Kohlmann, disclosed that a Pentagon official had cut a secret deal. Under its terms, the man who was captured while fleeing the U.S. invasion of Afghanistan and spent more than five years at this offshore detention center agreed to:

• Refrain from talking to the media for a year.

• Forever waive any profit from telling his story.

• Renounce any claims of mistreatment or unlawful detention.

• Voluntarily submit to U.S. interrogation and testify at future U.S. trials or international tribunals.

"If the United States were not ashamed of its conduct, it wouldn't hide behind a gag order," Wizner said. "The agreement said he wasn't mistreated. Why aren't we allowed to judge for ourselves?"

Hicks' Marine defense attorney cast him as a hapless soldier without a cause and urged a 20-month sentence, arguing that he should get credit for his five years and four months in detention as an "enemy combatant."

The short, stocky Hicks stood ramrod straight in a charcoal suit and tie, with a trim haircut, after he admitted to taking four al-Qaida training courses before the September 11 attacks. At one point, he admitted, he personally asked Osama Bin Laden why al-Qaida had no English-language training manuals.

"His heart wasn't with al-Qaida," said Marine Major Dan Mori, his Pentagon-appointed attorney. He called Hicks a "wannabe" soldier who ran away from home after the Australian army rebuffed his bid to enlist.

"He guarded a tank, he sat in a trench and he got bombed," Mori said.

Countered Marine Lieutenant Colonel Kevin Chenail, the prosecutor who sought a maximum seven-year sentence: "Other confused lost souls might follow in his footsteps."

Besides, Chenail said, Hicks willingly rejoined Bin Laden's forces a day after the 9/11 attacks. "He knew America was coming after al-Qaida; he wanted to help them out."

At his arraignment four days ago, in a crumpled tan prison uniform with straggly hair down his back, Hicks looked a disheveled, disheartened man. In contrast, he looked relieved Friday morning while soberly answering two hours of questions from the military judge with, "Yes, sir."

Sunday, February 17, 2008

WHEN DID WAR BEGIN? WHERE'S BATTLEFIELD?

When did the war on terror begin? Is the globe really one big battlefield? Can one gunman's firefight be another man's terror? Or, is it like Supreme Court Justice Potter Stewart's definition of pornography: People know it when they see it.

At Guantánamo's military commissions, the definition of the ongoing war on al-Qaida (when it started, who is immune from prosecution) is emerging as a core issue for military judges and eventually U.S. officers who will sit in judgment on alleged terrorists swept up in the Pentagon's global war on terrorism.

Prosecutors say the war began long before the September 11, 2001, attacks on the United States, and have charged captives here in conspiracies dating back to the mid-1990s.

Defense lawyers argue that the Pentagon has fashioned a definition of a new kind of war to suit its military commissions and carry out offshore justice.

That's because, says defense attorney Charlie Swift, a former U.S. Navy officer, "There is no war crime outside of war."

The issue is not new. Attorneys and politicians have been arguing the extent of President Bush's power since Congress passed its Authorization for the Use of Military Force a week after the 9/11 attacks.

The administration at first used the AUMF to launch its late 2001 assault on Afghanistan to topple the Taliban, hunt down Osama Bin Laden and dismantle al-Qaida's training camps. But White House lawyers have since cited it as justification for a range of activities, from extending the military's reach beyond the Afghan theater to legalizing the intelligence community's eavesdropping, interrogation and detention powers.

Now a test of the war powers is emerging in the al-Qaida conspirator case of Salim Hamdan, a Yemeni who admits he was a driver in Bin Laden's six-man motor pool in Afghanistan.

Ahead of a late May trial date, Hamdan's lawyers are asking a military judge, Navy Captain Keith Allred, to throw out or at least reduce the charges against the father of two with a fourth-grade education.

They argue that the charges are too broad, retroactive and in some instances redundant.

Prosecutors say the driver was a trusted al-Qaida member who helped Bin Laden elude capture, a sometime bodyguard and occasional arms courier who was an al-Qaida co-conspirator in everything from the 1998 U.S. embassy bombings in East Africa to the October 2000 suicide bombing of the USS Cole to the September 11 attacks. They do not say, however, that he actually helped plan the attacks.

At pretrial arguments, Allred asked when the Pentagon is alleging that Hamdan joined the conspiracy.

After a brief huddle, prosecutors for the Justice and Defense departments announced Hamdan's start date: February 1996, when U.S. evidence suggests Hamdan stepped into Afghanistan on his first trip from his native Yemen.

He has admitted that he went to Afghanistan answering a call to jihad to fight with Muslims in Tajikistan, to defend Islam, but not from the United States. Once in Afghanistan, he says, he took a job driving Bin Laden for an income, not ideology.

Moreover, it was not until August 1996, six months after Hamdan arrived in Afghanistan, that Bin Laden felt sufficiently entrenched there to issue a "Declaration of Jihad against the Americans."

The Pentagon's first round of charge sheets, withdrawn after the original commissions were ruled unconstitutional, mentioned the declaration prominently in all its war crimes cases, perhaps suggesting that by then the United States and al-Qaida were already at war.

But the current charge sheets neither name the war nor define the battlefield. Rather, they identify the embassy bombings and Cole and 9/11 attacks as among the war's hostilities.

Defense lawyers for Salim Hamdan discuss strategy at Andrews Air Force Base, Maryland, before leaving for Guantánamo Bay. From left, retired Navy Lieutenant Commander Charlie Swift, civilian lawyer Joseph McMillan of the Perkins Coie law firm, and Navy Commander Brian Mizer, the lead defense counsel, December 3, 2007. (Carol Rosenberg/Miami Herald)

At a recent hearing, the judge seemed to be grappling with the overarching question. He asked lawyers on both sides: "Which branch of government is charged with determining when hostilities began?"

Swift replied that in the absence of a declaration of war by Congress, the courts must decide.

Justice Department lawyer Jordan Goldstein said it would cover the period before, on or after the September 11 attacks, adding that "9/11 was not the start of hostilities. It was in fact the point where it was hard to ignore that we were at war."

Amnesty International rejects the notion of a global war on terror entirely.

Rather, it sees U.S. wars limited to two specific theaters — Iraq and Afghanistan, where the United States had previously armed and trained mujahideen fighters resisting the Soviet invasion.

Amnesty International attorney Jumana Musa, who has been tracking the military commissions from the start, says the government cases don't offer a specific start date for the war. Instead, she said, based on various evolving commissions cases, the war began "sometime after they stopped funding the mujahideen and before the September 11 attacks. You can't be funding the guys you are at war with."

An outspoken critic of the system, Musa said the open-ended war theory allows the United States to hold the detainees indefinitely without charges, as enemy combatants, while arguing that because of the ongoing war they can't disclose interrogation techniques or charge them in civilian courts.

Defense lawyers for Guantánamo captives accused the prosecution of, in a sense, shaping the war to fit each detainee's circumstance. The case of Canadian Omar Khadr, accused of throwing a grenade at age 15 that killed an American soldier in a firefight in Afghanistan, alleges a war crimes conspiracy dating back to 1997, when his father moved the family from Toronto to Afghanistan.

"According to a recent government filing, Omar allegedly began 'conspiring' with al-Qaida to commit 'war crimes' as a 10-year-old child," Khadr's defense lawyer, Navy Lieutenant Commander William Kuebler, said in an email.

Ridiculing the government's case, he added: "Omar's 'war' has consisted of being shot in the back, while wounded, after a four-hour bombardment, followed by years of illegal detention, coercive interrogation, and a planned trial for war crimes, which will likely result in a life sentence for little more than surviving the firefight in which he was shot."

Monday, July 28, 2008

REPORTER'S NOTEBOOK: A CHILLING DRINK

Several dozen media members brought in by the Pentagon to watch a day or two of the first U.S. war crimes tribunal since World War II got a ghoulish surprise when they went in search of drinking water at Camp Justice.

Carol Rosenberg

Bottled water in Tent City, where reporters are kept, is chilled in a 3,470-pound shipping refrigerator meant for the dead.

It is marked "MORTUARY" on the side and has shelves to accommodate eight body bags being airlifted by the U.S. Air Force.

It's all part of the Expeditionary Legal Complex, which can be dismantled and moved elsewhere should either presumed presidential candidate make good on his pledge to close the prison camps at Guantánamo.

Stacks of chilled water in a modular morgue, May 9, 2008. (Carol Rosenberg/Miami Herald)

An escort who briefs visiting news media assured journalists that the $32,000 ADR-300 mortuary had never been used for its intended purpose.

Whistling Dixie: Also a surprise, particularly to the foreign media, was what appeared to be a Confederate flag flying above Tent City.

U.S. military escorts explained that it was actually the state flag of Mississippi. An Air Force engineering unit called The 172nd (nicknamed "The Prime Beef") is in charge of keeping Tent City functioning. It hails from Jackson.

Driver 'tuned out': In the al-Qaida world of driver Salim Hamdan, exhortations to martyrdom and railing at the infidels can become mind-numbing. Or so claimed several FBI agents who testified at the trial of Osama Bin Laden's driver, the Yemeni with a fourth-grade education.

"Mr. Hamdan pretty much got tired of hearing the same thing over and over again," said FBI Agent George Crouch Jr. And so, he "tuned out."

New press room: For two days, Guantánamo got to show off its $49,000 war court media room, a Hollywood-style set built inside an abandoned airfield's hangar, which is a crude copy of the Pentagon's podium where Defense Secretary Robert Gates takes questions.

With nearly three dozen reporters on the island (the vast majority flown in for two days) many of the seats were, for the first time, filled during a question-and-answer session with the prosecutor.

By the weekend, the facility that the Pentagon says can host up to 60 journalists was down to only 11: four newspapers, three wire services, one radio reporter and an audio-video team from *This American Life,* which came to Guantánamo for gavel-to-gavel coverage of the Hamdan trial.

Tent City has 20 tents capable of sleeping 120 in the media section. Saturday's occupancy meant each media member could have his or her own six-man tent, with nine to spare. Media minders sleep in Navy housing.

Snapshot to Sana'a: The driver on trial as a terrorist didn't get a veto of his court sketch, but he got a glimpse.

An attorney told sketch artist Janet Hamlin that the Yemeni captive was eager to see her drawing. With permission of the guards, she held it up during a recess.

Hamdan studied his likeness, then flashed a grin and thumbs-up, a contrast to his somber demeanor in front of the U.S. military jurors.

Speculation centered on the fact that the media would show his likeness around the world, something like a snapshot sent home to the wife and kids in the Yemeni city of Sana'a.

A sketch of Salim Hamdan at his trial with Navy Captain John Murphy and the military jury at upper right, July 22, 2008. (©Janet Hamlin sketch artist)

Tuesday, September 23, 2008

SOLITARY CONFINEMENT FOR CATEGORY OF ONE

Some days, America's lone convicted terrorist at Guantánamo amuses himself by calling out "All rise," like a court bailiff, as guards pass his cell.

Mostly, Salim Hamdan passes the time with photos of family from home in Yemen.

It has been six weeks since a military jury made Hamdan a war criminal for working as Osama Bin Laden's $200-a-month driver in Afghanistan, and the Pentagon has yet to say precisely when his 66-month prison sentence ends. Or where he will go.

What to do with Hamdan illustrates how much the Pentagon is still improvising war-on-terror detention policy — six years after the Bush administration opened the prison camps. For now, he is segregated, the only prisoner in a corridor set aside for convicts at Camp 5.

But until someone else is convicted at the first war crimes tribunals since World War II, Hamdan, 40, is a category of one.

"A Detainee Socialization Management Plan will be implemented," says Army Major Rick Morehouse. The goal: "To avoid linguistic isolation and solitary confinement."

So the military says it will offer Hamdan "Movie Night." Guards say soccer and nature videos are popular with many detainees.

Also, the military plans to send Hamdan a government-hired linguist each day for what Morehouse calls "social conversation" and allow him four, three-hour visits a week.

Why it has taken so long to implement the program, or when it will start, the military will not say.

"One reason why you don't see a lot of long-term planning for this issue is that the commissions process itself has really been lurching from one problem to the next," says Columbia University law professor Matthew Waxman, the first of three deputy assistant secretaries of defense for detainee affairs to serve the Bush administration.

He was not surprised to learn about the dilemma of what to do about Hamdan. Earlier planning had focused on multiple convicts, he said, not just one.

At issue is how to interpret the Geneva Conventions, an issue that has dogged this offshore detention and interrogation center from the start.

On the one hand, the treaty that seeks to regulate warfare worldwide forbids holding POWs in the company of convicts.

But above all, the conventions are meant to make sure captives are held humanely. Which is why prison camp commanders have insisted for years that there is no such thing as solitary confinement at Guantánamo. Even for a category of one.

"This has been a make-it-up-as-you-go-along system from the very beginning," says Miami defense attorney Neal Sonnett, who watches the Guantánamo trials for the American Bar Association.

Perhaps planning has "hit snags," suggested Waxman, noting that the trials envisioned in the months after 9/11 to offer "swift justice" were met by "a series of legal challenges and diplomatic objections that not only slowed it to a near standstill but made it difficult to plan ahead."

Moreover, he said, the trials have at times been at odds with other administration goals since 9/11, such as gathering intelligence on al-Qaida and building coalitions with nations like Britain that from the start derided the Guantánamo trials.

Hence, the CIA kept the alleged 9/11 plotters in secret custody for years, slowing progress toward the complex conspiracy trial of alleged mastermind Khalid Sheik Mohammed and four alleged co-conspirators.

Monday, November 3, 2008

BIN LADEN VIDEO-MAKER GETS LIFE

A military jury convicted Osama Bin Laden's media secretary of war crimes for creating an al-Qaida recruiting video that prosecutors argued incited suicide bombers. Within hours, the jury sentenced him to life in prison.

The convict, Ali Hamza al Bahlul, about 40, responded by breaking his weeklong boycott of the trial with a 50-minute anti-American monologue.

He declared his devotion to Allah, berated the United States for the plight of the Palestinians and, noting his election-eve conviction, announced that radical Islam's war with the West would persist with whomever succeeds President Bush.

"We have fought and we fight and will fight any government that governs America," said Bahlul. He waved a poem he wrote in Arabic in praise of the September 11, 2001, attacks, *The Storm of the Airplanes.*

Until he was convicted, the Yemeni father of four had declined to mount a defense and sat silently, occasionally smiling at the mention of his handiwork.

The jury of nine Navy captains and colonels from the Army, Air Force and Marines had taken only four hours to find him guilty on all charges.

They deliberated on sentencing for only 45 minutes, less time than the prisoner in tan jumpsuit and sneakers took to rail at them.

No one testified during the no-contest trial that Bahlul, from Yemen's Red Sea region, ever fired a shot at Americans during his 1999-2001 tenure in Afghanistan.

Nor was there evidence that any of the 9/11 hijackers saw his video, *The Destruction of the American Destroyer USS Cole*.

But the Pentagon argued that Bahlul conspired with al-Qaida, supported terror and solicited murder by creating the two-hour video that spliced fiery Bin Laden speeches with Muslim bloodshed and stock news footage of the aftermath of the 2000 suicide bombing of the $1 billion warship.

In all, prosecutors called 16 witnesses: three former jihadists, prison camp interrogators, forensic experts and two victims of the USS Cole attack, notably the father of one of the 17 sailors killed on October 12, 2000, off the coast of Yemen.

Two men came up alongside the warship aboard a vessel packed with explosives in Aden harbor, waved, then detonated themselves and their load.

"Our son and his 16 mates were minding their own business, refueling in a supposedly friendly harbor and weren't out to hurt anybody and were viciously attacked and murdered," said Gary Swenchonis Sr., his hands shaking and voice trembling after using a cane to reach the tribunal's witness stand.

His son, Gary Jr., 26, of Rockport, Texas, was a Navy petty officer and firefighter. The father said the video was especially troubling because it promoted "propaganda, hate, violence" — values his family abhorred.

"He was raised, in short, to respect all people of religious beliefs and that violence was wrong," Swenchonis said. "If you had to go to war, you went to war for your nation. And you wore a uniform."

The Yemeni watched from the defendant's table expressionless.

In seeking the maximum life sentence, the lead prosecutor, Army Major Dan Cowhig, called Bahlul's video "a virus that this man had released on the world."

Swenchonis' father said all you have to do is surf the web to see it.

"The message that video sends every time it is played is blood, blood, destruction, destruction." said the prosecutor, asking the jury to sentence Bahlul to life imprisonment.

Monday, July 12, 2010

YOUNGEST CAPTIVE PLAYS LAWYER

Canadian Omar Khadr was captured eight years ago, nearly dead after a firefight with U.S. forces in Afghanistan. He was 15 and grew into manhood behind Guantánamo's razor wire.

Now, a strapping 23-year-old, he appears before an Army judge to tackle a thorny question: Is Guantánamo's youngest and last Western captive equipped to defend himself on war crime charges punishable by life in jail?

The Toronto-born Khadr, in an act of disgust and defiance, fired his lawyers. Sometimes, he says he'll be his own lawyer; sometimes, he says he'll boycott the tribunal.

"It's absurd to think, having spent a third of his life in confinement, that he would have enough ability to represent himself," says veteran Miami criminal defense attorney Neal Sonnett, who has worked for greater due process at the war court.

"He obviously has missed out on an education and he certainly is not in a position to understand the rules or to know anything about possible strategy."

A crossroads moment, it is happening because Obama administration reforms to the military commissions give a suspect more power to defend himself in a court that does not distinguish between juvenile and adult.

War court veterans have watched Khadr become what Canadian family lawyer Dennis Edney calls "a young man in an adult's body" since he first appeared at the court in January 2006.

In April 2006, he stunned war court observers by haltingly reading a handwritten statement rife with spelling errors and sought to fire his lawyers. His opening: "excuse me mr. jugde."

Burly, bearded and standing more than six feet tall, Khadr has had a dozen U.S. lawyers, some of whom were fired and others who quit. But the latest firings come at a crucial time — two months after his defense team called ex-intelligence forces to describe the teen's black-hooded, shackled treatment and stretcher-bound interrogations in Afghanistan. U.S. military doctors had saved him and his eyesight from bullet and shrapnel wounds.

Defense attorneys Barry Coburn and Kobie Flowers, now fired, sought to show that Khadr as a 15-year-old captive was coerced into confessing that he threw a grenade that killed an American army medic.

Undated International Red Cross photo of Omar Khadr obtained by the Miami Herald.

Then, Khadr sat next to his team when an interrogator testified that he frightened the teen with a rape scenario. Alex Neve, secretary general of Amnesty International Canada, saw Khadr sometimes engaged in his defense, sometimes weeping.

"Many days," Neve said by telephone, "this is a young man who experiences a great deal of anxiety and distress and physical pain and no doubt the legacy and aftermath of the eight years of detention and the effects of torture. None of that equips him to be someone who is able to look out for his best legal interests."

But Canadian counsel Nate Whitling, a Khadr legal advisor, said the firings were long in coming.

"He just doesn't want to participate in this charade anymore," said Whitling. "He thinks it's an unfair process and he's just done playing their game, basically."

Whitling disagreed with Canadian reports that said Khadr fired his team in disgust because they brought him government offers of a plea agreement in exchange for decades in prison. Defense lawyers are obliged to present any prosecution proposal to their client.

But he said Khadr is in no way prepared to handle his own defense. He hasn't even asked for a copy of the Handbook for Military Commissions. Secretary of Defense Robert Gates signed the rule book in April. Unless Canada intervenes, and a federal court there has again ordered the Stephen Harper government to do so, the Pentagon plans to assemble a jury of senior military officers to hear Khadr's terror trial in August.

Khadr, the son of a now-slain al-Qaida financier, is accused of conspiring with the terror group to plant mines to kill U.S. forces during the 2001 invasion of Afghanistan. The boy was captured, shot twice through the chest, in a U.S. commando air and land assault on a suspected al-Qaida safe house in July 2002.

He is also accused of murder in violation of the laws of war, a crime created by Congress. Prosecutors allege he hurled a grenade that fatally wounded U.S. Special Forces Sergeant First Class Christopher Speer, 28, of Albuquerque.

The case is perhaps more controversial than any at Guantánamo. Critics call it the West's first war crimes trial of a "child soldier" and argue that the United States should have rehabilitated him — not interrogated him and held him with adults.

UNICEF head Anthony Lake, who was President Bill Clinton's national security advisor, is among the latest in a long list of international law experts to urge the Obama administration to stop the trial.

Khadr has at times simply refused to show up, confronting both the judge and camp commanders with the dilemma of whether to use a tackle-and-shackle technique to force him into court.

But neither the Canadian boycotting his August trial nor defending himself would reflect well on Pentagon justice, said Sonnett. Rather, he said he hoped the judge, Army Colonel Patrick Parrish, "will have a nice conversation with him and talk him into accepting his lawyers and cooperating with his lawyers so that he has competent representation."

In fact, Sonnett said on reflection that he could imagine no scenario in which a Guantánamo defendant was equipped to defend himself. Most of the captives arrived in 2002.

"The military commissions are flawed enough," said Sonnett. "If they now have to proceed with people acting as their own lawyers, the flaws are going to be exacerbated and any results are at risk of being accused of being an injustice and a kangaroo court."

Sunday, October 31, 2010

'CHILD SOLDIER' GETS 40 YEARS, WILL SERVE 8

A military jury gave teen terrorist Omar Khadr a symbolic 40-year prison sentence for killing an American commando in Afghanistan, unaware that the United States agreed to send the Canadian home next year.

Khadr, 24, looked straight ahead when the jury foreman announced the verdict. The widow of his victim, Tabitha Speer, 40, cheered "yes," and then wept.

"He will forever be a murderer in my eyes," Speer said, adding that the 40-year sentence was a vindication.

The Guantánamo military commission, she said, provided a sense of finality along with assurances that Khadr would never be allowed to enter the United States or ride on an airplane.

The Pentagon staged closing arguments in the case, shielding the seven-officer jury from details of the plea bargain that capped his prison sentence at eight years — one in Guantánamo and, at most, seven more in Canada.

That means Khadr could be free by age 32, if not earlier under Canadian parole provisions.

Jurors were told only that Guantánamo's youngest captive had pleaded guilty to five war crimes, including hurling the grenade that mortally wounded Sergeant First Class Christopher Speer, 28, during a July 2002 assault on an al-Qaida compound. Khadr was 15.

The prosecution sought a 25-year sentence. Defense lawyers recommended repatriation.

Canadian attorney Dennis Edney of Edmonton in a hangar outside the war court, August 12, 2010. (Carol Rosenberg/Miami Herald)

In a rebuke, the jury said he should be imprisoned until age 64.

Khadr also admitted that, in the days ahead of his capture, he planted mines intended to maim or kill U.S. and allied forces. He was captured near dead, treated by U.S. forces and sent to Guantánamo soon after his 16th birthday.

Canada has balked publicly at the repatriation proposal.

But an exchange of diplomatic notes between the U.S. and Canadian governments, signed October 23, included this:

"The Government of Canada is inclined to favorably consider Mr. Khadr's application to be transferred to Canada to serve the remainder of his sentence," or whichever portion Canada's National Parole Board decides is required.

It was signed by the Canadian Embassy with no name attached.

The Pentagon's chief war crimes prosecutor, Navy Captain John F. Murphy, said he made the eight-year plea deal with Khadr to secure the certainty of a conviction for the victims of the so-called "child soldier."

He cited Khadr's youth at the time of the crime, calling him a "minor."

"I hope he will be rehabilitated in the future," said Murphy.

Former Army Sergeant Layne Morris, who lost an eye in the firefight that captured Khadr, said he was concerned that an eight-year sentence put the Canadian "on frankly the fast track to freedom" at "the prime of his life."

Khadr's Canadian attorney, Dennis Edney, lambasted the military commissions process, which has so far yielded five convictions, three through plea bargains.

"We may choose to believe that through his plea Omar finally came clean and accepted his involvement in a firefight when he was 15 years of age," he said, "or that this was one final coerced confession from a victimized young man who was in the wrong place at the wrong time because his father placed him there."

As a convicted war criminal, Khadr was to be moved to a single cell in a maximum-security lockup where the prison camp staff segregates its convicts.

He had spent the last two years in Guantánamo's most relaxed camp, sleeping at night in a bunkhouse with four other captives and by day praying and dining with at least a dozen at a time.

The Pentagon's Chief Defense Counsel, Marine Colonel Jeffrey Colwell, said Khadr's coming harsh conditions are "outweighed by the fact that he knows he's going home."

"There's closure here today," the Marine said, adding that Khadr's 40-year jury sentence "was hard for our team to swallow."

Chapter 5

9/11 TRIAL

Some furniture was still wrapped in plastic as the military showed reporters the new courtroom, February 3, 2008. (Carol Rosenberg/Miami Herald)

Sunday, February 3, 2008

COURT CAN SILENCE CAPTIVES WHO TELL SECRETS

The military unveiled a new state-of-the-art court capable of trying six alleged terrorists simultaneously — and silencing them from the outside world, if they try to spill state secrets.

The military offered a comprehensive look at its new court, part of a $12 million razor-wire-ringed legal complex that arrived by cargo plane and barge in prefabricated parts. Unlike a more ambitious plan to build a $125 million compound on the site overlooking Guantánamo Bay, the new compound can be dismantled and shipped back stateside once trials are done.

"We got it up in six months at a fraction of the cost," said Army Colonel Wendy Kelly, director of operations at the Pentagon's Office of Military Commissions.

Architecturally, the bunker-style building is a bland structure impenetrable to electronic eavesdropping.

Inside, it has an up-to 20-seat jury box for the U.S. military officers who will be assembled from around the world, case by case, to sit in judgment; typical judges' and prosecution tables, plus a bank of defense tables where six captives can sit at computers on faux leather chairs, unshackled but guarded by soldiers.

It also has a 30-seat adjacent room, behind a tempered-glass window, where observers can hear the proceedings on a broadcast basis — and a kill-switch where a security officer or the judge can cut the sound in case someone divulges a state secret.

There is no blackout capacity or curtain, meaning the media, legal observers, dignitaries and family members who might attend a trial could watch but not listen.

Such measures could be necessary if the Pentagon presses ahead with plans to try alleged 9/11 architect Khalid Sheik Mohammed or any of the other 13 high-value detainees who arrived at this base in September 2006 from three-plus years of secret CIA custody.

The agency has classified the interrogation techniques it used on the men (in secret sites, somewhere overseas) as national security secrets. Were one to blurt out his treatment at trial, the judge or security officer could simply stifle their voices.

It is inside razor wire along with five separate windowless cells where lawyers can meet clients who could someday include the alleged architects of the 9/11 attacks and other suspected senior al-Qaida leaders.

Thursday, June 5, 2008

ALLEGED PLOT MASTERMIND: 'MARTYR ME'

One by one, the U.S. military brought five accused 9/11 conspirators before a war court judge, and each one rejected his free-of-charge American lawyers. Two said they welcomed death.

"In Allah I put my trust," said reputed al-Qaida kingpin Khalid Sheik Mohammed.

Asked by the trial judge whether he understood that conviction could earn him a death sentence, Mohammed replied: "This is what I wish — to be martyred."

It was the first appearance of the alleged senior al-Qaida leaders, whom the United States has held secretly and interrogated overseas since their capture in 2002 and 2003.

They are accused of conspiring with Osama Bin Laden to orchestrate the four U.S. airline hijackings that toppled the World Trade Center, shattered the Pentagon and slammed into a Pennsylvania field on September 11, 2001, killing 2,973 men, women and children.

All were brought from the prison camps several miles away to the special maximum-security war court, and sat one behind the other.

Observers were able to watch the proceedings at special viewing sites, but on several occasions the audio feed was muted.

In one instance, Mohammed's nephew, Ammar al Baluchi, sounded like he was about to describe the circumstances of his capture.

The CIA has classified as state secrets the captives' time as "ghost prisoners" at clandestine overseas prisons, and the details of their interrogations, during which Baluchi's uncle was waterboarded.

In another, Yemeni Ramzi Bin al Shibh started explaining to the judge, Marine Colonel Ralph Kohlmann, why he had been taking "psychotropic drugs" since arriving at Guantánamo along with the other men in September 2006.

All the men sat in white tunics with their heads covered. Only Bin al Shibh, 36, was in shackles, with his leg irons bolted to the floor.

He allegedly tried to join the September 11 suicide squads, and obtain flight training in Florida, but failed to get a U.S. visa from Hamburg, Germany.

"I've been seeking martyrdom for five years. I tried for 9/11 to get a visa. And I could not obtain that visa," Bin al Shibh said in rejecting his defense lawyer. "If this martyrdom happens today, I will welcome it. God is great, God is great."

The hearing was meant to be an arraignment, a formal reading of the charges in advance of legal motions, discovery of evidence and a proposed September 18 opening of trial.

But the day was remarkable — a 9 a.m. to 6:30 p.m. court session, including two prayer breaks — in which each man rejected the two to four military and civilian attorneys sitting beside him.

The director of the American Civil Liberties Union, Anthony Romero, watched from the spectator's gallery in a fury. He had been building a death penalty defense fund and pool of criminal defense lawyers to help the military lawyers.

"It was one of the saddest days in American jurisprudence," he said. "The word 'torture' was used so abundantly and the legal process continued."

He blamed Pentagon haste to get the men to trial before the end of the Bush administration. Defense lawyers were not given sufficient time to forge attorney-client relationships "with men who were tortured for five years," before the arraignment, he said.

The Bush administration says it does not torture.

Some of the men rejected the legitimacy of commissions, in which U.S. military officers serve as judge and jurors. Saudi Mustafa al Hawsawi, who allegedly funneled funds for the terror plot, went last and appeared to be echoing the others who came before him.

Kohlmann ruled that three understood their rights enough to serve as their own attorneys: Mohammed, 43, known to the CIA as KSM; his nephew, Baluchi, who spoke near-perfect English and explained he was qualified as a "Microsoft-certified computer engineer;" and Walid Bin Attash, 30, a Yemeni who allegedly trained some of the 9/11 hijackers at an Afghanistan camp.

At one point, after earning the right to defend himself, Bin Attash interjected with a question: "If we are executed, will we be buried in Guantánamo or sent back to our home countries?"

Kohlmann didn't answer.

Mohammed struck a radical Muslim note in rejecting the court.

"I will not accept anybody, even if he is Muslim, if he swears to the American Constitution," he said, vowing to follow Islamic *Shariah* law and scorning the U.S. Constitution "because it allows for same sexual marriage."

The nephew, accused of sending money to the suicide squads, sounded more secular in his repudiation of the free legal services.

"I am in the wrong court. I am not a criminal. My case is political," he said. "Even though the government tortured me free of charge for all these years, I cannot accept lawyers under these circumstances."

Kohlmann withheld a decision on whether to let Bin al Shibh and Hawsawi act as their own lawyers, like the others, while keeping their Pentagon-appointed counsel as legal advisors.

Hawsawi's attorney, Army Major Jon Jackson, told the judge that he believed his client was intimidated by the others. He asked that his trial be severed from the others.

All the men had grown beards in captivity.

But Mohammed's appearance was the most striking. The Pakistani looked 20 years older than the disheveled man in a T-shirt who was rousted from his bed in the widely published photo from his 2003 capture. This Mohammed was tidily attired in pristine white tunic and turban and had grown a massive, mostly white, bushy beard that reached his chest.

He spoke in the broken English he learned as an engineering student in his 20s in North Carolina.

The eavesdrop-proof courtroom was specially designed to mute the alleged terrorists' audio feed, if they divulged national security secrets such as their treatment in CIA custody.

The CIA director, Air Force General Michael V. Hayden, has confirmed THAT agents employed a controversial technique called waterboarding on Mohammed. But he has not said where, nor has he specified other special interrogation tactics.

"I do not mention the torturing. I know this is a red line," Mohammed told the judge.

Sunday, April 29, 2012

JUDGE HAS HANDLED TOUGH CASES BEFORE

When President George W. Bush proposed razing Iraq's Abu Ghraib prison in 2004, this American Army judge declared it a crime scene and forbade its demolition. When five years later President Barack Obama asked the Guantánamo war court to freeze all proceedings, the same judge refused the brand-new commander in chief's request.

He's Colonel James L. Pohl, who has appointed himself to preside at the war crimes trial of the five men accused of orchestrating the September 11 attacks.

Chief Trial Judge James L. Pohl. Courtesy of Office of Military Commissions)

It's not that Pohl is unaware of rank after three decades in the Army. It's simply not relevant in this colonel's court.

Here's how he scolded a prosecutor when the prison commander, an admiral, was late for court to testify after lunch recess in January: "Witnesses should be waiting either in the trailer at the back or outside," the judge bristled, "and I really don't care what their rank is."

A soldier since the '80s and a judge since 2000, Pohl has had judicial oversight of some of the most notorious Army cases of the post-9/11 era.

• He presided at the trials of nine soldiers found guilty of abusing detainees at the Abu Ghraib prison.

• He decided that U.S. Army psychiatrist Major Nidal Hasan should get a death penalty trial for the 2009 shooting spree that killed 13 soldiers and wounded dozens more at Fort Hood, Texas.

• In September, however, he found the opposite at a show-cause hearing for Army Sergeant John Russell. Unlike Hasan, Pohl ruled, Russell had "an undisputed mental disease or defect" that made it "inappropriate" to pursue a capital case for allegedly killing five troops at the combat stress center at Iraq's Camp Liberty in May 2009.

• Pohl also presided at the so-called "mercy killing" trial of an Army captain, a tank commander, who killed a critically wounded insurgent in May 2004 and was captured on an aerial drone's videocam doing it.

Now, at a moment when most 60-year-old colonels are retiring from service, Pohl is chief military commissions judge, and has chosen to take on two of the most high-profile trials of his career: the 9/11 trial, and the trial of a man who allegedly engineered al-Qaida's 2000 USS Cole bombing.

Each case seeks the death penalty. Each is to be heard by a military commission, the tribunals that Bush had created after September 11 and that Obama ordered reformed upon taking office.

On Saturday, Pohl will face off for the first time with Khalid Sheik Mohammed, who bragged that he masterminded 9/11 for al-Qaida — wading into the case that's been a lightning rod for criticism that the court was created to cover up torture.

"All judges should be like him," says Indiana Supreme Court Justice Steve David, a retired Army colonel.

Pohl "takes what he does very seriously but not himself. He is fair and firm with a great sense of humor and a keen mind. If I were prosecuting or defending, he would be a great choice for judge."

He's by far the most experienced military judge currently in the Army, adds retired Marine Lieutenant Colonel Guy Womack, a veteran military defender of Pohl courts-martial from the Green Zone in Iraq, Germany and the United States, notably the Abu Ghraib case.

There, Pohl caused a mini-stir by refusing a guilty plea by Private First Class Lynndie England, the soldier photographed with a detainee on a leash. At her hearing, another soldier testified that England was ordered to pose for that picture, casting doubt on her admission of conspiracy. Pohl ordered a trial. She was found guilty.

Womack also described Pohl as one of the military's most methodical and careful crafters of judicial rulings to make sure they stand up to appellate scrutiny, a skill set he likely acquired in the early 1990s while working at the government appellate division in Falls Church, Virginia, defending Army convictions.

When he got the Abu Ghraib case, said Womack, Pohl kept "all of them, which is typical" — a practice Pohl has repeated at Guantánamo by handling all the trials of the former CIA captives.

Womack called Pohl's judicial style "dictatorial," and said the judge preferred to meet defense and prosecution attorneys in chambers, out of earshot of the public and off the record, before each day to map out how the session would proceed.

Of the 9/11 trial, said Womack, "Colonel Pohl would be the judge of choice for this case either because he doesn't want to be reversed, or because he wants to mean well. You need a strong judge; a weak judge would never get it done."

At the same time, he has shunned the spotlight.

Pohl wouldn't be interviewed for this profile.

He travels incognito, in jeans and polo shirt, no colonel's uniform for him. And he has stood in line to check in for the war court charter flight from Andrews Air Force Base undetected by reporters, legal observers, enlisted troops, even some lawyers going to Guantánamo, too.

An ex-Army prosecutor calls him "ego-less." David calls him "humble," and, oddly for a man so private, "someone that could do those commercials for Dove soap for men. He is very comfortable in his skin!"

Omitted from Pohl's terse court biography is that he was sworn in as a judge on May 19, 2000, after completing the Army's "Military Judge Course" with perfect scores on his final exams and graded practical exercises. That makes him the longest serving judge currently in the U.S. military. His biography also does not mention that he's been retained past his retirement date, October 1, 2010, and serves in a special status that requires renewal each year.

At Guantánamo, it's hard to spot him around the base, where he mostly splits his time between the court and his quarters. On a sticky evening in April, military lawyers donned crisp uniforms and civilians put on suits and ties to climb a hill to the old tribunal building and meet the judge in his chambers.

They found Pohl in jeans and loafers, no socks, and a pink sports shirt.

By gavel-down the next morning, he was in his Class Bs, the new Army uniform with a gold stripe down the trousers, topped by a black robe, commissions business attire.

Sometimes, you can see him at dinner in a corner booth at O'Kelly's pub. But, unlike the lawyers and reporters, who mingle and make small talk, he keeps the company of his staff, and he doesn't linger at the bar.

Judge Pohl comes to the 9/11 case from the peculiar position of having been passed over for promotion to general and retained past retirement, meaning "he's got nobody he has to please," says retired Lieutenant Colonel Victor M. Hansen, who spent 20 years as an Army lawyer and now teaches at New England Law School.

Hansen says Pohl has the judicial independence to throw out a case for insufficient evidence, no matter how high profile. "He would not bat an eye, and sleep like a baby that night."

Guantánamo's death penalty cases present Pohl with grave issues in a still-evolving system.

CIA torture is alleged. Some of the accused were waterboarded, threatened at gunpoint, sleep deprived, hung by their wrists, had their families threatened. A jury of U.S. military officers decides guilt or innocence, life or death. It's Pohl's job to decide what charges go to the jury and to make sure no evidence derived from abuse or worse is used at trial.

Pohl has yet to tip his hand on what he'll do if he's confronted with proof that U.S. agents tortured a captive. By international law, it's a war crime.

He has told defense lawyers it'll be their job to instruct him on how to regard the treatment, what rules apply, and it'll be his job "to follow the law and the preferences given to me by counsel and as I interpret it."

Hansen predicts that Pohl "will take the prosecution through the wringer" to make sure no "derivative evidence from coerced confessions comes in."

Earlier in their careers, Hansen was an Army prosecutor who worked opposite Pohl, who was taking a turn as defense attorney, typical of the Army legal career track. Hansen predicts the judge will be "tough on both sides" at the 9/11 trial.

"He's lived as a defense counsel in the Army, when you've got the whole prosecution against you. And so he's very good on keeping the government's feet to the fire."

Lawyers who've watched Pohl for years say he sweats the details, and demands the same of those who come to his court.

Pohl's an intensely private man.

Friends likewise declined to answer the most innocuous human interest questions. Not even what he does when Army plays Navy, a football rivalry that's a rite.

Public records show that James Lancaster Pohl earns $10,557 a month plus a housing allowance. He turns 61 next month.

He has served a stint in Korea, at least five years in Germany and is now based at Fort Benning in Georgia, where he registered as a voter in September 2008.

He's voted once since, on November 4, 2008, the historic elections that put the first African American in the White House.

He's a 1974 graduate of UCLA, where records show he got a bachelor of science degree in psychology. He went up the road to Malibu's Pepperdine University to get his law degree in 1978, and was admitted to the California Bar after Thanksgiving that year.

Several friends mentioned his hilarious sense of humor, which you only glimpse at court.

Once, a defense attorney invoked the estimate that it costs $800,000 a year per Guantánamo detainee and called it "a monument to waste."

Pohl retorted: "Let's say it is robustly resourced."

When a Saudi in his court pulled out a poster showing Obama's pledge to close Guantánamo, the judge dryly asked the man's attorney whether this should be marked as evidence.

"For as many big cases as he's had, that he's tried, the man really is ego-less," said former Army Major Christopher Graveline, who prosecuted the Abu Ghraib case and left the military in 2006. "It's never about him, it's about doing the process and trying to reach a fair result."

So when Pohl was holding hearings in Baghdad and President Bush remarked back home that Abu Ghraib prison should be demolished, the judge ruled for defense attorneys that the place needed protection.

"He gave a restraining order to the president and didn't bat an eyelash," said Graveline, who called it unprecedented and seemed genuinely dumbfounded by the order even now. "It wasn't like a chest thumping thing for him. He said, 'This is a crime scene and we're going to allow them to take a look at it.' "

In the same hearing Pohl ordered numerous officers in the military chain of command, notably the Central Command's chief, Army General John Abizaid, to undergo questioning by defense lawyers trying to make the case that the guards were following policy by posing detainees for humiliating photos. (They weren't, and all the soldiers were convicted.)

"I was shocked," Graveline said. "I was a captain at the time. I had to go back and tell my boss!"

The judge drew the line, however, when lawyers asked to question Defense Secretary Rumsfeld and Stephen Cambone, his undersecretary for intelligence.

Pohl ruled the defense had not drawn a clear enough line to the political hierarchy to merit a subpoena. But, he told them, if they could make a better case for it later, he'd reconsider the request — not unlike what he's been telling defense lawyers in the USS Cole case when their motions fail.

It was his handling of the Cole case that confounded the freshly minted Obama administration.

Just hours in office, Obama sent word to the Pentagon that he was suspending the trials at Guantánamo to review all the cases.

Obama had campaigned on a promise to close the prison in Cuba, and prosecutors filed motions to delay the arraignment of Abd al Rahim al Nashiri, who'd been waterboarded by the CIA.

Bush-era lawyers had approved death penalty charges in the dwindling days of the administration, and had served Nashiri on Christmas Eve. A statutory 30-day speedy trial clock was ticking.

And Pohl ruled against the new president.

"The Commission is bound by the law as it currently exists not as it may change in the future," he wrote. A continuance, he added, would "not serve the interests of justice."

The Pentagon had an out: It could withdraw the charges, without prejudice, and preserve the option to try Nashiri later. A Defense official ultimately did that. But not before a mini-maelstrom over Pohl's motives.

Anthony D. Romero, executive director of the American Civil Liberties Union, blamed Bush administration holdouts for "exploiting ambiguities in President Obama's Executive Order as a strategy to undercut the president's unequivocal promise to shut down Guantánamo." Former USS Cole Commander Kirk S. Lippold countered that the judge had delivered "a victory for the 17 families of the sailors who lost their lives on the USS Cole over eight years ago."

An online bulletin board for the military law community posted the development with the headline, "Army Judge Pohl Sticks it to Obama Administration."

Lawyers who had worked with the judge weighed in, and disagreed.

Pohl had applied the law, as written, to the government motion and could not find a reason to grant it. "On its face, the request to delay the arraignment is not reasonable," he had ruled.

Classic Pohl, it reflects the judge's penchant for noting the political and then arguing it's irrelevant.

At a hearing weeks after Obama was elected, but before he took office, Pohl announced the obvious:

"This court is aware that on January 20 there will be a new commander in chief, which may or may not impact on these proceedings." Meantime, he advised, everyone should stay focused "unless and until a competent authority tells us not to."

Guantánamo has a court like no other. It gets turned off and on by a charter flight carrying staff, and follows its own rulebook, not the Uniform Code of Military Justice used to try American soldiers. In between court sessions, Pohl issues instructions by email. He's announced that he'll accompany Nashiri prosecutors and defense lawyers to Yemen this summer, as deposition officer overseeing sworn testimony from Yemenis who can't be subpoenaed to the war court in Cuba.

"Location does not matter to Judge Pohl," said Graveline. "I know he's gone to Afghanistan, he's gone to Iraq. In that sense, he's very Army." He's held court at a forward operating base in Baghdad's Sadr City, the mostly Shiite slum that often simmered with anti-American unrest.

Once, during an Abu Ghraib hearing, the courtroom building shook with the thud of insurgent mortars striking inside Camp Victory in Baghdad. Pohl told everyone "to stop in place" for a few moments; the attack over, he ordered court to resume.

The Pentagon is bringing up to 60 reporters for the coming arraignment.

Pohl's made clear from the bench that he's a proponent of transparency but will close the court if the rules require it.

"I don't think he worries about the media scrutiny or the military scrutiny," said Hansen. "But he doesn't want to make a bad ruling or a rash ruling."

Plus, said Hansen, "He's certainly not afraid to ruffle feathers, to call it like he sees it and not necessarily worry about the long-term consequences."

At the end of the day, those who know him say, Pohl will play the role of referee at Guantánamo through the prism of three decades of service to the Army that honors judicial independence guided by what the rules created by Congress and the White House require.

Says Graveline, the Abu Ghraib prosecutor: "Judge Pohl knows what the law is — that's military law and U.S. law — and he follows the law. There's always evolving areas of law, but we try to analogize it to bedrock principles of justice, and it always goes back to, is this a fair process?"

Defense attorney Womack, who argued opposite Graveline, says that Pohl is capable of delivering that kind of justice. "He

knows the law. He has a strong personality. And you can't have
referees that vacillate."

Saturday, May 5, 2012

ARRAIGNED AGAIN, BUT SILENT AND DEFIANT

Accused 9/11 mastermind Khalid Sheik Mohammed and his
alleged co-conspirators put on a show of defiance during a mara-
thon war court arraignment, sitting mute rather than answering
their U.S. military judge's questions ahead of their trial on charges
of planning the terror attacks of September 11, 2001.

At no time did the five men enter pleas — dashing hopes that
they'd cut short a trial process potentially lasting years by admit-
ting their guilt or confessing to the crime in a bid to get a fast track
to martyrdom.

Instead, the military judge struggled to get through the basics
of starting the clock toward the capital murder trial, provisionally
scheduled for a year from now, by unilaterally assigning Pentagon-
paid defense attorneys to the five men accused of orchestrating the
worst terror attack on U.S. soil.

"Why is this so hard?" the judge, Army Colonel James Pohl,
declared in exasperation.

The five accused men allegedly trained, advised and financed
the 19 hijackers who commandeered airliners and then crashed
them into the World Trade Center, the Pentagon and a Pennsylvania field, killing 2,976 people. All could get the death penalty, if
convicted.*

The day began with guards carrying one accused terrorist, alleged 9/11 trainer Walid Bin Attash, into the maximum-security
courtroom at about 9 a.m. strapped into a restraint chair. The
judge said guards chose to put the captive in restraint because of
his behavior outside the court. There was no additional explanation.

The long session concluded more than 12 hours later with the
chief prosecutor, Army Brigadier General Mark Martins, and other
prosecutors reciting the 87-page charge sheet in English — and a
translator echoing each paragraph in Arabic because the accused
refused to don headphones for simultaneous translation. In between the accused slowed the process by not only accepting each

of the judge's offers for three prayer calls that required recesses in the long hearing but by also adding extra prayers in the midst of the proceedings.

From left, Mustafa al Hawsawi, Ammar al Baluchi, Ramzi Bin al Shibh, Walid Bin Attash, and Khalik Sheik Mohammed, pray at their arraignment, May 5, 2012. (©Janet Hamlin sketch artist)

At one point, Ramzi Bin al Shibh, the alleged organizer of an al-Qaida cell in Hamburg, Germany, got up from his defendant's chair and began to pray. He stood, arms crossed on his chest, then at one point got on his knees. The guards didn't move and the court watched in silence until he finished.

The rare Saturday war court session was the first appearance of the five men since January 21, 2009, a day after the inauguration of President Barack Obama. Since then, Obama has worked with Congress to provide the men with greater protections. But the Pentagon-paid defense lawyers wouldn't stick to the script, either, instead peppering the proceedings with a litany of procedural protests — about a lack of resources, about presumptive classification requirements, and about allegations of abuse of their clients at the detention center, miles from the war court compound called Camp Justice.

Mohammed was attired in a turban and what appeared to be a white gown. His massive beard looked reddish, apparently from henna, rather than the speckled gray of a few years ago.

The prison's command staff "does not provide detainees with hair dye," said Navy Captain Robert Durand, a spokesman, in response to a request for an explanation. He added that the detention center "conducts safe, humane, legal and transparent care and custody of detainees."

All day long, Mohammed refused to answer the judge's questions. And, with one exception, his four alleged collaborators fell in right behind him. Some appeared to be reading the Quran rather than responding to the judge's questions.

The Heritage Foundation's Cully Stimson, a longtime war court observer and reserve Navy judge, described it as "coordinated chaos." Mohammed, Stimson said in an exchange via Twitter, "wants to control the courtroom."

But Mohammed's demeanor was in dramatic contrast to his appearance at the previous arraignment, June 5, 2008, in the case that was started under President George W. Bush but was withdrawn by Obama while he reformed the military commissions with Congress.

Four years ago, the self-described architect of the September 11 attacks disrupted the proceedings by reciting Quran verses aloud and declaring that he welcomed the death penalty.

"This is what I wish — to be martyred," he told the first judge on the earlier case, a Marine colonel.

That occurred less than two years after Mohammed's arrival at Guantánamo from more than three years of custody in secret CIA prisons, during which he was subjected to 183 rounds of waterboarding and other aggressive interrogation techniques.

In this court appearance, the only verbal outburst came from Bin al Shibh, who blurted at one point that the prison camp leadership was just like Moammar Gadhafi, the slain Libyan dictator.

When the judge tried to hush Bin al Shibh, explaining the accused would be given a chance to speak later, the Yemeni replied: "Maybe they are going to kill us and say that we are committing suicide."

Defense lawyers said, alternately, that the men were protesting prison camp interference in the attorney-client relationship;

something that happened that morning involving Bin Attash's prosthetic leg during his transfer from his cell to the war court; being strip-searched before arriving at the court complex; and their treatment in years of CIA custody prior to their September 2006 arrival at Guantánamo.

Outside the war court, Tara Henwood Butzbaugh holds a picture of her brother, John Henwood, who was working as a bond trader on the 105th floor of Tower One of the World Trade Center and was killed during the 9/11 attack, May 4, 2012. (Walter Michot/Miami Herald)

"These men have been mistreated," declared Pentagon-paid defense counsel Cheryl Bormann, Bin Attash's attorney, a civilian who specializes in death penalty cases.

Bormann stunned spectators by turning up at the compound in a black *abaya*, cloaking her from head to toe — covering her hair, leaving only her face showing.

With the exception of Bin al Shibh's outburst, the men adopted looks of disinterest throughout the hearing. During recesses, they spoke animatedly between themselves and across the five rows they occupied in the courtroom, at times laughing and smiling.

For a while, Mohammed's nephew, Ammar al Baluchi, leafed through a copy of The Economist. He handed it back to Mustafa al Hawsawi, sitting in the defendant's row behind him during a recess. The nephew, a Pakistani, and Hawsawi, a Saudi, are accused in the charge sheets of wiring money to the September 11 hijackers.

Pohl questioned Bin Attash's military attorney, Air Force Captain Michael Schwartz, about whether Bin Attash would sit peacefully if the restraints were removed. Midway through the morning, the judge instructed him to be released. He sat for the rest of the day in an ordinary court chair, but didn't appear to be following the proceedings.

At issue early in the hearing was whether the accused 9/11 conspirators would accept their Pentagon-paid defense counsel, a key preliminary step to holding an arraignment. The defense lawyers sought, first, to argue motions at the court alleging inadequate defense resources, prison camp interference in the attorney-client relationship and restrictive conditions imposed on their legal duties.

Pohl would have none of it. He insisted that the issue of appointment of counsel come first.

Then, one by one, the judge read a script to each of the accused, spelling out each man's right to a Pentagon-paid legal team. Pohl periodically asked each of the men whether he understood what was being said.

None replied, so he noted over and over again for the record, "Accused refuses to answer."

And, then one by one, the judge unilaterally appointed their Pentagon-paid attorneys to defend them.

Book editor's note: By the time of this arraignment, prosecutors had named 2,976 9/11 victims, three more than in the original charges.

WHAT NOT TO WEAR: GUANTÁNAMO EDITION

Accused 9/11 mastermind Khalid Sheik Mohammed wanted to wear paramilitary-style woodland-patterned camouflage clothing to court.

His nephew wanted to sport the same cap he used to pose for a Red Cross photo.

A series of documents unsealed at the Pentagon reveal a source of tension at the arraignment of the September 11 accused at Guantánamo — the men sought to wear what the prison camps commander considered alternately unsafe, culturally inappropriate or disruptive attire. And he forbade it.

Now, lawyers for the five men who face a death penalty trial are appealing to the chief military commissions judge to stop the camps commander, Rear Admiral David B. Woods, from interfering with their clients' court wardrobe.

The challenge to the authority of Woods, who runs the camps that house 169 prisoners, is the latest in a series by defense attorneys who argue that the career Navy officer, whose specialty is intelligence jamming, has interfered with the court process by having his forces go through the captives' attorney-client mail. Woods, who will be replaced at the U.S. Navy base later this month, has countered that security is paramount.

Now, in an affidavit, the admiral explains how he and the colonel in charge of the prison camp guard force went through the accused's proposed wardrobe (provided by their Pentagon attorneys, most uniformed officers) and rejected everything but the white gowns and prison camp uniforms that they wore to court for the unusual Saturday arraignment.

As a result, the most traditionally clad person in court was a secular attorney, Cheryl Bormann from Chicago, who donned a black *abaya*, a shapeless head scarf and gown that covered her hair and left only her face exposed.

Bormann, paid by the Pentagon to defend accused al-Qaida deputy Walid Bin Attash, said she was respecting her client's Muslim sensibilities and at one point scolded women on the Pentagon prosecution team to watch their hemlines.

The hearing spanned 13 hours and began with attorneys bitterly complaining that the five men accused of organizing, training and funding the September 11 hijackings were refused their choice of attire.

Khalid Sheik Mohammed, once the judge had ruled in his favor, sits at a defense table wearing a camouflage vest during the third day of a pretrial hearing, October 17, 2012. The judge, Colonel James Pohl is at top right with his court security officer beside him. (©Janet Hamlin sketch artist)

In the instance of the alleged mastermind, Woods wrote, Mohammed's lawyer presented a jacket, hunting vest and fabric for a proposed turban all made of "woodlands camouflage print" — shown with a label calling it a "Ranger's Vest" in a court document. Woods said he forbade it because of "security and good order and discipline concerns, and because they were inappropriate courtroom attire."

War crimes defendants at World War II tribunals in Tokyo and Nuremberg were able to wear military-style clothing to their trials, said Mohammed's attorney, Army Captain Jason Wright. Mohammed sought to wear "militia-style" clothing in the Laws of Armed Conflict sense of the term, as a paramilitary organization.

Two of the accused sought to wear traditional Afghan caps and vests, no camouflage. Lawyers bought them in a Virginia shop called Halalco that specializes in Muslim products. And in each instance Woods rejected that choice of attire because "such vests are traditionally only worn during the winter or in colder climates."

Jay Connell, the attorney for Mohammed's nephew, known as Ammar al Baluchi, said the cap that his client wasn't allowed to wear to court was the same as the one he wore to pose for the Red Cross. Those photos have turned up on websites sympathetic to al-Qaida. Neither contained any messages, he said, describing Baluchi's proposed wardrobe as "banal."

All five of the men who got to Guantánamo in 2006 from CIA custody were allowed to wear their skullcaps to court, Woods said in the affidavit, "in recognition of their cultural and religious significance."

And they were allowed to bring their prayer rugs with them, unfurling them inside the maximum-security courtroom during breaks.

But Woods wrote he was forbidding "clothing that is inconsistent with the decorum and dignity of a court proceeding whether in the United States or the Middle East."

Plus, no vests allowed. Or anything with pockets, "a potential means of removing unauthorized items from the courtroom."

"Excessive clothing could potentially complicate the guards' ability to gain control of a detainee."

Guards brought four of the September 11 defendants to court unshackled. Bin Attash was brought in a restraint chair like those used for force-feeding prisoners, with his prosthetic leg detached due to an unspecific episode prior to the hearing. Eventually he was freed.

Bin Attash lost a leg in fighting in Afghanistan before the September 11 attacks and also planned to dress paramilitary style for court. His lawyers got him a "foul-weather jacket of the Desert Camouflage Uniform print," similar to those worn by U.S. Coast

Guard members at the war court, according to Woods' affidavit. "It was not culturally appropriate courtroom clothing," Woods said.

Woods' spokesman did not immediately respond to a request for comment, including whether the admiral consulted with the judge, an Army colonel, on what would constitute "culturally appropriate clothing" in his court.

At the May 5 hearing, the judge, Colonel Pohl, said he was willing to take up the issue. "The rule is they are entitled to wear appropriate non-prison garb attire," Pohl said, adding that if Woods made "some arbitrary and capricious decision on that, let me know about it and I will revisit it."

The motion seeks to do just that. It argues that the men are still suffering from their treatment in CIA custody (Mohammed was waterboarded 183 times) and that Woods' "arbitrary, unpredictable and standard-less denial of the detainees' right to wear appropriate clothing" to court "replicated the psychologically disruptive nature of the CIA procedures."

Also, they argue that Woods is prejudicing the case against them. Forbidding them "clothing customarily worn by belligerents within the context of hostilities under the laws of armed conflict reverses the presumption of innocence," they say. Mohammed is the self-described former chief of operations of al-Qaida and has called himself a revolutionary just like George Washington.

At the prison camps they are held as the enemy. But at the war court they are afforded a presumption of innocence, according to the Pentagon, one reason why earlier judges have urged defendants not to wear their prison uniforms to court. But one of the accused, Saudi Mustafa al Hawsawi, wanted to wear an orange jumpsuit, which Woods forbade, citing "institutional and security concerns."

Only certain captives are kept in orange jumpsuits, the admiral wrote, and Hawsawi is not among them.

But orange jumpsuits have been seen at the war court before: Afghan teen Mohammed Jawad, since released after a federal judge ruled him unlawfully detained, was arraigned in March 2008 in an orange jumpsuit and ankle shackles, demonstrating he was uncooperative with his captors. And two years earlier Binyam Mohamed donned a traditional Pakistani tunic and trousers, a *shalwar khameez,* that his lawyer had had dyed jumpsuit orange in London for his arraignment. Mohamed has since been released to live in Britain, and cleared of all charges.

Hawsawi's attorney, Navy Commander Walter Ruiz, said the Saudi wanted to wear the orange jumpsuit because it "more accurately reflects his status as a political prisoner in relation to war hostilities rather than the softer and less accurate 'detainee.' " It was provided, he said, by a founder of the Code Pink anti-war group, Medea Benjamin.

Thursday, January 31, 2013

REMOTE CENSOR SURPRISES JUDGE

The military judge presiding at the September 11 trial mil ordered the government to unplug any outside censors who can reach into his courtroom and silence the war crimes tribunal.

Only a court security officer sitting in court, at the judge's elbow, has the authority to hit a mute button on the proceedings if there's a suspicion that national security information could be spilled, Judge Pohl announced.

At issue was a mysterious episode Monday when the sound to spectators was suddenly replaced by white noise in court after 9/11 mastermind Khalid Sheik Mohammed's attorney David Nevin said the word "secret."

Nobody inside court did it. The judge erupted in anger, and appeared surprised that "some external body" had the power to prevent the public from listening to the proceedings — which are broadcast in the spectator's gallery on a 40-second delay.

"This is the last time *that* will happen," the judge said Thursday. "No third party can unilaterally cut off the broadcast."

The court was just beginning to tackle a defense request that the judge issue a protective order on whatever remnants exist of the CIA's secret overseas prison network. President Obama ordered those facilities closed upon taking office.

Defense lawyers say the five men now charged as the alleged plotters of the September 11, 2001, hijackings were tortured at those places. The chief prosecutor, General Martins, says no evidence obtained other than voluntarily will be used at their death penalty trial.

Army Brigadier General Mark Martins, the chief prosecutor for military commissions, briefs the press after the arraignment of the alleged 9/11 plotters, May 6, 2012. (Walter Michot/Miami Herald)

Pohl never once mentioned the CIA, the agency that controls information about what happened to alleged mastermind Mohammed, whom agents waterboarded 183 times, and his four co-defendants. Instead, he referred to the "OCA" (short for the original classification authority), a generic term for any agency of the U.S. government that stamped a document or declared a program Top Secret.

"This is the last time that an OCA or any third party will be permitted to unilaterally decide if the broadcast should be suspended. The OCA, any OCA does not work for the commission and therefore has no independent decision-making authority on how these proceedings are to be conducted."

On Tuesday, civilian 9/11 prosecutor Joanna Baltes cast the role of the OCA as an approved extension of the military commissions.

"The OCA, original classification authority, reviews closed-circuit feed of the proceedings to conduct a classification review to ensure that classified information is not inadvertently disclosed," she said in a note to the judge.

It was not immediately clear if the judge would order the prosecution to present a witness to swear that outside censor buttons had been unplugged. Defense lawyers asked the judge to have the war crimes prosecutor certify it, once done.

The drama of the day occurred out of earshot of the five men accused of conspiring in the September 11 hijackings. Mohammed and the others chose not to attend the hearing, a pretrial prerogative the judge has granted them. The outside censorship episode occurred on the first day of proceedings after the judge formally approved the 40-second audio delay in the September 11 trial, rejecting an American Civil Liberties Union argument that it transformed a live court into a "censorship chamber."

The way the Guantánamo war court works: Spectators watch the proceedings live inside a soundproof room at the back of the court, hearing the audio 40 seconds later. If the court security officer functioning as a censor deems what is being said is a national security secret, he pushes a button and obscures the sound with white noise.

A red emergency light then spins in court to signal to everyone inside the tribunal chamber that the outside world can no longer hear them.

White noise has silenced the court three times since Mohammed and his fellow defendants were arraigned on May 5, and in each instance the judge or prosecutor concluded it was not legitimately censored, or "closure" as the lawyers and judge refer to it. All three instances occurred while defense lawyers were speaking — two of them U.S. military officers arguing to the judge in uniform.

Wednesday, April 16, 2014

DELAYS FRUSTRATE 9/11 VICTIMS' FAMILIES

Frustration simmered into suspicion as relatives of September 11 victims attending stalled hearings here accused a jealous Justice Department of conducting an FBI probe of 9/11 defense lawyers to derail the long-awaited war crimes tribunal.

"These things just don't happen. It's not some rogue FBI agent. This had to be approved from the highest level of the FBI to do this," said Don Arias of Panama City, Florida, a former Air Force officer and New York City firefighter whose brother Adam was killed in the World Trade Center on September 11, 2001.

"Some could even say that this was done purposely to derail these hearings and to force it back to federal court," he told reporters. His sister Lorraine added, "It looks like a well-orchestrated snafu. We're going to stall now for them to be investigated. A reappointment process could drag it out another year or more."

The latest, 10th round of hearings stalled on the revelation that two FBI agents questioned a security officer on one 9/11 defense team, then had him sign a nondisclosure agreement, an incursion into attorney-client confidentiality that defense lawyers call "chilling."

The war court was dark a day after the judge, Colonel Pohl, issued a bench order to anyone who ever served on the defense teams of the September 11 case, past and present, to admit if he or she was "contacted or interviewed by agents of any federal government agency," regardless of any nondisclosure agreement.

At issue for the FBI, apparently, is who gave The Huffington Post and a British TV channel an unclassified 36-page jailhouse commentary "Invitation to Happiness," by the alleged 9/11 mastermind Khalid Sheik Mohammed. It skewers American values and society.

The military has held nine rounds of pretrial hearings since the five accused were formally charged in the case May 5, 2012. Defense attorneys and prosecutors are still haggling over what law applies to the death penalty case and what will constitute trial evidence against five men who spent years in secret CIA prisons.

The judge has yet to set a provisional trial date and the Pentagon has yet to designate a site at the base to carry out any death sentences.

Charlie Clyne of New York lost his wife, Susan, an insurance executive, in the World Trade Center, leaving him to raise their four kids. He declared the proceedings "a farce."

"These parasites did it," he said. "Why the dog and pony show? They're guilty. Let's try them, fairly. And then kill them. Take them out to the Bronx Zoo — no, I'm serious — feed them to the lions."

Suburban Bostonian Claudia Jacobs, whose brother Ariel was killed in the attack, didn't necessarily buy into the conspiracy but did describe the less than three hours of court before the FBI probe froze the proceedings as eye-opening.

As she sat in the courtroom watching the alleged 9/11 plotters through thick glass, and listening to the proceedings on a 40-second delay, an old adage came to mind:

"What you should never see made is sausage and legislation," she said. "I would add 9/11 hearings to that. It's frustrating and long and I understand it has to be the process. But it is also at the same time quite painful not to have this thing resolved before now."

Wednesday, April 20, 2016

TRIAL BY SKYPE?

The Obama administration is proposing to hold parts of the Guantánamo trials by video feed and let war court judges outsource some legal decisions to secondary military judges in a bid to speed up the war court.

The Pentagon submitted the request to Congress on April 14, coincidentally just after the Miami Herald published a leaked report on potential toxic hazards at the war court compound in Cuba, Camp Justice.

Rather, Navy Commander Gary Ross said that the proposed Military Commissions Act Amendments of 2016 are "designed to improve the efficacy, efficiency, and fiscal accountability of the commission process." They are "fully in alignment with the interests of justice and consistent with our American values of fairness in judicial processes."

As long as there's no jury present, under the new vision, a judge could convene a hearing elsewhere and let the accused terrorists participate, Skype-style. Ross cast it as "another tool" for the military judge "to facilitate the scheduling and convening of hearings." The idea is "to provide flexibility at the military judge's discretion to convene hearings without requiring all necessary participants to travel to Guantánamo Bay, Cuba."

A veteran death penalty defense attorney on the September 11 case, Jay Connell, called the idea unworkable "because everyone has a right to be present at their own trial." He reminded that the Pentagon prosecutor has argued in court that the alleged 9/11 plotters should be required to attend all pretrial hearings. The trial judge allows them to waive attendance after an initial appearance.

Sign at Camp Justice, November 4, 2014. (Walter Michot/Miami Herald)

The new rules would authorize a military judge to take a war crimes guilty plea by video feed.

Criminal defense attorney Michael Tigar, who has never practiced at Guantánamo Bay, said that similar remote hearings were "floated through the Federal Criminal Rules Committee" about two years ago and rejected. "The Confrontation Clause has to do with physical presence."

"I think it's a terrible idea. We want the judge to look the defendant in the eye," said Tigar, professor emeritus at the law schools of Duke and American University. He quoted a colleague, the late criminal defense attorney Michael J. Kennedy, as nicknaming the scheme "Defendants Electronic Access Terminal Housing," whose acronym is DEATH.

Another proposed change would permit a trial judge to assign a secondary military judge to "rule upon one or more collateral or other motions before a military commission," according to the request the Pentagon sent Congress.

Approaching hurricanes, a communications break, discovery of a secret CIA mute button at the war court and a sick lawyer have all derailed hearings after a Pentagon plane shuttled participants from Andrews Air Force Base to Cuba — including the judge and attorneys, court stenographers, linguists, paralegals, couriers, journalists and September 11 victim observers.

The new proposal is the opposite of a withdrawn Pentagon order to speed up the trials by having judges live at the Navy base. A Navy judge ruled the order an attempt to unlawfully influence the court, and Pohl froze the 9/11 trial until the Pentagon rescinded it.

Officials could not put a price tag on the proposals. The prison and the war court cost $455 million in 2015, according to the Department of Defense. With 80 war-on-terror captives currently at Guantánamo, 10 of them with war court cases, that works out to $5.56 million a year per prisoner at the detention center staffed with 2,000 Pentagon personnel.

"Holding a trial without a defendant present would not produce a conviction that would hold up on an appeal," said Connell, who is paid by the Pentagon to defend Ammar al Baluchi, 38, nephew of accused 9/11 plot mastermind Khalid Sheik Mohammed.

Virtual presence at a hearing would only permit the accused to see what a camera shows. It's one thing to take testimony from a witness remotely, Connell said, but quite another to have the defendant participate in a Skype-style setting, something the Pentagon is already using for Guantánamo detainees to ask for release before a federal review board.

For those parole-like hearings, the Pentagon lets the captive's lawyer go to Guantánamo to sit with the prisoner asking for freedom.

But adopting that formula for video-fed trial hearings would deny the accused "a host of intangible factors," Connell said, "such as the relationship between the defendants and the judge and the other lawyers."

Tigar, who has represented a long string of unpopular clients from Oklahoma City bomber Terry Nichols to Abbie Hoffman and a lawyer in the Chicago Seven case, said some might consider remote viewing of pretrial hearings, not the jury trial itself, as "just a trivial departure."

"But the Sixth Amendment doesn't have a footnote that says, 'Oh, by the way, trivial departures are OK,' " he said.

Tuesday, May 31, 2016

MILITARY JUDGE SHOUTS DOWN KSM

Accused 9/11 mastermind Khalid Sheik Mohammed began complaining to his military judge, and the judge shouted him down in a brief, at times baffling, episode at the war court.

At one point, Mohammed, 51, inexplicably announced in Arabic "this is a nuclear bomb in the world," as related through a court interpreter, after the judge threatened to eject him from court. After court, Mohammed's attorney, David Nevin said he thought the remark "referred to the World War II bombing of innocent people in Hiroshima in Japan," and called it "a placeholder for the idea that the United States has done harmful acts."

Pohl reminded the alleged terrorist known as KSM that his Pentagon-paid lawyers speak for him in court. "He's an American," Mohammed replied, as Pohl continued to try to shut him up. "They're American."

Mohammed, facing a death penalty tribunal whose date has not yet been set, has mostly let his lawyers speak for him. But he chimed in at the end of lengthy legal arguments over a proposal to take sworn videotaped testimony here in October from elderly and infirm relatives of people killed on Sept. 11, 2001.

The war court prosecutor wants to preserve the testimony for use at trial, and the sentencing portion if Mohammed is convicted of war crimes. Mohammed is accused of hatching the plot and dispatching the 9/11 hijackers who killed nearly 3,000 people in New York, Pennsylvania and at the Pentagon. He accused Pohl of "not being neutral."

Mohammed was clad in his typical war court attire: a woodland pattern jacket atop a traditional white robe, a white turban on his head. His beard, as usual, was dyed bright orange. Before Mohammed could elaborate the judge shouted him down to be quiet, adding that he will not tolerate defendants talking without permission in his court.

Chapter 6

FOREVER PRISONERS

Army guards escort a detainee into Camp 5, October 18, 2011.
(Petty Officer Kilho Park/U.S. Navy)

Tuesday, June 28, 2011

AFGHAN MAN COMMITS SUICIDE

An Afghan man who was found hanging from a bedsheet at Guantánamo was held by the Pentagon as an "indefinite detainee" — an Obama administration designation originally conferred on 48 captives at the prison camps in Cuba.

Department of Defense officials have not released the list of indefinite detainees. Nor have they notified the men of their status as ineligible for either trial or release among the captives currently held in Guantánamo.

But a Pentagon spokesman, Dave Oten, confirmed that the May 18, 2011, death of a captive known to his lawyers as Hajji Nassim and to the Pentagon as Inayatullah reduced the indefinite detainee tally.

"It's a sad case, a very sad case," said his Miami attorney Paul Rashkind. A federal public defender, Rashkind had been on the Afghan's case for about a year. He said, though he had never been told of his client's status, he might have been able to persuade the government otherwise.

"We were hopeful that we would be able to complete a psychiatric profile of him and present that information to the government in the hopes they would release him," said Rashkind.

The Pentagon had claimed that Inayatullah was an al-Qaida emir in Iran who planned and directed the group's terror operations. He got to Guantánamo in 2007, one of the last detainees sent there. Rashkind countered that the captive was never known as Inayatullah anywhere but in Guantánamo, never had a role in al-Qaida and was in fact named Hajji Nassim and ran a cellphone shop in Iran near the Afghan border.

Guards discovered him early May 18 dangling from bed linen in a prison recreation yard in what the U.S. Southern Command described as a "suspected suicide." Rashkind said his client had a history of psychological problems and spent long stretches in the prison's psychiatric ward.

The lawyer had several times obtained permission to bring a private civilian psychiatrist to the base to help with the case of the 37-year-old captive. Rashkind said he had no doubts the death was a suicide.

In February, the military said Awal Gul, 48, another Afghan indefinite detainee, collapsed and died of an apparent heart attack after working out on an exercise machine in a Camp 6 recreation yard. He had been held as a one-time Taliban official.

The remains of both men were repatriated within days of their deaths for burial in Afghanistan.

Monday, June 17, 2013

LAWSUIT UNMASKS 'INDEFINITE DETAINEES'

The Obama administration lifted a veil of secrecy surrounding the status of the detainees at Guantánamo, for the first time publicly naming the four dozen captives it defined as men too dangerous to transfer but who cannot be tried in a court of law.

The names had been a closely held secret since a multi-agency task force sifted through the files of the Guantánamo detainees in 2009 trying to achieve President Obama's order to close the detention center. In January 2010, the task force revealed that it classified 48 Guantánamo captives as dangerous but ineligible for trial because of a lack of evidence, or because the evidence was too tainted.

They became "indefinite detainees," a form of war prisoner held under Congress' 2001 Authorization for Use of Military Force. In essence, they became forever prisoners of a forever war on terror.

The Department of Defense released the list to the Miami Herald, which, with the assistance of Yale Law School students, had sued for it in federal court. The Pentagon also sent the list to the House and Senate Armed Services Committees, a Department of Defense official said.

According to the list, the men designated for indefinite detention are 26 Yemenis, 12 Afghans, 3 Saudis, 2 Kuwaitis, 2 Libyans, a Kenyan, a Moroccan and a Somali.

Human rights groups denounced the existence of such a list.

Amnesty International's Zeke Johnson called "fundamentally flawed" the notion of classifying captives as indefinite detainees. "Under international human rights law," he said, "all of the detainees should either be charged and fairly tried in federal court, or released."

Human Rights First's Dixon Osburn hailed release of the list through the Freedom of Information Act: "It is fundamental to democracy that the public know the identities of the people our nation is depriving of liberty and why they are being detained."

Some of the men on the list are currently on hunger strike and being force-fed at the prison — for example, Kuwaitis Fawzi al Odah, 36, and Fayez al Kandari, 35, and Yemeni Abdel Malik Wahab al Rahabi, about 43, who in March, according to his lawyer David Remes, vowed to fast until he got out of the prison "either dead or alive."

Guards and detainee as seen through a window from Camp 5, January 20, 2010. (Carol Rosenberg/Miami Herald)

Two men on the list are deceased. Both Afghans, one committed suicide with a bedsheet in a recreation yard at Guantánamo's Camp 6 for cooperative captives and the other died of a heart attack, also in Camp 6. So now the 166 captives at Guantánamo actually include 46 indefinite detainees.

Two former CIA captives, held apart from the majority of Guantánamo's prisoners as high-value detainees are also listed as indefinite detainees: Mohammed Rahim, an Afghan man, and Hassan Guleed of Somalia.

Administration officials have through the years described a variety of reasons why the men could not face trial: Evidence against some of them was too tainted by CIA or other interrogation torture or abuse to be admissible in a court; insufficient evidence to prove an individual detainee had committed a crime; or military intelligence opinions that certain captives had received suicide or other type of terrorist training, and had vowed to carry out an attack on release.

In all, the list identifies 34 candidates for prosecution. Army Brigadier General Mark Martins, the Pentagon's chief war crimes prosecutor, said recently that fewer than those 34 men will be charged because of federal court rulings that disqualified "providing material support for terror" as a war crime in most if not all Guantánamo cases.

At Human Rights Watch, senior counterterrorism counsel Andrea Prasow called the list "a fascinating window into the Obama administration's thinking circa January 2010" but both flawed and somewhat irrelevant today.

"Many of the detainees designated for prosecution can only be prosecuted in civilian court," she said. "So unless Congress lifts the restrictions banning their transfer they are effectively 'indefinite detainees.' "

She also noted that the Obama administration was reportedly considering transferring five Afghan Taliban to custody of the Qatari government in exchange for the release of U.S. POW Bowe Bergdahl.

The Wall Street Journal named the five men and all appear on the list as indefinite detainees: Mullah Mohammad Fazl, Mullah Norullah Noori, Mohammed Nabi, Khairullah Khairkhwa, and Abdul Haq Wasiq.

One man categorized in 2010 as a possible candidate for prosecution was Saudi Arabian Mohammed al Qahtani, 37, once suspected of being the absent "20th hijacker" in the September 11 plot. He was so brutally interrogated at Guantánamo that a senior Pentagon official excluded him from the Bush-era 9/11 war crimes charge sheet. That official, Susan Crawford, told The Washington Post's Bob Woodward that Qahtani's treatment amounted to torture.

Editor's Note: The Miami Herald's Carol Rosenberg, with the assistance of the Media Freedom and Information Access Clinic at the Yale Law School, filed suit in federal court in Washington in March for the list under the Freedom of Information Act. The students, in collaboration with Washington attorney Jay Brown, represented Rosenberg in a lawsuit that specifically sought the names of the 46 surviving prisoners. Hours before the release of the names, U.S. District Court Judge Gladys Kessler had set a July 8 deadline for the government to update the court on its classification review. The Justice Department gave the list to Brown, who in turn gave it to Rosenberg.

Wednesday, November 5, 2014

FORMER 'FOREVER PRISONER' GOES HOME

A Kuwaiti aircraft carrying a long-held captive left Guantánamo Navy base before dawn, sealing the first repatriation of a "forever prisoner" whose dangerousness was downgraded by the U.S. government parole board.

Fawzi al Odah, 37, was held for nearly 13 years in Cuba, starting off in the crude outdoor Camp X-Ray. He was never charged with a crime.

His release was the first since President Obama's controversial May 31 transfer of five Afghan Taliban prisoners to the custody of Qatar in exchange for U.S. Army Sergeant Bowe Bergdahl, a war prisoner of a Taliban affiliate.

It also came within a day of midterm elections roiled by debate over Obama's ambitions to close the offshore prison. In Kansas, Republican Senator Pat Roberts had campaigned on a pledge to prevent relocation of the detainees to the U.S. military prison at Fort Leavenworth. He won as the GOP took control of the Senate for the first time in eight years.

"Fawzi bears no ill will against the United States despite his long incarceration," said his attorney, Eric Lewis. "He wants to get on with his life."

Odah, though never charged, was among the most high-profile prisoners because his name appeared in U.S. Supreme Court cases and his father doggedly campaigned for his release.

"We are a very, very tight family," Odah's father, Khalid, told the Witness to Guantánamo project, adding that his wife had left their eldest son's bedroom untouched throughout his long absence.

The father, a former Kuwaiti Air Force officer, said his son was a school teacher in a region near the Afghanistan-Pakistan border before his capture by bounty hunters who handed him over to the Americans.

The U.S. military considered him to be a member of al-Qaida who was captured in Pakistan after fleeing Afghanistan through the Tora Bora mountains after the 9/11 attacks. The parole board approved his repatriation in July on a promise from Kuwait that he would take part in a minimum yearlong rehabilitation program.

Kuwait had long sought the return of all its citizen detainees. So much so that the emir personally asked Obama and President Bush before him to release them. When Odah went before a parole board this summer, a senior Kuwaiti diplomat attended a closed circuit viewing of the public portion of hearing.

Odah's attorneys were among the earliest and most persistent challengers of Bush's right to lock him up as an enemy combatant. He was named in two U.S. Supreme Court cases that gave detainees the right to file habeas corpus petitions. His attorneys then argued his case before a federal judge and lost in September 2009.

Monday, March 28, 2016

GUANTÁNAMO LIMBO

Mustafa al Shamiri spent most of his years at Guantánamo wrongly described as an al-Qaida trainer and facilitator, a captive of consequence, until his first parole-style hearing revealed an astonishing admission. An intelligence review "discredited" the most damning parts of his dossier in his 14th year of U.S. military detention. He was mistaken for someone else with a similar name.

Within weeks, the Periodic Review Board concluded he was a low-level fighter, not a leader, who could leave Guantánamo, preferably to an Arabic-speaking country to ease him into a new life. Today, two months after that decision, the 37-year-old Yemeni is still in custody, awaiting a country to take him.

But he is one of the lucky ones. Another 40 captives who also were deemed ineligible for release in 2009 have yet to have their fate decided by the board. Can they go or must they stay?

It wasn't supposed to work that way. When President Obama ordered the Department of Defense on March 7, 2011, to set up inter-agency reviews for Guantánamo detainees, something the International Red Cross had long advocated, those detainees not charged with a crime and not cleared to go with security arrangements were supposed to get a first hearing within a year.

Now at the current rate, says attorney Shane Kadidal of the Center for Constitutional Rights, "it seems utterly implausible that they can complete these hearings before the end of the president's term." Kadidal has gone before the board once with a client who was ultimately cleared to go.

And these are baseline hearings that decide not that a captive can leave — just whether the State Department can start looking for a country to take him in. Once a destination is arranged, a second intelligence analysis ensues to determine if a would-be host country offers robust enough security arrangements.

A Pentagon spokesman, Navy Commander Gary Ross, said all Guantánamo detainees entitled to an "initial hearing" should get one "by the end of the fall." After a hearing the board decides each case, a process that in one Yemeni's case has gone on eight months.

A Justice Department lawyer, Joseph Folio, told a federal judge that the process was hampered by the need to create a bureaucracy to handle Obama's order and complicated by the participation of multiple agencies in it.

As for the inertia, Kadidal says some people in the Pentagon may have purposely slowed the process. Not that they're wedded to keeping these specific last detainees. Instead some at the Pentagon want to preserve the military's authority to hold detainees in an offshore prison, if unintentionally but inevitably "perpetually trapped in a legal quagmire that does not clean itself up."

Or as Kadidal put it: "Bureaucracies have their own sort of agendas."

Government officials have blamed a variety of factors, including the complicated task of combing through intelligence agencies' files. Their task is to sort fact from fiction in a place that in some instances may not have gotten it right for years, as the story of Shamiri illustrates.

As anonymous as Shamiri was before his hearing, Mohammed al Qahtani is infamous.

He was suspected of being the would-be 20th hijacker in the September 11 plot and interrogated in such a ruthless fashion that someone leaked his interrogation log to Time magazine in 2005. By 2008, a senior Pentagon official rejected his prosecution in the joint trial of five men accused as 9/11 plotters.

"We tortured Qahtani," Pentagon war court overseer Susan Crawford told journalist Bob Woodward in early 2009. Yet a federal task force sorting through the Guantánamo files for the new Obama administration included Qahtani on a January 22, 2010, list of trial candidates.

Now 40, the Saudi citizen has never been charged. And he only just recently was assigned a hearing to decide whether he'll present a significant continuing security threat to the United States. If so, because he's not charged, he could be added to the list of indefinite detainees, a forever prisoner, ineligible for release.

"There hasn't been the urgency that one would expect" for something that Obama ordered done, said Kadidal, a lawyer representing Qahtani. That was the president's second order to get something related to Guantánamo done within a year. The first, issued January 22, 2009, was to sort through the captives' files and close the detention center. On that day the prison held 242 captives. Now there are 91.

Of the 24 detainees who have gotten full board hearings, 20 men once considered trial candidates or forever prisoners have been approved for release, with security arrangements.

Just four who were reviewed were still considered too dangerous to let go. Forty captives have yet to get their first hearings.

While the board hasn't finished reviewing all the forever prisoners, it has begun looking at men once considered as possible candidates for trial who are still not charged. Among them: Diarist Mohamedou Ould Slahi, 45, whose lawyers sued in federal court to get him a hearing.

Justice Department attorney Folio said at a November 24, 2015, federal court hearing that Slahi "remains in line, like dozens of other detainees at Guantánamo, to receive a PRB hearing." In one mysterious instance, the board heard from Salman Rabeii, 36, a Yemeni, eight months ago but has yet to decide his case. In contrast, the board cleared fellow Yemeni detainee Ayyub Ali Salih, 37, in five weeks.

American University law professor Steve Vladeck, who routinely studies the board decisions, is likewise a critic of the glacial pace of the process. He blames, in part, "internal resistance and obstructionism" by bureaucrats who don't want the prison closed.

But what Vladeck sees as remarkable about the enterprise is not how few have gone through the process but that the majority of those evaluated actually have been approved for release — after spending years on a list deemed too dangerous to be let go.

In that regard, the process appears to have vindicated critics of Guantánamo who argue that U.S. intelligence was overwhelmed or ignorant in assessing its captive population in the first dozen or so years. Some who probably should still be there were let go during the years when the Bush administration mostly repatriated about 530 captives, he says. And some who are still there probably could have been released years ago.

"From a politics and rhetoric perspective we should be past the point where anyone can say the 91 folks at Guantánamo are 'the worst of the worst,' " Vladeck says. "A handful of them might be. But plenty of them aren't. That's not a matter of speculation. It's the president's own PRBs that are saying that."

Defenders of the process say the board's bureaucracy picked the most straightforward cases first, tipped the scales toward those likely to be allowed to go. Vladeck says that's even more damning. "Even if they picked the easy cases first, what does it say that there are 'easy cases' at Guantánamo at this point in time? After 14 years in the blink of an eye they get cleared by the PRB."

Book editor's note: As this edition went to press, the review board had approved the indefinite detention of 12 "forever prisoners" and had yet to hear or decide 28 captives' cases.

Thursday, March 31, 2016

A BIN LADEN BODYGUARD LOSES BID FOR RELEASE

The Guantánamo parole board has upheld the detention of a Yemeni "forever prisoner" profiled as a former Osama Bin Laden bodyguard despite pledges by former President Jimmy Carter's Atlanta-based Carter Center to help the man succeed in his transition to life after 15 years in U.S. custody.

The board wrote in a short decision that it could not recommend the release of Muhammed al Ansi, 40 or 41, given "the significant derogatory information regarding the detainee's past activities in Afghanistan." It was dated March 23, 2016.

At a February 23, 2016, hearing, Atlanta lawyer Lisa Strauss said that she had enlisted the Carter Center to help the Yemeni if he were resettled in another country. Strauss, whose only detainee client is Ansi, said that he has long respected "American culture," something she learned from nearly 300 hours of meetings with him at the base across eight years.

In that time, she said, they discussed "movies, television, food, magazines, and my situation as a working wife and mother." He also "loves," she said, the *Fast & Furious* movies, the Atlanta-based zombie TV show *The Walking Dead* and National Geographic.

Ansi got to Guantánamo in January 2002 as one of 30 men who had fled Afghanistan and had been captured by Pakistani forces. They were believed to have been Bin Laden's bodyguards. Many of those so-called "Dirty 30" have since been released.

An October 2015 U.S. intelligence assessment said that Ansi went to Afghanistan in 1999, joined al-Qaida, swore an oath of allegiance to Bin Laden "and served as his bodyguard." It added suspicions that Ansi had probably fought U.S. forces at Tora Bora and was at one time possibly considered for a suicide mission. At Guantánamo, it said, he has been mostly a well-behaved prisoner.

A U.S. military officer assigned to help Ansi make his case for release told the board that the Yemeni had studied math, science, English, Spanish, life skills, computers, health and art in his time at the U.S. Navy base.

Under the Periodic Review Board system, he is entitled to another review in six months. The board said it would conduct that file review and urged the captive to continue working with prison medical staff to continue dealing with an unspecified chronic health condition.

Strauss said in her offer of assistance by the Carter Center that the philanthropic organization had similarly helped a captive who was repatriated in 2007, during the Bush years, to an unidentified country where "it was questionable whether he would be welcomed."

TOO DANGEROUS TO LET GO, AT 68

The Guantánamo parole board has rejected a plea for freedom from the prison's oldest war-on-terror captive, a 68-year-old Pakistani businessman, citing the prisoner's past ties to al-Qaida and declaring him too dangerous to release.

Saifullah Paracha told the national security board March 8, 2016, that his preference was to rejoin family in Pakistan or go to the United States, where he lived from 1970 to 1986.

Instead, the board cited his "refusal to take responsibility for his involvement with al-Qaida" and his "refusal to distinguish between legitimate and nefarious business contacts."

The board also invoked "the detainee's past involvement in terrorist activities, including contacts and activities with" Osama Bin Laden and the alleged mastermind of the 9/11 attacks, Khalid Sheik Mohammed. It said Paracha had a role in "facilitating financial transactions and travel, and developing media for al-Qaida."

Paracha's lawyers have long described him as a once wealthy Karachi-to-New York import-export specialist who was lured to a Bangkok meeting in July 2003, ostensibly to see some Kmart buyers. It was an FBI-orchestrated sting, and Paracha was flown to Afghanistan for 10 months and then to Guantánamo.

Paracha "cannot show 'remorse' for things he maintains he never did," attorney David Remes told the board in March, describing him as a "model prisoner." Now, Remes says Paracha "will try to address the board's concerns in his file review in October."

Wearing the white uniform of a compliant prisoner, Paracha spoke to the board near Washington, D.C., by teleconference from the base. He said in a statement that he was "duped" into visiting Afghanistan and handling certain finances as part of charity work he did. He said he met Bin Laden in Paracha's role as chairman of a Karachi TV broadcasting studio, and sought an interview, which the studio never did get.

Former Pakistani businessman Saifullah Paracha posing for the International Red Cross, 2009. (Courtesy of attorney David Remes)

An intelligence assessment prepared for the board said Paracha met Bin Laden in the early 2000s and later worked with KSM to facilitate financial transactions and develop al-Qaida propaganda. It alleged that before his capture, Paracha (who has never been charged with a crime) did research on chemical, biological, radiological and nuclear materials and "offered operational suggestions to al-Qaida."

Example advice included how to smuggle explosives into the United States, something "that al-Qaida planners probably did not take seriously."

Paracha denied doing the research. "I never worked with anybody to harm anyone in my life," he wrote the board.

Paracha's prison profile cast him as "very compliant" with the guards and espousing "moderate views and acceptance of Western norms" in his more than 11 years at Guantánamo. A 2009 task force listed Paracha as a possible candidate for trial although he has never been charged either in federal court or at the military commissions.

The April 7, 2016, Periodic Review Board decision effectively rebrands him as an indefinite detainee in the war on terror, a "forever prisoner." The official board language declared that "continued law of war detention of the detainee remains necessary to protect against a continuing significant threat to the security of the United States."

Chapter 7

GITMO, IT'S A BASE, TOO

The view across the bay from the naval station, March 30, 2009. (John Van Beekum/Miami Herald)

Sunday, November 17, 2002

CUBANS' 6-MONTH SLEEPOVER SPANS DECADES

It was supposed to be a safe haven for six months. Now, 40 years later, dozens of Cuban day laborers have grown old in what they thought would be temporary residence in this U.S.-controlled corner of Cuba.

Theirs is a curious Cold War subculture — an aged, dwindling population of Cuban workers who chose to side with the U.S. Navy in the early, chaotic days of Fidel Castro's revolution.

Rather than move on and resettle in the United States, these exiles have continued to work and live at Guantánamo with special Pentagon dispensation, some still shunning offers of U.S. citizenship, in a limbo-like existence, while they wait to go home.

Meantime, these Cubans live in Navy housing, rent-free. They get the best Department of Defense healthcare, cost-free.

Most have retired on U.S. government pensions, but about a dozen still work. One bags groceries for tips. Another walks each morning from his bachelor suite to his clerk's job at a Navy supply office. Two are waiters at the Bay View restaurant, a nightspot on this mostly sleepy 45-square-mile base where sailors and the 64 special Cuban residents live in suburban-style white stucco housing.

Although they have been community fixtures for years, their story is seldom told. After months of requests, the Navy finally let the Miami Herald get a rare glimpse inside the lives of these Cubans who live with a special Pentagon status: "Long-Term Visitors." *

The Cubans include Paulina Wilson, 70, who as a nanny and housecleaner left her two children in her mother's care on the Communist side in 1962. She remarried and raised two more children here and these days runs the Navy Hospital's linen room, neither ready to retire nor to move on.

Paulina Wilson, 70, and her son Dennis Miller pose for a portrait at The Cuban Club restaurant that Paulina's now deceased second husband started, August 2, 2002. (Patrick Farrell/Miami Herald)

"It feels like Cuba because it's Cuban land," she said, explaining why she has spurned suggestions that she relocate stateside.

And there's Ramón Ramírez, 59, who helped his grandfather deliver fruits and vegetables on a boat that plied the Guantánamo River. He moved in on December 28, 1959, after he realized that his grandfather was right, communism was coming to Cuba. He was 17.

"My grandfather said, 'If you want to stay alive or out of jail, you'd better stay here,' " Ramírez said. He has visited the United States, but always comes back to the base known as Gitmo because, after four decades, it has become home.

"We have the only geriatric Navy housing anywhere," said Navy Captain Robert Buehn, the base commander. "Don't look for any regulations that cover this. It's a funny place. It evolved this way, and we're just trying to take care of the people the right way."

The oldest of the "temporary guests" are 90 and 91, housebound widows who require visiting nurse care. Once a month, a Navy volunteer takes them to the graves of their husbands, who died and were buried on the base.

The youngest member of the base's Cuban community is José, 5, the son from a recent union between a septuagenarian Cuban waiter called "Boxer" and a Jamaican contract worker who is less than half his age. Because of his father's status, the boy can live on the base through high school.

One of the men has for years taught judo and karate to Navy children.

Another resident is Gloria Martínez, 69, a grandmotherly figure who can be found most days working for tips at the checkout line of the Navy Exchange, Gitmo's grocery store.

Like many, Martínez said she stayed, at first, because she thought the upheaval would be over soon. Her husband, a former army officer loyal to Fulgencio Batista, who ran Cuba before Castro, had already sought sanctuary on the base. So on April 23, 1961, she drove right inside, after using a bogus identification card to pass a Cuban police checkpoint.

Everyone, it seems, thought the U.S.-Castro crisis would last "about six months."

Her husband, she said, was to serve as a scout for any counter-invasion of Cuba's eastern provinces. But the invasion never happened. So he worked as a base janitor and builder, saving money to one day move to Hialeah, Florida. He was killed in an electrical accident while working on a house there during a visit. She buried him in nearby Opa-locka, and, although their daughter and son have since moved to Florida, she said, after 40 years, Gitmo feels most like home.

"I'm afraid to live in the States alone," she said. "It's too crazy driving in Miami. If Cuba opens, I will go back and take the buses."

U.S. forces first came to Guantánamo in 1898, during the Spanish-American War. Five years later, Presidents Tomás Estrada Palma and Theodore Roosevelt signed the first lease agreement to establish this U.S. Navy repair and refueling station. Over time, it became a magnet for Cuban workers, notably in the 1950s among young people who moved to nearby Guantánamo City and Caimanera from Batista's hometown of Banes.

Working with Americans was, for some, a family tradition. Some of their parents had worked for the American-owned United Fruit Co. in Banes, and so they came to work as everything from ditchdiggers and translators to cooks and clerks.

Old-timers recall that the pay was good. Many earned 25 cents an hour.

When Fidel Castro came to power in 1959, he and other revolutionaries wanted to break the $2,000-a-year lease signed in 1934. They cast the base as an enemy interloper — an unwanted corner of colonialism in the Caribbean. The exiles recall that police pressured workers to quit their jobs or, worse, spy on their bosses and co-workers. Cuban gate guards subjected workers to humiliating strip searches.

By 1964 Castro's anger had boiled so much that he cut off two-way vehicle traffic from the Cuban land that abuts Guantánamo — and accused the Americans of stealing Cuban water. The Pentagon countered by building a desalination plant and the base has made its own water since then.

Navy commanders also made their commuter workers a standing offer: Stay and sleep in barracks until the U.S.-Cuban rift is settled.

Edgar Lewis, 78, who had worked on the base since 1943 as a translator, accepted the offer on February 26, 1961.

Edgar Lewis, 78, peeks from behind his screen door at his Guantánamo Bay Navy base home, August 2, 2002. (Patrick Farrell/Miami Herald)

"I was having my little problems with the Cuban police. I never started out thinking it would be so long. I lost my father, lost my mother over there. I never saw them before they died."

But life, he says, has steadily improved. After the 1962 Cuban Missile Crisis, the workers moved from their barracks to a trailer park. Then in the 1980s they got the same housing as Navy families.

Today he and his wife, Loleeta, a Jamaican who works as a clerk at command headquarters, occupy a four-bedroom home in a neighborhood called Caribbean Circle near Gitmo's mostly brown golf course. Their daughter, Monique, 21, lives in Jacksonville.

Lewis recalled the base's boom-and-bust history, from its height during the Cold War with more than 10,000 forces to support an artillery battalion, tank platoon and DC-9 squadron.

Lewis was already retired by the mid-1990s when Gitmo became awash in tent camps for more than 45,000 Haitian and Cuban boat people who were intercepted en route to Florida. He was earning a government pension and refining his stroke on the golf course when Washington ordered a downsizing that closed up housing and cut the base population to 2,400 in late 2001.

Now, about 6,000 people live at U.S. Navy base Guantánamo, both U.S. forces and contract workers.

In January, the Pentagon found a new purpose for Gitmo — America's offshore detention center for international terror suspects from Afghanistan's Taliban militia and Osama Bin Laden's al-Qaida movement.

"The United States is in a state of war right now," Lewis said. "This place is essential."

The frigate USS Samuel B. Roberts after refueling and resupply at the base, April 2, 2009. (John Van Beekum/Miami Herald)

By cultural measures, this place is less Cuban than many corners of Miami. There are no *cafecito* counters, and meals are spicy at The Cuban Club, a base restaurant where Jamaicans work in the kitchen, and the menus are in English.

Dennis Miller, 39, runs it. He was born and went to school on the base, where he still lives with his Cuban-born mother, Paulina Wilson, who has worked in the Navy hospital linen room for 35 years. His father died years ago, as did his kid brother, who had moved to Miami and was killed in a train accident.

Now Miller says he prefers the solitude of Gitmo to the fast life of, say, Miami, which he has visited. "This is my home. I feel comfortable here."

So does his Santiago-born mother, who decided to stay in 1962 to earn money as the nanny to Navy officers' children and find a way to send some back home to the daughter and son she had left with her parents.

"They told me that they thought it would last for six months, maybe," Wilson recalled. "I'm still waiting for those six months."

Meantime, she has missed her parents' funerals and has only spoken to her two Cuban-side children by telephone through a third-country hook-up. "They're married now. They have their own children now. God give me the strength."

But, she said, she has made good on her plan to ship a share of her earnings to family in Castro's Cuba. Twice this year, she sent $600, via Canada.

"I'm glad that I'm here and I can help them. If I couldn't help them, it wouldn't be worth it," she said.

Work is one reason that Harry Sharpe, 72, stays. He runs the buffet line at the Mongolian Barbecue at the Bay View restaurant, where he pulls down a $2,200-a-month salary and gets two weeks of paid vacation.

It's a big improvement over the 12 cents an hour he earned his first day of work — March 30, 1953 — first pushing a wheelbarrow, then polishing brass plates in a command office. Another incentive, he said, is that housing has been free ever since July 30, 1963, when he finally moved in.

"My goal is to go back to Cuba and live when Castro leaves or when the U.S. lifts the embargo, so I can get my pension there," said Sharpe, who is three years away from full retirement.

Sharpe has obtained U.S. citizenship and a home in Pensacola, Florida. And he has family scattered in the United States and Cuba. U.S.-born nephews Shannon, Sterling and Lewis Sharpe were NFL players. Two other nephews, the sons of a different brother, are doctors at a government-run hospital in Havana.

Yet, he has a 30-foot boat at Guantánamo and gets free medical care that saw him airlifted to Walter Reed Medical Center near Washington for a thyroid condition. So he is in no hurry to leave. If the Cuban system is unchanged when he retires, he says, he might move to Detroit, where a brother lives.

"Pensacola's too slow for me," he explains. "And I don't much like Miami. It's too much 'Cuba' there. Everybody's the boss there.

They're going to go back and take over. They've been saying that for 40 years."

Meantime, the Navy is grappling with increasing concern for the Cubans' deteriorating health, first recognized in a 1991 Navy command directive that authorized officers to "provide for the geriatric needs" of this special community.

Several have been flown to U.S. Navy facilities for surgery. Six receive meals-on-wheels, delivered from the hospital's kitchen. Among them is a woman with advanced dementia and no next of kin.

Soon, Buehn said, the Navy will assign a sailor full time to oversee their needs. Now the work is done ad hoc by his staff and Spanish-speaking volunteers.

Buehn said some of the last 64 may yet move away, to join adult children who have grown up and moved to the United States, mostly to Florida.

"Many have places they can go," he said. "But they like it here. It's Cuba still."

Book editor's note: After this story was written the Navy rebranded the Long-Term Visitors as Special Category Residents.

Sunday, March 5, 2006

FEW BURIED HERE WERE AMERICAN

They include women and children, merchant mariners and civilian contract workers who never went home. Some of those buried are unknown.

"Baby boy Theodore, Haitian refugee," declares one grave marker at the sun-speckled grounds of the Navy-run Cuzco Beach Cemetery.

Another marks the last resting spot of Antonia Negron Valle, who died in 1928 at age 29, and her unnamed child.

The Miami Herald was allowed a rare visit inside the cemetery not far from a 19th-century Spanish-American War beachhead. And it reflects a different image of Guantánamo than that of terrorism suspects held captive or U.S. Marines standing guard.

At first glance, this place seems a miniature of Arlington National Cemetery. But few of the 300-plus people interred were Americans, and fewer still were members of the U.S. military.

The oldest grave dates to 1906, three years after the base was formally established.

The most recent arrival was Edgar Lewis, an elderly Cuban citizen, who had stayed to work on the base amid U.S.-Cuban tensions in the 1960s and never did get to go home.

The base cemetery, March 31, 2009. (John Van Beekum/Miami Herald)

There's also a turn-of-the-20th-century U.S. sailor, William King, who was born in May 1884 and died April 22, 1906, eight years after the Marines landed in the Spanish-American War.

And there's Gertrude Myers Russell, whose headstone says she was a civilian employee. She died November 19, 1922, at age 29.

A walk through the cemetery — off the beaten path, behind a no-go security zone — tells a story much different from that of the one that catapulted this base to international controversy. The cemetery has no war-on-terror prisoners, nor are there any recent fallen American service members, who by policy and practice return home to U.S. soil.

Rather, one section of the cemetery recalls the huge 1990s rafter crisis when upward of 45,000 Haitian and Cuban boat people fled political crises in their homelands. The Cubans were given sanctuary in tent camps until the Clinton administration renegotiated its Cuban migration policy with Havana. Haitians waited out a political crisis in their country, and most were ultimately repatriated.

"Unknown Haitian Refugee," declares a grave marker, engraved with a Christian cross. It has no age and no name of the person who died, only a poignant passing date: July 4, 1994.

The cemetery, which reflects a blend of nationalities, is the military's crisp answer to the civilian burial plots that were scattered around the base before consolidation in the 1940s. It reinterred remains from different sites overlooking the Caribbean as well as on a site once called McCalla Hill, not far from the place where enemy combatants face war crimes charges.

Today the base is a high-security zone with air and sea craft coming and going through a delicate coordination between the U.S. military and its Cuban counterparts.

And the cemetery is cut off from the main portion of the base. It is miles from the McDonald's, out of view of the war crimes court and open to base personnel once a year, on Memorial Day.

In the meantime, the graves hint at an earlier era, when gates were open, two-way traffic flowed freely, and seafarers visited.

For instance, one headstone belongs to a merchant mariner named Olaf Z. Olson. The marker doesn't say when he died, but he lies near another merchant mariner, a Greek captain called Anthony J. Coumelis, who was laid to rest in 1942 at age 45.

Cuzco Beach is also the final resting place for Juan Zarazabat, 33, whose marker says he was a Cuban contractor when he died, for reasons unknown, in June 1943, during an era of amiable U.S.-Cuban relations. Then, when thousands of Cubans commuted to the base each day for work.

Another headstone belongs to Miguel Tam of China, described as a civilian employee who was born October 15, 1906. He died, according to his marker, on May 7, 1962. By then U.S.-Cuban political tensions were roiling, and the year would see the Cuban Missile Crisis.

By the time civilian worker Ramon Guerra Pinero of Spain died at age 65 on January 23, 1965, the base was a self-sufficient entity desalinating its own water and producing its own electricity in defiance of Fidel Castro's demand that U.S. forces leave.

Georgiana Hurley, a Jamaican civilian, was born October 17, 1908, and died March 19, 1996, after the families of U.S. sailors were evacuated from the base to make way for Cuban rafters, or *balseros*, who fled the island.

Sign at back of base cemetery designates a separate section for Muslims that has yet to be used, March 3, 2009. (John Van Beekum/Miami Herald)

Less is known about others buried here. One marker identifies its occupant simply as Mrs. Walters, perhaps because of the 1940s cemetery consolidations, which swept up remains from now-lost locations called the North Toro and Caracoles Point cemeteries.

Another declares simply, "Vincent, civilian."

Thursday, January 21, 2010

HAITI EARTHQUAKE RELIEF MISSION

A dirt lot behind the war court the Bush administration built is now a landing zone. If the Cuban government agrees, U.S. military helicopters could ferry earthquake relief supplies straight into Haiti, a 170-mile dash directly over Cuban soil.

Relief flights now land night and day at the base runway, both cargo planes and helicopters on shuttles to Port-au-Prince and U.S. Navy vessels off the coast of Haiti to help after its devastating January 12 earthquake.

Friday was meant to be a bittersweet date — President Obama's missed one-year deadline to empty the Pentagon prison camps. In its place, there was an air of elation and purpose that the military was helping out in an unambiguously good assignment.

"You see the look, the smile on a parent's face if you ease the suffering of an injured child, that's more exhilarating at the moment than walking the block in a detention camp," said Rear Admiral Thomas Copeman, the prison camps commander. "Not to say that walking the block is not an extremely important mission for the United States. But probably not as gratifying as saving somebody's life."

Helping Haiti is the latest assignment for this outpost better known for the prison camps controversies and the Hollywood hit, *A Few Good Men*, set in the Cold War.

In that drama, the Cubans were the enemies across the 17.4-mile minefield that divides the two sides. This time, Havana swiftly approved medical evacuation flights straight through Cuban airspace to Miami for U.S. victims evacuated from Haiti.

Now, the Cuban government has provisionally approved U.S. military relief flights going straight to Haiti rather than having to continue to zigzag around Cuban soil, said Navy Captain Steve Blaisdell, the base commander. The Federal Aviation Administration, he said, is ironing out the agreement.

"Clearly Haiti has eclipsed everything else in the short term," said Blaisdell, "independent of any other things that are swirling around."

Meantime, a tent city that could house 12,000 or more migrants is slowly rising on base in case any Haitians are intercepted off their shore and can't be immediately repatriated. The Department of Homeland Security and a troop force from the U.S. Army South in San Antonio would handle an influx.

But, the U.S. Coast Guard says, photos of Haitians taking to rafts so far show victims sailing away from the earthquake-stricken capital for safe haven in rural portions of the country.

To keep it that way, the U.S. has sent the Navy: a floating hospital, the USNS Comfort, and triage and treatment centers aboard the USS Bataan and aircraft carrier Carl Vinson, to handle casualties at sea, close to home, and stem an exodus.

Here, troop rotations are continuing. But family visits are canceled to make space for more troops and federal agents.

The prisoners, who are forbidden to speak to reporters, learned long ago from news reports that the Obama closure deadline would be missed. Staff say they more recently saw protesters in orange jumpsuits from London to Washington condemn the United States as the prison camps entered their ninth year.

They learned of the earthquake in Haiti the same way and discovered live — on al-Jazeera's English-language network — that Cuba was under a tsunami watch that included the clifftop prison camps on the edge of the Caribbean.

"They asked, 'Where's the manual? What are our instructions?' " said Zaki, a Muslim American who acts as intermediary between the military and detainees as the prison camps' cultural advisor.

Saturday, December 24, 2011

RADIO STATION ROCKS IN FIDEL'S BACKYARD

Drive through this base dotted with a McDonald's, golf course and outdoor cinema featuring first-run movies and you could be in anywhere America.

But switch on the radio in this one-station town and the location is inescapable. "Radio Gitmo," goes a jingle in a nod to the economic embargo, "We're close but no cigar."

This station's motto is "Rockin' in Fidel's Backyard."

It's emblazoned on T-shirts, key chains, tote bags and beer-can covers — classic public-radio fundraising fare. Except these poke fun at the Cuban *comandante* who's been telling the U.S. Navy to get out since the 1960s.

Each item bears the motto, along with a likeness of Fidel Castro in a green military cap. And, though he claimed to kick the habit years ago, he's chomping on a cigar — a caricature stubbornly locked in time, not unlike the U.S. grip on Guantánamo.

Successive U.S. administrations have considered it a strategic location. So the Navy maintains it as a small town with a port, prison and airstrip of 6,000 or so occupants, from U.S. troops and contract workers to sailors' spouses and kids.

Navy Petty Officer First Class Tim Tolliver of Chicago, left, Petty Officer Third Class Ace Rheaune of Southbridge, Massachusetts, center, and Commander Jeffrey Johnston, the base public works officer, Radio Gitmo, March 30, 2009. (John Van Beekum/Miami Herald)

For residents who don't want to tune in to Spanish broadcasts of *Radio Reloj* from across the minefield, there's Radio Gitmo, with its mix of country music in the morning and hip-hop programming at night, mostly streamed in from elsewhere.

It offers public service programming, too, such as reminders to use sunblock while snorkeling and to designate a sober driver when out drinking. A sailor announcer adopts the audio persona of a talking iguana to warn people against feeding wildlife. A more solemn announcer advises listeners to be aware of their surroundings, avoid terror attacks.

Still, the station's lobby is a popular spot. Its gift shop, a pair of bookshelves, offers hooded sweat shirts for $40 and a Fidel figurine whose head bobbles for $25. Travel mugs and bottle openers go for $10, all of it for fun, not profit.

Proceeds are going to help the nine seniors at the high school fund their class trip, an eight-day cruise, and also cut the costs for junior-enlisted to attend the Navy and Marine Corps balls, says Chief Petty Officer Stan Travioli, who runs the station.

By far, the $15 T-shirts are the best-selling items.

Soldiers on deployments of a year or less send them to the kids back home. Off-duty troops sport them at the beach. A British newspaper correspondent was picking one up for her husband recently when a counterman at the Guantánamo McDonald's walked in to buy two.

During war crimes hearings, escorts shuttle observers from Camp Justice, where the Pentagon puts them up in a crude tent city powered by cacophonous generators, to buy the kitsch. More likely than not, they're souvenirs of something they've never heard.

Drummer Derek Berk got his Radio Gitmo regalia, gratis, when his Detroit-based indie rock band, The High Strung, played a couple of concerts and spent a week kicking around the base.

Berk literally did rock in Fidel's backyard: "There's not any combat going on down there," he says. "We're just occupying our area." He considers his souvenir a treasured addition to his T-shirt collection, political correctness not a concern.

"I think it's just kind of funny," he says.

"Is it PC for our Army to make fun of their so-called enemy? I feel like silliness is OK."

Sailors at the radio station don't use the motto as a radio jingle, just in case it might offend the neighbors. And it's simply not known how those in Havana view it, if at all.

Neither the motto nor the broadcasts have come up in monthly meetings with a Cuban military officer along the fence line, said Navy Captain Kirk Hibbert, the base commander.

Radio Gitmo bobblehead figurine of Fidel
Castro, March 27, 2009. (John Van
Beekum/Miami Herald)

The U.S. military opened the channel of communication in
the 1990s, to let one side alert the other to activities that may
alarm the other's troops. At the meetings, commanders have given
advanced notice of training at the firing range, fireworks on the
Fourth of July and the first arrival of al-Qaida suspects in 2002.

The radio station and its quirky motto were already around
when Hibbert got to the base in 2010. He "never gave it much
thought," he said, until a reporter asked about it.

"I don't see myself sitting in Fidel's backyard," he replied
good-naturedly. "I see myself as the naval officer in charge of
Guantánamo Bay."

ENERGY CONSCIOUS BASE STRIVES TO GO GREEN

Solar-powered lights serve as sentries where U.S. Marines once faced off along the Cuban frontier. Some Navy cops now ride bikes rather than gas-guzzling patrol cars in the searing Caribbean sunshine.

In this corner of Cuba that is better known as a lab for Pentagon justice and interrogation, the U.S. Navy has been quietly engaging in more low-profile offshore experimentation — seeking environmentally friendly alternatives to reduce its whopping $100,000-a-day fossil fuel dependence.

It's a Navy-wide goal to halve dependence on fossil fuels by 2020. But the greening of Gitmo comes with a particular challenge.

The base that today houses 6,000 people makes all its own electricity and desalinates its own water. It has done so ever since the 1960s when Rear Admiral John Bulkeley, then base commander, faced down Fidel Castro and disconnected the naval station from Cuba's water and power supply.

Now everything from diesel fuel to spare parts arrives by ship or aircraft, more than tripling the price of power, according to base estimates.

"From my perspective certainly the greening of Gitmo is important," says Navy Captain Kirk Hibbert. National security is paramount, he said, but the Navy mandate to curb consumption "has an effect on almost everything we do here."

Hibbert is the base commander who put a pair of Navy cops on bike patrol rather than sit inside air-conditioned sport utility vehicles, an $800-a-year savings that sends a symbolic message. And it's been on his watch that a contractor has started building a huge solar array behind the base's high school.

Guantánamo can strike visitors as a small slice of Americana, with its trailer parks and tract housing, a hilltop church, McDonald's, cinemas and schools. But it's a base behind a Cuban minefield with the Navy controlling who may come and who may go and who gets water and electricity.

Commanders like to compare it to a ship at sea, except this one is towing "The Most Expensive Prison on Earth."

Three of four base wind turbines, May 5, 2012. (Walter Michot/Miami Herald)

By base estimates, it costs $32,000 a day, or $11.7 million a year, to keep the lights on and water flowing to the 171 captives at the Pentagon's prison camps and the 1,850 U.S. forces and contractors who work there.

The Department of Defense set up the detention center a decade ago, temporarily, at a time when the Navy was already tinkering with energy efficiencies.

In 2005, a Massachusetts firm installed four 270-foot-tall windmills on Guantánamo's highest hill with visions of capturing up to 25 percent of the base's power consumption from the Caribbean trade winds. But that analysis did not anticipate the never-ending nature of detention operations, a venture that tripled the base population and sent construction costs soaring, from the coastal prison camps to the crude war court compound built atop an abandoned airfield.

"We get a lot of attention here because we are such an expensive base in the Navy," says Arthur Torley, a senior civilian worker at the base version of a small-town Department of Public Works. "Gitmo, to me, is even more of a priority because of the expense. They would much rather spend money fixing planes and ships than dumping fuel into Gitmo."

So his workers use a fleet of 24 solar-powered minis, squat little electrical vans with panels on their roofs. They arrived this summer, and can go about 35 miles before needing a charge, just about right for a week's worth of work on a 45-square-mile base.

Hibbert cautions against seeing the base as a site for random experimentation, of "just taking stuff and throwing it up against the wall and seeing what sticks." Because it's remote, and because importing goods and services is so expensive, the Navy engages in "a lot of analysis" ahead of time to figure out what might work.

But Guantánamo's location in the tropics straddling a bay does make it fertile ground for innovation.

• Two Florida firms put in a 1,200-panel solar array behind the base high school, just below the scrubby nine-hole golf course. It should produce 430,000 kilowatt hours a year and power the gym, which doubles as a hurricane shelter.

• There also have been email exchanges about whether the base could grow algae, as biofuel, inside a floating field of wastewater discharged into the bay. "NASA scientists are exploring this technology," says base spokesman Terence Peck.

Solar array installation with Guantánamo golf course in background, February 9, 2012. (Carol Rosenberg/Miami Herald)

• In 2007, a Public Works officer bought a bioreactor off the internet and tried his hand at extracting fuel from used cooking oil. It was abandoned after eight months.

• The Navy put in artificial turf at Cooper Field, the outdoor sports complex, to save on the fuel for desalinating water for the baseball diamond and soccer pitch.

Guantánamo is also the first Navy base in the southeast region (stretching from Texas to South Carolina to Cuba) to introduce mock utility bills.

Since the military picks up the troops' tab, the faux bills are meant to shock sailors and their families into conserving by estimating base household power costs. They come in at nearly 3.5 times the price of an average U.S. household.

The bills have had the desired "wow!" effect. Guantánamo human resources worker Ambroshia Jefferson-Smith felt her stomach turn in October when she got her $1,021.79 mock bill for a month of power at the single-story ranch-style house she shares with her 15-year-old son, five television sets and a cat.

"It's like coming home when you have been on holiday and getting that big credit card bill," she said. "You don't see anything tangible there, and you realize you have consumed a lot of electricity and water."

By her estimate, the bill would be seven times the sum she would pay back home in Mississippi. So now she makes sure all the TVs are turned off, including the one on the backyard patio, and turns up the AC thermostat before she heads to work.

Another military unit has joined the movement.

The Marine major in charge of the force that monitors the 17.4 miles of fence surrounding the base let the Public Works Department replace a third of the floodlights with solar-powered LEDs. They're still on the electrical grid in case of too many gloomy or rainy days. But they haven't needed the grid yet.

"I don't know what they're doing along the Mexican border," said Torley. "But the Marines were on board with all the energy stuff. They couldn't tell a difference."

Sunday, September 14, 2014

IS GUANTÁNAMO PART OF THE USA? IT DEPENDS ...

U.S. troops blare *The Star-Spangled Banner* across this base each morning at 8 o'clock sharp. Fireworks crackle overhead on the Fourth of July.

Marines control the fence line opposite Cuba's minefield and American sailors check visitors' passports or Pentagon ID cards as they arrive by plane.

So why then did U.S. officials recently advise some Chinese journalists who report from Washington that, by traveling to Guantánamo as guests of the Pentagon, they would see their visas to visit and work in the United States expire?

The answer is that, while the U.S. Navy base functions like an extension of the United States, sometimes it is and sometimes it isn't — mostly to the benefit of those in government.

Consider this: Department of Defense contractors who work and live at Guantánamo and don't set foot onto U.S. soil for more than 30 days a year get a tax break, like any American living and working abroad.

Army guards at the prison don't get the tax exclusion, but they do get $425 a month in allowances, imminent danger and hardship duty pay, plus $250 a month if they leave family behind.

Those dollars buy time scuba diving, Pizza Hut delivery and drinks in the base bars, all Navy-run enterprises, as are the free rides home to avoid the base's drunk-driving checkpoints.

Navy base and prison guests are put up in two-story townhouses that ooze Americana. They have patios for barbecues, a downstairs powder room for guests, private laundry rooms. But over at Camp Justice, the place where the Pentagon is trying to put on the death penalty trials, visitors are put up in a crude tent city evocative of Bagram air base in Afghanistan circa 2001.

It all creates a certain dissonance, says retired Army Lieutenant Colonel Chris Jenks, who observed some September 11 pretrial hearings recently, his first foray back to "the battlefield" since leaving service and becoming a law professor at Southern Methodist University in Dallas.

At one moment, the West Point grad said, you can see families at McDonald's or the bowling alley or taking a sunset sail on the bay. But the war court compound where he was put up was so reminiscent of his last forward operating base in Iraq that one morning he groggily reached for his M16 in the latrine tent, and briefly panicked because it wasn't there.

Guantánamo, he says, is made up of "puzzle pieces from three or four sets" that don't fit together.

Navy Chief Petty Officer Bill Mesta, the base public affairs officer, flips burgers in the backyard of his suburban-style Navy-issue housing, March 28, 2009. (John Van Beekum/Miami Herald)

Jenks is a former infantryman turned lawyer in the JAG Corps who has handled detainee abuse and friendly fire cases and looks to precedent and the law to try to parse the question.

"If you look at the lease, it's America as long as we want it to be America," he says. "I'm not sure how that functionally is any different than Puerto Rico."

In 1965, he said, the U.S. declared the outpost a special maritime jurisdiction and brought a Cuban to federal court in Miami for the machete killing of another non-U.S. citizen on base. For that crime, Guantánamo was subject to the prosecutorial jurisdiction of the United States. Since the Bush administration chose to imprison war-on-terror captives seized around the globe, it has sought to make sure the opposite applies.

That's why moments before boarding a U.S. military charter to Guantánamo at Andrews Air Force Base (the place where the Pentagon parks the president's plane, Air Force One) an airman warned two Chinese journalists that going to Guantánamo would amount to entering a foreign country, and their single-entry work visas would be invalid upon their return.

They were invited by the Office of the U.S. Secretary of Defense to report on some war crimes hearings and were scheduled back a week later, on a nonstop flight.

They didn't go.

Had they gone, they could've purchased a souvenir plastic cup at the base commissary for $6.99, duty free by federal code covering "articles of foreign origin" at GTMO, the military's shorthand for the base. A study in schizophrenia, the souvenir is stamped "GTMO. USA. CUBA. "

It is for this base of about 6,000 residents that the U.S. military is building a $40 million undersea fiber optic link to Florida so data can reach the Pentagon as swiftly as any office on U.S. soil.

And while there has been a continuous American presence at Guantánamo Bay since U.S. forces took it in a Spanish-American War battle in 1898, it's technically leased territory. From Cuba, whose landlord, Fidel Castro, told the tenants to go home long ago.

The U.S. government says it's a tenant barricaded behind a Cuban minefield and, as though to prove it, cuts a check each year for $4,085 — rent, based on a 1934 treaty made public by President Franklin D. Roosevelt.

It's a one-way transaction. The Cuban government does not cash the checks.

Babies born to Americans at the base hospital are automatically citizens. A diplomat from the U.S. Embassy in Kingston, Jamaica, the closest to the base, periodically visits to process paperwork for Guantánamo's American babies, says Kelly Wirfel, the Navy base spokeswoman.

But that's not a privilege passed along to Filipino or Jamaican guest laborers who work as waitresses at the Irish Pub or clean the officers' guest quarters. Were one to get pregnant at Guantánamo, she'd probably get a ticket home to avoid the issue of her baby's citizenship.

Which is why nobody was willing to speculate on that baby's theoretical nationality. Would that baby be Cuban? Guantánamite? Stateless?

Guantánamo is not like Puerto Rico, says the State Department's Bureau of Consular Affairs. It's more like a U.S. embassy (with school, golf course, church and prison), and babies born to non-citizens at embassies aren't entitled to citizenship, either.

And that pretty much reflects the pick-and-choose approach that's become all the more pronounced as the war court hears pretrial motions in six death penalty cases.

Defense attorneys are asking the military judges to decide which portions of the U.S. Constitution apply at the court that George W. Bush built and Barack Obama froze, then reformed to exclude some, but not all, self-incriminating statements made in the years before the men got lawyers.

Habeas corpus? Yes, because the U.S. Supreme Court said so in the landmark 2008 Boumediene v. Bush decision. "In every practical sense Guantánamo is not abroad," Justice Anthony Kennedy wrote for the majority. "It is within the constant jurisdiction of the United States."

Ex post facto? At least sometimes, because a federal appeals court decided recently that Osama Bin Laden's 9/11-era "media secretary" couldn't be convicted in 2008 of providing material support for terror in 2001 because Congress created it as a war crime in 2006. Separately, a military court of appeals panel in the same case has ruled out his First Amendment free speech right to produce an al-Qaida recruiting video, one of his crimes.

Confrontation? That's still playing out at the war court, where defense lawyers are arguing to exclude the hearsay evidence of a man who was interrogated by the FBI in Yemeni custody in 2001, then killed by a missile launched from a U.S. drone 11 years later.

"I always feel silly doing this," said Cheryl Bormann, defense attorney for a Yemeni man accused in the 9/11 plot, as she filled out a U.S. Customs form aboard a Miami Air charter hired by the Pentagon to shuttle lawyers from a war court hearing.

She had left Andrews Air Force Base two weeks earlier on a nonstop Pentagon flight to the U.S. Navy base, never left U.S.-controlled territory, and was now returning to Andrews.

"The reason that we're filling out those stupid forms is they want to pretend this isn't the United States," she said later. "As though those forms are going to help an argument down the line that Guantánamo Bay, Cuba, is a foreign country; and somehow their establishment of this commission in a foreign country can avoid U.S. law. And I think they're wrong on all counts."

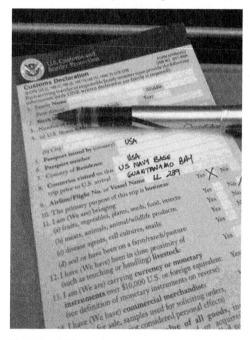

Miami Herald illustration

She calls it pick-and-choose patriotism.

"It's America when the environmental protection laws prohibit us from killing an iguana or committing drunken driving," she said.

"But it's not America when they can get away with paying less than minimum wage" to the Jamaicans or Filipinos who clean the officers' guest quarters. "It's not America when they want to violate American law regarding torture. And it's not America when they avoid applying the Geneva Conventions."

So what did she write as the country she visited prior to her return to Andrews Air Force Base?

"Guantánamo Bay Naval Air Station."

Bormann wrote not the name of the entire base, where a secret prison has jailed her client since 2006. She wrote in the airport — a seafront airstrip a ferry ride away from the courthouse where she is defending an accused terrorist.

Chapter 8

HUNGER STRIKES

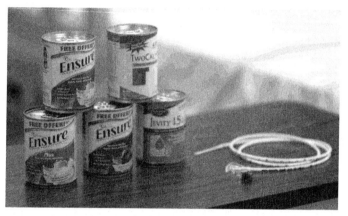

Dietary supplements and a tube typical of those the military says are used to feed detainees, April 2, 2009. (John Van Beekum/Miami Herald)

Thursday, February 28, 2002

PRAYER PROTEST SPARKED FIRST FASTS

Nearly 200 suspected al-Qaida and Taliban fighters staged a hunger strike and threw their gear outside their chain-link cells at Camp X-Ray in a growing protest against their Caribbean confinement.

For about 45 minutes, commanders reported, about 150 prisoners defied their guards and shouted in Arabic, "God is Great," and, "There is no God but Allah."

So serious were the midmorning disturbances that heavily armed Marines surrounded the camp containing 300 suspected international terrorists.

But by dinner, a speech by the prison operation commander and a change in policy regarding turbans appeared to have temporarily calmed the situation.

Marine Brigadier General Michael Lehnert went to the camp to deliver a personal address to both prisoners and guards over a public address system.

In a reversal of policy, Lehnert advised the prisoners that they could turn their towels into turbans. He also told them they'd be moved to cells with running water in two months and "they will be judged fairly at a time in the future," said the general's spokesman, Marine Major Steve Cox.

Commanders said the hunger strike was a protest against the behavior of a U.S. soldier who removed a captive's turban during prayer Tuesday.

Refusal to eat began on Wednesday in scattered parts of the detention center. In all, 107 prisoners refused breakfast and 194 refused lunch Thursday.

Thursday night, after the general's address, only 88 refused their dinner – rice, beans, bread, milk and an apple.

Medical personnel said they were monitoring the prisoners' health and had recently weighed all of them. They are prepared to force-feed the prisoners by intravenous drip if they become dangerously dehydrated, said Navy Captain Al Shimkus. The first sign of significant dehydration could be at least three days away.

"Rest assured, there will not be a detainee who starves here at Guantánamo Bay," Cox said. "That's just not going to happen. We are responsible for their health and welfare."

Disturbances broke out in about half of the cells at 9:45 a.m. Thursday, Cox said. Some prisoners shoved their sleeping mats, sheets and towels out of their cells.

Military commanders then mobilized the heavily armed Marines. Soldiers inside Camp X-Ray are not armed. Army MPs, who act as the jailers, carry only a canteen, walkie-talkie and shackles.

The widespread unrest was the first major security problem at Camp X-Ray, which received its first 20 prisoners on January 11. Declared at capacity with 300 captives on February 15, it has only 20 vacant cells, which are used for isolation.

Problems began when an Army MP noticed that a prisoner had fashioned a turban for his head out of a towel or sheet. Captives had been permitted to wear only white knit, military-issue skullcaps as head coverings.

The guard told the prisoner to remove it and then had a translator issue the order.

But the captive was on his knees, said Cox, fully absorbed in Muslim prayer, so he did not hear the order. Several guards went inside his cell, shackled and handcuffed him, then removed the head covering.

The guard, said Cox, "was focused on the headdress, not the larger issue. It was unfortunate that he followed the proper procedure in the midst of the prayer."

Lehnert later told U.S. troops at Camp X-Ray that they would get additional sensitivity training.

In an earlier confrontation, about a dozen prisoners chanted, "*Allahu Akbar* [God is Great]," after another guard mistakenly kicked a Quran during a surprise inspection.

Cox attributed the headdress affair to an underlying tension that stems from the prisoners' uncertainty about their fate.

"They want to know what is going to happen and when it's going to happen," said Cox. "We give them the honest answer: We don't know at this point." Decisions are in the hands of policymakers in Washington.

Amnesty International said the protest was a reflection of the prisoners' "legal limbo."

A spokesman urged the United States "to acknowledge that all of the prisoners are covered by the Geneva Conventions and to ensure that they are granted due process rights, including the right to challenge their continued detention."

Sunday, March 3, 2002

WHY THE U.S. WON'T LET PRISONERS STARVE

Why not let the terror suspects starve to death?

News of the five-day hunger strike has provoked Americans from soldier to citizen to wonder aloud why the U.S. military is going to extraordinary efforts to keep alive those refusing to eat among the 300 prisoners. Members of the U.S. military gave a range of explanations for not letting their al-Qaida and Taliban prisoners die.

They are an intelligence resource. The Pentagon decided to transfer the prisoners here, an 8,000-mile trip from Afghanistan, for interrogation by federal agencies and military intelligence to get greater understanding of Osama Bin Laden's al-Qaida network. "Certainly, they are providing valuable information for the war on terror," said Marine Major Steve Cox hours before a first-ever visit by FBI Director Robert S. Mueller.

Information gathered in five wooden, windowless buildings outside Camp X-Ray is fed into an intelligence clearinghouse off the island, Cox said, and sifted through with other pieces of information as part of a huge puzzle on international terror networks. The military wants these prisoners fit and cooperating with their interrogators, not hooked up to intravenous lines, kept alive by Navy medics.

It's the humane thing to do. "We intend to keep them alive because they are human beings," says General Lehnert, overall commander of the nearly 2-month-old prison project. He added that the hunger strike "is a problem. I'm not going to try to diminish it." Commanders say their mandate includes caring for the captives' overall welfare, from their physical health to their spiritual needs. Whatever their motivation, the general said, starving themselves to death "is not one of their basic rights."

The world is watching. Human rights organizations have been critical of a Bush administration policy decision to deny the detainees POW status, and the accompanying rights that it brings. Beyond that, European and Arab countries looked on with concern at Pentagon photos released in mid-January that showed the shackled and blindfolded prisoners kneeling in a holding pen. Officers are keenly aware of world criticism on how the U.S. military is treating these men.

Doctors don't stand by and let patients die. Some of the Navy's finest medical professionals are at Guantánamo to tend to the suspected terrorists. Medical professionals associated with the tent hospital that treats the prisoners have said, repeatedly, that they are giving the prisoners the same quality care that they would give their own U.S. sailors.

The captives are not in charge. Military Police say the prisoners may be less interested in martyrdom than testing their captors. Many MPs are reservists called up from civilian prison-guard duty. And they say hunger strikes are a typical jailhouse technique to assert control over their lives. "This is no surprise," said Army Colonel Terry Carrico of Fort Hood, Texas, the chief MP, effectively the camp warden. So far, he said, it has not been a real challenge to the guards, who by Sunday had shuttled six prisoners to receive intravenous drips on nine separate occasions.

At the height of the food strike, 194 skipped lunch Thursday. By the weekend it had settled into a solid one-quarter of the 300 prisoners refusing nutrition. Only 13 of the detainees have thoroughly stuck with the hunger strike over the past five days, military officials said.

Sunday, March 24, 2013

FOOD FIGHT AT CAMP 6

It's lunchtime on the communal cellblocks for cooperative captives, and detainees dressed in tan and white camp uniforms are steadfastly refusing the guards' offer to wheel in food carts.

Only if a prisoner pulls shut a gate to a chute called a sally port can a soldier lock it remotely and send in the meals. And one by one, every block but Delta Block refuses. Some captives call out that they don't want the food.

Over at Charlie Block, an angular-looking detainee is stubbornly ignoring his guards, sitting at an empty stainless-steel picnic table, watching footage from Mecca on Saudi TV.

Within an hour, the guards systematically trash a lunch that looks like it could feed 100. Unopened juice bottles go in the garbage first, then Styrofoam boxes of pita bread and special dietary meals. Buffet tins of stewed tomatoes, rice and sweet-and-sour stir-fried beef follow.

It's hunger-strike time at Guantánamo. And while the military and its captives dispute when it started and how widespread it is, it was clear from a three-day visit to the prison-camp compound that the guard force is confronted with its most complex challenge in years.

Guards trash communal lunch for dozens of detainees at Camp 6 prison for cooperative captives, March 20, 2013. (Carol Rosenberg/Miami Herald)

By this weekend, the U.S. military had defined 26 of the 166 captives in the detention center as hunger strikers. Eight were being fed nutritional shakes through a tube snaked through a shackled captive's nose to his stomach. Two were hospitalized, getting nutrition through a tube and intravenous hydration as well. Lawyers for the captives quote their clients as counting dozens more as long-term hunger strikers, who are getting weaker by the day.

Communal captives are no longer cooperating with guards at the once-showcase Camp 6. They've covered the cameras inside their cells. They've quit going to art classes. Both sides report frequent fainting spells (the military calls them "Code Yellows") although the prison spokesman says they're fake, staged for visitors.

More men are being moved out of communal confinement to the maximum-security prison, where up to 125 can be kept in 8-by-12-foot cells and where it's easier to conduct tube-feedings. But the Camp 5 commander, an Army captain who wouldn't give her name, decided it would be too disruptive for a reporter to observe lunch being served there. To watch a guard pass a lunchbox through slits in the cell doors at the disciplinary block, the captain concluded, was too "high risk."

Although it's camp policy to prevent a captive from starving himself, the prison staff talks about the possibility that a hunger-striking captive will be found dead one day.

Lawyers for the men say the strike was sparked in early February by an unusually aggressive search of prisoners' Qurans that to them amounted to desecration. Prison staff says no Qurans were disrespected, no policy changed.

All sides blame long-simmering frustration with President Obama's inability to deliver on his promise to close the facility.

The prison's Arab-American Muslim cultural advisor, a Department of Defense employee, says he and the chief guard, Army Colonel John Bogdan, have been trying to negotiate with the detainees. But it may be that nothing short of an airplane ticket will end the deadlock.

"They are serious," says the advisor, who goes by Zaki. "They have lost hope."

Says Army Captain Jason Wright, the lawyer for a 30-something Camp 6 Afghan hunger striker called Obaidullah: "There's no constructive engagement" in the standoff over handling of the Quran. "There just appears to be a stalemate."

In years past, captives staged hunger strikes in single-occupancy cells where meals went in, containers came out and camp staff could closely monitor consumption.

This protest began in Camp 6, the place where in better times the military would boast that up to 130 cooperative captives could eat and pray in groups, play soccer and go to class. Troublemakers were removed one at a time.

They pointed to perks like PlayStations, food pantries and wristwatches that helped keep the captives cooperative. The detainees were inside the cellblocks, with guards watching through cameras, and posted just outside.

The Army captain in charge of Camp 6 since January said all the cellblocks but one had refused their food carts for "around three or four weeks," and were subsisting on snacks such as pita bread and peanut butter that were stashed in their pantries or thrown over recreation yard walls from Delta Block.

The captives are still drinking water. But the communal meals ended weeks ago, complicating the calculation of how many meals in a row a particular detainee has missed.

Guards now are keeping checklists, trying to track a captive snacking or slipping into a food pantry. It's an increasingly complex task because the commanders say the no-longer cooperative captives of Camp 6 have covered the cameras in their individual cells with empty cereal boxes, making it hard to look inside.

"All they can do is watch TV and movies and play PlayStation. It's pretty boring for them now," said the Army captain, who gave his first name, John. "The pantries are getting thin. It's now just beginning to be a problem."

The strike is by no means universal.

On Delta Block, a chubby elderly prisoner closed the gate and received the lunch cart. He systematically unloaded buffet trays into Delta's designated food pantry. Minutes later, other Delta captives filed inside.

Before the big hunger strike, captives could be seen kicking a ball at Camp 6, August 8, 2012. (Walter Michot/Miami Herald)

From a distance, some of the men in Camp 6 seem slim, their clothes clearly baggy as they can be seen standing on cellblock scales to check their weight. The elderly captive who unloaded the food cart at Delta Block, however, had a potbelly.

Commanders point to scraps of pita bread and used individual portions of peanut butter in trash bags otherwise filled with empty water bottles at the exits of supposedly hunger-striking cellblocks, and snicker that the captives are cheating and eating.

Still, the boycott of the popular arts and life-skills classes is total, camp commanders said. Soccer games are rare.

Camp 6 has stopped requesting items from the detention camp library. But the chief librarian, who gives his name as Milton, said four copies of the last *Twilight* episode are still in circulation, as well as *John Madden NFL 2013* and *NBA 2K13,* for the PlayStation mounted inside each Camp 6 cellblock.

Defense attorneys who speak with the captives paint a far more desperate picture. They wrote to Defense Secretary Chuck Hagel, saying that their clients report frequent fainting spells and some captives coughing up blood.

Kuwaiti captive Fayez al Kandari, 35, told his lawyer he was down to 108 pounds this past week, and lost 32 pounds in his hunger strike.

"His cheeks were sunken and sallow. He was exhausted," said Ohio federal public defender Carlos Warner. Warner said Kandari's waist looked like that of the lawyer's 6-year-old child. (A military weight chart released years ago says Kandari was five feet six inches and 136 pounds when he arrived at Guantánamo in 2002.)

The Pentagon staff is at times dismissive of the claims. "Nobody's coughing up blood. They're using ketchup or biting their tongues," said Zaki, the cultural advisor. But they are also concerned that somewhere in the communal camp a captive may be stealthily managing to starve himself, out of sight of the cameras and checklists the military uses to scan physiques at prayer time.

"It's all about using the hunger strike as the weapon," said Zaki, blaming a hard-core group in detention for a decade or longer as inciting others to forgo food. "We might be hit with one behind hidden cameras, that one suddenly dies."

The Navy prison camps spokesman, Captain Robert Durand, said "stealth hunger strikers" are a concern. Captives who openly refuse meals agree to be led off to a tube-feeding while none of the others are watching.

But some detainees may be trying to thwart the system, Durand said, by accepting a meal and not eating it.

Most numbers are guarded secrets at the detention center, where about 1,700 Pentagon troops and contractors are assigned to feed, watch and manage the 166 captives. But a visit made clear that the communal camp was being slowly drained and the maximum-security prison is slowly filling. By Thursday, the Camp 5 commander estimated occupancy at her 125-cell lockup at "a little under half."

In her camp, she said, some are eating and "some of them aren't." What would stop the fasts? "They want to be released," she replied. "That's pretty much the only thing I've gotten."

Relations started to sour in Camp 6 around the time of this year's presidential inauguration.

These men were among those being force-fed at Guantánamo in 2013, according to their lawyers, who got notice from the Justice Department. Top row from left: Yemeni Tariq Ba Oda, Saudi-born UK resident Shaker Aamer, Yemeni Mohammed al Hamiri. Bottom row from left: Kuwaiti Fayez al Kandari, Yemeni Yasin Ismael and Yemeni Samir Moqbel.

Throughout Obama's first term, the one that started with a pledge to close the detention center by January 2010, Camp 6 was presented as a model POW-style prison — and the lockup for many of the captives cleared for release by a 2009 task force. Now, about 90 captives are cleared for release but are still in Guantánamo because of a combination of congressional restrictions and no place to send them.

On January 2, in an episode only disclosed two months later, a guard fired a round of rubber pellets into the $744,000 "Super-Rec" soccer field.

The irony is the yard was built with remote-controlled gates so guards wouldn't need to bring captives to the recreation yard. Less contact caused less friction, was the explanation. So each side could keep to itself.

Detainee writes in the communal area of Camp 6, October 29, 2010. (Petty Officer Elisha Dawkins/U.S. Navy)

But then a detainee scaled a fence to get the attention of a guard in a tower, and a guard pointed his rifle at him. The captive climbed down immediately, but other captives saw the guard with the rifle and hurled rocks at him. A ricocheting rubber pellet struck a Taliban elder in the throat, according to both military and attorney accounts, but he was not hurt enough to merit hospitalization.

Then in February, new Army guards at Camp 6 undertook a shakedown of the cells — something the detainees say through their lawyers was unusually aggressive in the seizure of personal items, from legal mail to family photos. The detention center said it was business as usual.

Unauthorized electronics were also seized — for example, a handheld game called a Nintendo DS that the spokesman, Durand, said wasn't approved for use. Commanders worry that clever captives were trying to rig up equipment and prepare "a propaganda video" to embarrass the prison, he said.

The captives launched a hunger strike, even if it was only partial at times, and notified an International Red Cross delegation in mid-February that it was underway. While one Red Cross delegate was in a Camp 6 recreation yard, according to multiple accounts, he was splashed with a mixture of feces and urine hurled by a detainee.

In the past year, congressional restrictions meant only five detainees left the prison. Two Uighurs ordered released by the courts years ago were resettled in El Salvador. Two convicts were repatriated to Canada and Sudan as part of court-approved plea agreements. And a Yemeni who had attempted suicide for years went home dead, after what the prison concluded was an overdose of hoarded drugs.

Not one of those men was living in Camp 6.

Tuesday, March 26, 2013

REPORTER'S NOTEBOOK: DESDEMONA AT GITMO

Navy medics giving tube-feedings to hunger strikers do it anonymously, just like every other member of the military at the prison camp complex.

Guards wear serial numbers in place of their name tapes. Commanders display acronyms, such as SMO, for the Senior Medical Officer, or OIC, for the Officer in Charge.

Carol Rosenberg

But to give it a personal touch, the Navy's medical staff for years wore pseudonyms to work to conduct the tube-feedings that the captives' lawyers say are forced and the military says are collaborative, with hunger strikers voluntarily getting strapped into a feeding chair.

One rotation took its monikers from colors, and another used birds, making it possible to see Petty Officer Purple or Lieutenant Sparrow in Navy uniforms.

The current Navy medical crew has a more literary approach, borrowed from Shakespearean characters. The men and women sailors moving around the blocks last week included Desdemona, Gertrude and Malvolio.

One sailor tagged as Bertram explained good-naturedly that the name belonged to "a donkey," suggesting somebody had read the wrong CliffsNotes. Bertram was a cavalry officer in *All's Well That Ends Well* who behaves like an ass, while Bottom ends up as a donkey in *A Midsummer Night's Dream*.

Tuesday, July 9, 2013

FORCE-FEEDING VIDEO GONE VIRAL

In a brutal video that's gone viral, rapper-actor Yasiin Bey, aka Mos Def, is clad in an orange jumpsuit and recoils against restraints as a doctor tries to put a feeding tube up his nose. He resists. He sobs. He wriggles out of his restraints.

It's the latest production by a London-based law firm determined to get its captive clients out of Guantánamo. But there's a problem, says Lieutenant Colonel Todd Breasseale, the Pentagon spokesman for Guantánamo policy, "It doesn't comport with our procedures."

Breasseale, who's never actually seen a Guantánamo force-feeding and earlier in his career served as the U.S. Army's envoy to Hollywood, was at first reluctant to offer a review. "We don't provide commentary on theatrical productions," he said.

But, unlike other members of the U.S. military who wouldn't comment, he called it "a clever bit of cause marketing by Reprieve and the Guardian," the British newspaper that first posted it.

That's the point. Reprieve, the London-based nonprofit law firm that catapulted Guantánamo's hunger strike onto The New York Times' op-ed page with a prisoner's first-person account, has captured the public's imagination with the rapper's dramatization of a captive's force-feeding.

The lawyers released the video on the eve of Islam's holy month of Ramadan and, as it happens, hours before a U.S. District Court judge called Guantánamo's tube-feeding practice "painful, humiliating and degrading." The judge, Gladys Kessler, said she was powerless to act on the request of Syrian captive Abu Wa'el Dhiab, 41, to stop the Pentagon from force-feeding him.

Reprieve represents Dhiab and 16 other men at the prison where 106 captives were on hunger strike Tuesday, 45 of them listed for tube-feedings.

Lawyers for Dhiab and three other captives asked the federal court in Washington to stop the feedings. Kessler said the person with the power to do it is President Obama.

At the White House, spokesman Jay Carney defended the policy. "The president said in April, we do not want these individuals to die." Carney added that Obama "understands that this is a challenging situation," then referred reporters to the Justice and Defense departments for "specifics about the hunger strikers and then the litigation itself."

In London, Reprieve attorney Cori Crider said the video racked up 2 million hits in the first day. It also stole the thunder of the military's latest bid to ease tensions at the prison of 166 captives staffed by about 2,000 employees, who include Navy nurses, Army guards, contract linguists and librarians and a little-mentioned intelligence unit.

At 6 p.m. Monday, said Captain Durand, the military issued a "Ramadan pardon," excusing some disciplinary offenses and restoring "some privileges lost" for this, the 12th Ramadan at the prison camps in Cuba for most of Guantánamo's captives.

About 40 detainees, none of them hunger strikers, were released from nearly 90 days of lockdown, up to 22 hours daily in their solitary cells. The prison was letting some captives eat and pray together during Ramadan, provided they voluntarily went to their solitary cells to be locked inside for six hours a night.

Others could eat and pray together at times but were being locked in their cells 12 to 18 hours a day.

In a concession to Islam's month-long holiday, those being force-fed would get their tube-feedings after sunset and before dawn. "We have sufficient staff on hand to conduct enteral feeds at night," Durand said.

Reporters who visit the prison have so far been forbidden to see the twice-daily tube-feedings, to test military claims that most captives go willingly and sometimes agreeably chug a can of Ensure instead. News photographers can't show a captive's face as a condition of access to the camps. Force-feeding became a distant, daily numerical report from Cuba.

Enter Bey, a New Yorker who is also Muslim. He donned the orange jumpsuit of a detainee in June, said Crider, to make the four-minute video in a single day in London.

It shows a British doctor in turquoise scrubs lubricating a tube and then attempting to insert it into Bey's nostril, the doctor urging him to "relax." Instead, Bey tenses up as another doctor and unseen actors in black T-shirts try to restrain him.

In a portion of the video that military sources say could not happen at Guantánamo, the actor gets loose from his restraints. Bey wails and sobs, and calls it quits.

"It is me," he said. "Please stop. I can't do it."

Efforts to reach the rapper failed. Crider said he was in Morocco, unavailable for comment.

Friday, July 26, 2013

MEDICS: IT'S NOT TORTURE

Rapper Mos Def may have scored sympathy for the prisoners at Guantánamo with a brutal web video dramatization of a force-feeding. But in this corner of Cuba where U.S. troops are charged with managing the long-running hunger strike, fans are hard to find.

"I deleted his music off my iPod. I was a little upset about it," said Army Sergeant First Class Vernon Branson, 33, a watch commander at Camp 6, the steel and concrete prison where more than 100 prisoners went on hunger strike this year.

As of Friday, the military said, 68 captives were on hunger strike, down from a high of 106 amid apparently easing tensions for Ramadan, Islam's holy month. Of the 68, 44 were designated for tube-feedings of the type that the hip-hop recording artist who now goes by Yasiin Bey tried to portray in London in a demonstration organized by a British legal defense group.

Detention center troops interviewed this week expressed opinions ranging from resentment to indifference to the rapper's stunt. Reporters have asked to observe tube-feedings but were not allowed. So the question is: Where does the truth lie? Is it the depiction in the viral video and the lawyers' claim that their clients are being tortured? Or is it the insistence of the U.S. military that force-feedings are intended to preserve life, not inflict pain?

Sergeant First Class Vernon Branson, a career MP, was so disappointed in rapper Mos Def that he wiped an entire album, *True Magic,* from his iPod, July 25, 2013. (Carol Rosenberg/Miami Herald)

Several guards in Branson's MP unit got the tube-feedings out of curiosity, the sergeant said, "and took it like a champ."

"It's a life-saving tool if you ask me," said Branson. "We see it every day and we know it's not as bad as they make it out to be."

The captives' lawyers say their clients consider it torture — an agonizing, degrading introduction of nutrition that deprives of them of their right to protest their indefinite detention. They got U.S. District Judge Gladys Kessler to agree, although she ruled she does not have the authority to stop the military.

Yet 10 members of the Navy medical corps who do the feed-ings said in a series of interviews that they are proud of their service and pained by the portrayal that they are doing something inhumane. Detainees who don't want the tube, they said, have the option to eat. But, as U.S. military medical forces, they are determined not to let them starve.

"I never felt like I would be that person who would be persecuted for keeping a detainee alive," said Eric, a 24-year-old corpsman, the Navy's name for a medic. He helps evaluate the captives to see whose body weight is low enough to merit tube-feedings of a nutritional shake if they will not drink it on their own.

Navy nurses and corpsmen interviewed said they've routinely trained for nasogastric feedings by inserting tubes up their own noses or in fellow sailors or soldiers. They universally shrugged off tube-feedings as painless. All said they volunteered to deploy to the prison from such far-flung posts as Italy, Illinois and Washington, D.C. Several said they'd volunteer again, citing a range of reasons, from the beauty of the beaches to scuba diving to the camaraderie of service.

In the video that went viral, the rapper recoiled from the tube and wouldn't let a British doctor snake it up his nose. He resisted. He wriggled free of his restraints. He sobbed in a stunt that a Navy nurse who goes by Ensign Lodowick called "ridiculous."

The video is "the opposite of everything that goes on here," said Lodowick, 30, who spends his nights offering a captive designated for nutritional supplements a choice: Drink a bottle of Ensure, or take it through a tube snaked up your nose and into your stomach.

"It's not that painful. It's not that excruciating," he said on his way to a night shift at the prison where, for Islam's daylight fasting during Ramadan, the prison staff adopted an after-dark feeding routine.

"They're not begging for you to stop," a 23-year-old corpsman named Hannah chimed in.

To be sure, the troops say some of the hunger-striking prisoners become furious when women among the medical corps administer the so-called "e-feeds," short for enteral feedings. In one account, a captive slipped out of his restraints and slugged a nurse. The nurse was not made available for an interview.

A night shift nurse named Candice, a 32-year-old Navy lieutenant, said she has been spit on, cursed at and threatened with such angry prisoner glares that "I feel my soul is being sucked out."

But in her experience, by the time the guards have the detainees settled in the restraint chair, they cooperate and "guide," as she put it, wriggling their heads to help the tube find its way to their stomach.

"For the most part it's good patient interaction," she said.

This week, for the first time, nurses and corpsmen volunteered to be interviewed and did so inside an unused surgical ward not far from a poster that warned medical troops to think about security before they blog, tweet or post on Facebook. Each of them had seen the Mos Def video despite having to endure slow and balky internet access to do so.

Army Sergeant Lasima Packett, on temporary duty here with an Indiana National Guard public affairs team, said the video was a disappointment and her respect for the rapper diminished.

Captain Durand, the public affairs officer who has been defending the honor of the detention center throughout the hunger strike, drew a distinction. "I disagree with his portrayal and his performance," he said, "but I still like him as an actor and musician."

Tuesday, July 15, 2014

NAVY NURSE REFUSES TO FORCE-FEED

In the first known rebellion against the prison's force-feeding policy, a Navy medical officer recently refused to continue managing hunger-strike tube-feedings and was reassigned to "alternative duties."

A prison camp spokesman, Navy Captain Tom Gresback, would not provide precise details but said the episode had "no impact to medical support operations at the base."

"There was a recent instance of a medical provider not willing to carry out the enteral feeding of a detainee," he said by email. "The matter is in the hands of the individual's leadership."

Word of the refusal reached the outside world in a call from prisoner Abu Wa'el Dhiab to attorney Cori Crider of the London-based legal defense group Reprieve. Dhiab, a hunger striker, described how a nurse in the Navy medical corps abruptly refused to "force-feed us" sometime before the Fourth of July then disappeared from detention center duty.

A restraint chair typically used for forced-feedings at Camp 6, August 2, 2009. (John Van Beekum/Miami Herald)

Crider called the nurse, a man, the first known U.S. military "conscience objector" of the prison's 18-monthlong hunger strike, and said his dissent took "real courage." Dhiab, 43, is challenging the prison's force-feeding policy in federal court. He is Syrian and has been cleared for transfer since 2010 but can't be repatriated because of unrest in his homeland.

The Herald has not been able to determine the nurse's name or home base. Crider said Dhiab described him as a perhaps 40-year-old Latino who turned up on the cellblocks in April or May with the rank of "captain," suggesting he has two bars on his uniform.

Prison medical staff members come from the Navy, however, meaning the nurse is likely a lieutenant.

Last year, civilian doctors decried as unethical the Guantánamo military medical staff's practice of force-feeding mentally competent hunger strikers in a commentary in the New England Journal of Medicine — and urged a medical mutiny.

On the day the prison confirmed the Navy lieutenant's refusal, it had 149 detainees, an unknown number of them on hunger strike. The prison had a 147-member medical staff, "of which 83 are responsible for direct detainee care," Gresback said.

Retired Army Brigadier General Stephen Xenakis, a psychiatrist who visits the prison frequently for defense lawyers, said he had no firsthand knowledge of the episode but, based on his talks with Pentagon policymakers, the nurse should suffer no professional setback for having refused to do force-feeding.

Medical staff members are allowed to refuse by invoking medical ethics, he said, and should not be treated as insubordinate. Instead, the nurse should be allowed to continue providing healthcare to detainees, just not enteral feeds.

"They have said to us directly that if a provider objects for ethical reasons or other reasons," said Xenakis, "they would not suffer any adverse consequences."

Sunday, July 19, 2015

CAPTIVES MARK 14ᵀᴴ RAMADAN AT GUANTÁNAMO

It's edging toward dawn on a Ramadan morning at a communal prison building, and one by one detainees inside a cellblock clad in a jumble of white, beige and brown uniforms are brushing their teeth, getting ready for the daylong fast and to settle in for a day's sleep.

Yes, a day's sleep.

The military has upended much of its so-called "battle rhythm" of the day for this, the captives' 14th Ramadan at this remote base and the first for their U.S. Army guards. Lockdown, the time when each captive is locked in his cell for a guard sweep, usually happens from 2 to 4 a.m. Now it happens between 2 and 4 in the afternoon.

The rhythm of life — largely turned upside down — resembles earlier Ramadans here.

Art classes are still offered by day, but attendance drops. Lawyers still can arrange daytime, weekday visits, but few do. The cellblocks are abuzz with activity at night: Between long periods of prayer, captives click through free satellite TV in search of news or sheiks delivering sermons. Some still kick around a soccer ball late at night or before dawn when their bellies are full and the searing summertime temperatures dip. Hunger strikers are tube-fed after dark, and most medicine is delivered at night, too, in consideration of the daylight hours fast of the Muslim faithful.

Meals are delivered by dusk for breaking the fast. But this year, inexplicably, there's no lamb along with the traditional dates and baklava in the nightly *iftar* meal, something kitchen workers would highlight in past years as proof of their cultural sensitivity. The prison's cultural advisor blames "logistics" for the lack of lamb on the base which each week gets first-run movies on flights from Florida. Menus are no longer discussed.

Captives from two different cellblocks, separated by a fence, break their daytime Ramadan fast for communal evening prayers at Camp 6, July 7, 2015. (Walter Michot/Miami Herald)

Still, staff say the mood among the 116 captives is mostly mellow, bolstered by the pre-Ramadan release of six long-cleared Yemeni captives to Oman. Their departure raised to 33 the number men transferred since last Ramadan.

"They're always complying during Ramadan," says the prison commander's cultural advisor, a Muslim American whom the guards call Zak and the captives call Zaki. "Every year they hope it's their last Ramadan here."

The holy month of fasting and reflection has started for years here with the commander of the guard force issuing the "Ramadan pardon."

Belligerent detainees who have racked up hundreds of disciplinary days for hurling excrement or invectives or trying to kick their guards get a clean slate that presumes them cooperative and eligible to live in communal cellblocks. The exceptions are hunger strikers the military confines to solo cells for what it calls health and safety reasons, even those deemed "highly compliant."

No one will say how many hunger strikers there are because there's a military gag rule. But they do provide a different metric: The day before Colonel David Heath's pardon, 12 of the 116 were on disciplinary status, considered "noncompliant." By the 19th day of Ramadan four had broken enough rules to be back in disciplinary status.

One detainee — he's not identified — had more than 1,500 disciplinary days, according to the commander of Camp 5, an Army captain. Captives lose privileges on disciplinary days. His Ramadan slate was clean for less than 24 hours, according to several interviews with commanders.

The captive refused to leave a recreation yard, and a team of soldiers had to force him. Nineteen days later that "noncompliant detainee" had accumulated 273 disciplinary days, meaning that unless he's transferred out, he can't go to classes, get more than two books at a time, or eat and pray in the same space as others until sometime after April Fool's Day.

But on the 20th day of Ramadan, 112 of the captives were considered to be behaving — a stark contrast to remarks a week earlier by the Southern Command's Marine General John F. Kelly that Guantánamo's captives are "occasionally compliant but most often defiant and violent" and "among the most hateful and violent men on the planet."

"The pardon actually worked for some detainees," says the Army captain in charge of Camp 5, a veteran of the 2003 Iraq invasion. "Aside from these four, it's been very, very quiet. It's going very well."

Three brief, choreographed visits to the main lockups for about 100 of the captives seemed to support the commanders' claims of calm behind the razor wire. At Camp 6, where up to 20 captives live communally, guards now watch each block through one-way glass rather than from an enclosure on the cellblock.

Even the one disruption that reporters hear, after five captives in single-cell, maximum-security detention realize there are visitors, is tame by comparison to audio recordings that have emerged from the detention center in earlier years.

Detainee hangs laundry to dry at Camp 6, a communal prison, March 31, 2009. (John Van Beekum/Miami Herald)

"We don't have any rights," a captive called out. "And we haven't done any crime. Where is the American freedom?"

Other metrics seem to support the impression of little strife.

A senior Army officer who's forbidden to give out precise figures says fewer than 10 hunger strikers require tube-feedings.

At the psych ward, a Navy mental health specialist says in the prior week there had been just one "suicidal ideation," an expression of a desire to die. At least one detainee was an inpatient at the psych ward, called the Behavioral Health Unit (BHU), a place guards across the years have described as a destination for detainees who want a timeout from the other captives.

An unnamed Navy officer who runs the mental health program offers that instability in Yemen is a major mental-health stressor. About 70 of the captives are Yemeni, and they see their nation imploding on television, and get calls and letters from family describing the upheaval. "We spend a lot of counseling time dealing with that," the medical professional said.

The detainees "seem to be enjoying Ramadan," says Heath, calling the camps overwhelmingly "quiet and compliant. They are up most of the night and we adjust our schedules" with most medicine and meals distributed at night, including a midnight snack and early morning pre-dawn meal. "There's more prayers, there's communal prayer."

Then Heath offered a "success story."

A month before Ramadan, a well-behaved captive in the communal lockup asked a Navy medical staffer for one-on-one time with a troublemaker who had racked up disciplinary days in the maximum-security prison. They are friends of a sort, as Heath describes it, "a big brother type of thing."

So Heath approved. The two men are moved to the BHU for 10 days. They were locked in separate cells but spent time together in a recreation yard, essentially a cage, got counseling and based on the compliant "big brother's" say-so and observation were moved together back to the communal lockup.

So far, so good, Heath says.

Neither man's identity has been made public. But officers at the prison know them. The misbehaving captive had refused to follow guards' instructions daily, and was subjected to "daily FCEs," Guantánamo lingo for a Forced Cell Extraction, when a team of soldiers tackles, shackles and forcibly moves a noncompliant captive. "He was a pretty noncompliant detainee and that mentorship really helped," said the Camp 5 Army captain, who in civilian life is a corrections officer at a medium-security prison.

It's a single success story, casting a spotlight on the kind of captive-captor cooperation that was more routine before the big hunger strike erupted in 2013. But it may be a harbinger of a return to an earlier era of coexistence. Heath says he hasn't ruled out adopting a similar buddy system for other chronic troublemakers in the future.

Chapter 9

THE TROOPS

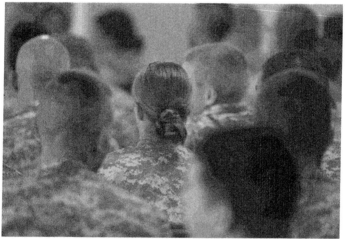

U.S. troops attend an awards ceremony at a chapel in the Detention Center Zone, November 4, 2014. (Walter Michot/Miami Herald)

Thursday, January 31, 2002

MUSLIM CLERIC AND U.S. NAVAL OFFICER

You're the first American Muslim cleric to minister to a prison camp full of suspected terrorists and one confides he has a weapon.

Do you keep the secret?

Or do you breach religious confidentiality?

If you're U.S. Navy Lieutenant Abuhena Mohammed Saifulislam you search for a third way to resolve the conflict between the crescent moon pin stuck in your left lapel and the lieutenant's bars on the right side of your uniform.

"I will say, 'Give it to me,' and not tell the general who had it," he says softly but firmly. "I'll make sure that he doesn't have it."

A 39-year-old lifelong, practicing Muslim, the soft-spoken immigrant from Bangladesh is navigating uncharted waters and juggling complicated loyalties — all while managing an international spotlight he has never experienced before.

As a U.S. military chaplain, his contacts with prisoners are governed by the same confidentiality as that of a priest, minister or rabbi in the clergy corps. Saifulislam is by training an imam, a prayer leader, who guides the faithful in Muslim prayer.

At Camp X-Ray, he is also serving the function of a muezzin, the person who announces the call to prayer, commonly from a tower called a minaret. In his case, he is using a public address system and recording the prayer for five-times-a-day broadcast.

Sometimes he laughs uncomfortably when questioned by journalists. Sometimes he looks bewildered. But mostly he's a busy man, trying to soothe Muslim sensitivities over the rugged chain-link-fence cells at Camp X-Ray.

Saifulislam arrived at the detention center for suspected terrorists on January 24 and made his debut by chanting the predawn call to prayer to wake alleged leaders of Afghanistan's Taliban militia and members of Osama Bin Laden's al-Qaida network.

Since then, he has emerged as their advocate, arguing that the U.S. military can safeguard its soldiers while adding a few amenities of everyday Islamic life.

Soon, he says, traditional white knit skullcaps will arrive for the captives to top off their fluorescent orange jumpsuits.

Saifulislam has also asked for some copies of the Quran in Urdu, a language of Afghanistan and Pakistan, plus large-type, Arabic copies for those with bad eyesight or those who read like elementary schoolchildren.

"These things are hard to find in America, and Gitmo is far, far away," says Saifulislam, a husband and father of a nearly 2-year-old daughter in California.

Until he emerged as the chaplain of choice for this special assignment from among only 14 Muslim clerics in the U.S. Armed Forces, he was the only cleric specifically assigned to a Marine Corps base, in Camp Pendleton, California.

Military recruiters building a Muslim chaplains corps spotted Saifulislam in 1993, while he was an enlisted man working as a payroll clerk in the Pentagon and studying part time to become a Muslim cleric.

He was commissioned as an officer in 1998, just a year after obtaining U.S. citizenship and nine years after leaving his homeland to study in America.

His role has a curious juxtaposition, which he sums up simply. Captives at Camp X-Ray are entitled to spiritual solace, he says, even though he doesn't accept radical interpretations that have led them to an unorthodox battlefield against the so-called "Great Satan," the United States.

U.S. Navy Lieutenant Abuhena Saifulislam during a brief assignment at Guantánamo to religiously handle the bodies of three captives who the military said committed suicide by hanging in Camp Delta, June 2006. (Carol Rosenberg/Miami Herald)

"I, of course, don't agree with their cause," he says, "and neither does the religion, Islam."

But after several days of four- and five-hour shifts inside the camp, hearing the prisoners' requests, he said exchanges have not dipped that deeply into the doctrinal.

Mostly, they ask about their fate, and when they might go home.

"I don't have any answer for them," he says.

Conversations between the cleric and the captives have taken place, one on one, in his native Bengali and Urdu. Others require the services of Arabic interpreters who, like Saifulislam, are U.S. military men in battle dress uniforms.

So far no one has asked him how a practicing Muslim can also wear the uniform of the U.S. Armed Forces. It was a question he had expected. But instead, he says with surprise, "They all want to speak with me. They all raise their hands" to catch the attention of the U.S. government's designated spiritual leader.

"If they don't trust me with their needs, they don't get it," he says, with a sigh. "I wish I had more time."

Tuesday, May 27, 2008

9/11 HERO TAKES CHARGE AT PRISON

On September 11, 2001, Navy Captain Dave Thomas plunged into the burning Pentagon and crawled through smoke and molten metal in search of a college buddy. The friend was lost, but Thomas emerged a hero for pulling other survivors from the wreckage.

Thomas is now a rear admiral and in charge of the prison camps housing 270 war-on-terror prisoners, among them the five men accused of orchestrating the attacks that killed his friend.

"Dave is a hero of 9/11. As 18,000 people were running out of the Pentagon after that airplane hit, he was one of the few people running in," said Admiral James Stavridis, head of the Pentagon's Southern Command, who presided at Thomas' installation.

Stavridis said he chose Thomas for the job because his "career and life are much bigger than a single moment in the Pentagon. But what that moment shows you is his integrity and instinct and grace under pressure."

For the record, the Defense Department decided months ago to make Thomas the eighth commander of the detention and interrogation program called Joint Task Force Guantánamo.

Unforeseen, however, was the extraordinary timing. A week from Thursday, the reputed al-Qaida kingpin Khalid Sheik Mohammed and four other former CIA captives will be brought to the Pentagon's war court complex here, miles from the prison Thomas now runs.

For the first time, a military prosecutor will formally charge them with war crimes alleging they conspired to dispatch, train and finance the September 11, 2001, suicide hijackers. Their charge sheet lists, name by name, the nearly 3,000 victims from the World Trade Center, Pentagon and a Pennsylvania field. Number 2,831 on the indictment is Navy Commander Robert E. Dolan, the buddy from Annapolis whom Thomas could not save.

In a brief first interview after taking command, Thomas, a lanky 50-year-old second-generation U.S. Navy officer, said that his 9/11 heroism was of no consequence and that he sees his one-year assignment like any other.

U.S. Navy Rear Admiral Dave Thomas, the commander of the detention center, leaves the base headquarters known as the "Red Roof Inn," March 31, 2009. (John Van Beekum/Miami Herald)

He rejected the notion that with the alleged perpetrators of 9/11 facing their first taste of military commission justice, there is a certain symmetry in his career.

"Whether they're some guy rolled up on the battlefield or the 9/11 conspirators, it's all the same to me," he said. "In all candor, I'm here to execute the policy of our government. There is no connection between 9/11 and this job for me."

What he did on September 11, 2001, was all instinct, he said, on what was "just a bad day for our country," not a formative experience in 27 years in the military.

"I am who I am, a trained sailor who sails ships at sea. You run toward your shipmate in times of trouble."

Historical accounts describe Thomas as forming an impromptu rescue party in the moments after American Flight 77 struck the Pentagon at 9:38 that morning. They crawled through smoke and rubble as molten metal and plastic rained down, slithered past live wires, never reached Dolan but helped others flee the disaster.

Never mind that in the terror of the moment Thomas ran toward the fire, not with the crowds away from it. Nor that the fire-scorched uniform he wore that day is now part of the Smithsonian Institution's American History collection.

"It's like commanding anything," he said of this one-year mission. "Take care of your people. Take care of your job."

Wednesday, October 14, 2009

GITMO REACTS TO OBAMA'S NOBEL PRIZE

Here in the land of limbo, the news of President Barack Obama's Nobel Peace Prize landed with more of a whimper than wild enthusiasm among those waging their part in the war on terror.

Most troops interviewed this week reflected the surprise of their commander in chief on waking to the news. More than a few hadn't heard about the award for the president who pledged to empty the prison camps here until they were asked about it.

"I've been fishing," said Navy Petty Officer 3rd Class Daniel LeBoy, 23, of Puerto Rico, a yeoman who was mobilized from a personnel job on a West Coast aircraft carrier.

Now he walks the cellblocks in Camps 1, 2 and 3 on 12-hour shifts and mostly shuns the news, he said. "But I think it's a great thing," he said, crediting Obama's campaign to "reach out to the entire world" with a message of friendship.

Others disagreed. "Someone else got gypped!" cracked Army Sergeant First Class Steve Rougeau, 52, of Orlando, a former corrections officer now with the Florida National Guard escorting visiting reporters.

"On the first day, everyone was surprised," Rougeau said. "I didn't know that he had done something on a grand scale. So many people deserve the peace prize who've done more than he has in his 10-month tenure."

Obama turned the spotlight on Guantánamo, and earned international admiration, on his second full day in office by pledging to empty the prison camps by January 22, 2010.

With 14 weeks to go and White House officials warning they may miss their own deadline, defense lawyers have reported that it has fed cynicism among the 221 remaining detainees. Most are approaching their eighth year in detention, most without charges.

"I would not be surprised if the common reaction is, 'What did he do to earn it?' " said defense attorney David Remes, who represents 17 Yemenis awaiting word on whether the Obama administration can reach a repatriation agreement with their government in Sana'a. "As far as they're concerned, he's all sizzle and no steak."

Still, the Nobel news did provide a distraction in the cellblocks. Word reached the men "the same day" through family phone calls, lawyers and the live TV some get, said a Jordanian-American named Zaki, the command staff's cultural advisor.

Arabic and Pashto language linguists who work at the camps got the first word not from news reports from Oslo but from the captives themselves, Zaki said.

"They see it as something good," he said. "The detainees are waiting, just like everyone else, to see what January 22 brings. We are all in limbo. We don't know."

Moreover, the prize is likely to feed the fascination with the new American president among the detainees who learned of his election the very same night in November and taunted their captors with chants of "Obama, Obama, Obama."

Since then, English copies of Obama's books, *Dreams of My Father* and *The Audacity of Hope,* have been in hot demand at the detention center library, reported Rosario, a civilian librarian.

Camp staff ordered 10 copies each about three months ago through the Pentagon's requisition program, she said. But they had yet to arrive, leaving the single copies in constant circulation.

What do they like about his books?

"Maybe because Obama traces back to a Muslim family," she said, then demurred. "We don't ask, and they don't tell."

The chief jailer, Army Colonel Bruce Vargo, learned about the prize the same day on the news. He declared himself "happy" for his commander in chief, then added a bit wistfully: "I wish I could win the Nobel Peace Prize."

Friday, June 17, 2011

WASTE WARS: CAPTIVES 'WEAPONIZE' EXCREMENT

When a fiddle player and her band toured the prison camps recently, guards told of a new devious and disturbing tactic confronting them.

A captive on a hunger strike had been jamming something foul up his nose to contaminate the pathway for nurses who insert a nasogastric tube to feed him a nutritional shake twice a day.

It was his own excrement. On the topic of bodily waste abuse, prison camp management "will not speculate on the motivations of this behavior," said Navy Commander Tamsen Reese, who confirmed the account of country artist Natalie Stovall.

The guards see it as a tactic to demean those tasked with keeping the captive alive, wrote Stovall in a blog post. "It means the medic putting the tube up his nose and down his throat must clean out the feces first." But Stovall wondered whether the prisoner was debasing himself as well.

Guantánamo guards have for years told visitors that the war-on-terror captives "weaponize" their body waste. They throw cups of urine and feces at troops in what soldiers and sailors call "a cocktail."

But this latest contamination tactic marks a new frontier here.

Still, the act of smearing feces is not unique to foreign captives accused of ties to al-Qaida. Earlier this month guards put an Oregon county jail under lockdown and called an emergency response team to pepper-spray an inmate who refused to eat, had covered himself with feces and wouldn't leave his cell and shower. He was removed for medical care.

In the late 1970s, hundreds of Irish Republican Army prisoners smeared excrement on the walls and emptied chamber pots of urine under cell doors at Long Kesh prison near Belfast to protest their captivity and conditions.

The phenomenon is "generally regarded as a sign of mental illness or abject desperation or both," says psychologist Craig Haney, whose expert testimony was recently cited by the U.S. Supreme court in a 5-4 decision that ordered the California corrections system to downsize the population in its unsanitary, overcrowded state prisons.

"As bizarre and distasteful as it may seem," he said, "they turn to one of the few things over which they have control. Their feces."

At Guantánamo, the gut-wrenching odor of excrement has for weeks wafted through the air vents of Camp 5, the state-of-the-art 100-cell maximum-security prison. It amounts to a kind of collective punishment that assaults the senses of compliant captives and their captors.

"Because Camp 5 is a modern detention facility with centralized air conditioning, the odor emanating from the conduct of a few detainees is noticeable throughout the building, both by guards and detainees," said Reese, the prison spokeswoman.

Reese confirmed the account of the country music artist who signed her blog entries, "Peace, love, fiddle." Stovall toured the prison while at the base to entertain the troops on Memorial Day weekend. The commander said hunger strikers have stuck other items up their nose to frustrate force-feeding — bread and toilet paper, for example. Using human waste, "has only recently been employed."

She also noted that the phenomenon of body fluid abuse is an old one with detainees smearing "feces, urine, blood, semen and saliva, or a combination thereof, not only on themselves but on the walls and doors of the cells, or have pushed it under their cell doors."

Haney, a psychology professor at the University of California-Santa Cruz, says such behavior is more prevalent in solitary confinement and Supermax-type settings where prisoners "are denied most or all forms of normal social contact."

By policy, the military doesn't clean up after the captives unless they push their filth out to the corridor. "Detainees are responsible for cleaning their own cells, and they do," Reese said.

"The guards will also clean the threshold when the detainee is out of the cell, on an as-needed basis."

LISTEN TO THE SOUNDS OF A CELLBLOCK

A detainee is angry inside a cellblock because there's a female soldier assigned to this midday watch. The captive covers his cell door window, breaking the rules and blocking the guards' view.

A male guard who sounds unruffled by the episode tries to settle him down.

Soldier: "What's going on, man?"

Detainee: "Why is she walking back and forth?"

Soldier: "That's 'cause she's working on this block."

Detainee: "She's bullshit. I'll start covering; don't make me start covering and ... do a lot of stuff that you guys you don't like.

"I want to call for prayer. Open the bean hole for prayer."

Soldier: "OK."

At the request of the Miami Herald, an officer put an audio recorder inside a cellblock to let the outside world hear a prisoner summon his fellow Muslim captives to prayer. It did capture the prayer call. A gentle wail wafted through a slit in a cell's steel door summoning the men of Camp 5's Charlie Block to *dhuhr* prayer.

But the recording also let the world eavesdrop, briefly, on life on a maximum-security cellblock. It was around 1 p.m. on the third Monday in Ramadan, for many of the captives their 11th Ramadan in U.S. custody.

"Allahu Akbar. Allahu Akbar. Allahu Akbar. Allahu Akbar. Ash-hadu anna la illaha illa Allah ..."

None of the men on this particular block have been convicted of a crime. Nor are any facing charges. The audio makes clear that most of the guards knew that the recording device was there. The captives did not.

It picked up crosstalk between captives and guards, who addressed their charges not by their names but by their detainee numbers.

It recorded chatter between the mostly Arab captives, who were shouting through the penitentiary-style cement walls and steel doors.

A guard makes his every three-minute cell check, Camp 5, March 31, 2009. (John Van Beekum/Miami Herald)

It captured the clanking of shackles as troops in combat boots quietly moved their charges from single-occupancy cells to the recreation yard where captives are kept in a labyrinth of chain-link fencing.

It offered up guards whispering into walkie-talkies wondering whether the prayer period had ended for all 20 to 30 captives in the 100-cell, $17 million, eight-year-old prison.

But mostly there are long passages of silence as the detainees went about their midday prayer.

Wednesday, July 15, 2015

SOLDIER CELEBRATES RAMADAN ALONE

While most captives are spending their 14th Ramadan at Guantánamo, an Army platoon sergeant mobilized with the California National Guard is celebrating her first here.

All are Muslims, away from home and family, for this holy month when the devout fast during daylight hours and devote themselves to prayer.

But that might be where the comparison ends. The soldier is a woman and the 116 captives are men. She chose Islam, came to Guantánamo for just nine months and, as the only Muslim she knows on base, prays alone. The prisoners were born to the faith, mostly share meals and prayer communally, and do not know when, if ever, they can go home.

While the military has upended prison life in consideration of their Islamic faith (delivering most meals and medicine to captives at night, force-feeding hunger strikers after dark) Sergeant First Class A, as she can be known, says her Ramadan is mostly imperceptible as she carries out her duties in charge of about 30 guards, from an office outside the razor wire that encircles the war-on-terror prisoners.

"I'm a soldier. My mission comes first," she said during an interview in a conference room not far from a prison compound.

The sergeant is a 47-year-old mother and grandmother who was raised in the Pentecostal Holiness Church but chose Islam 19 years ago. By then, she says, she had also chosen the U.S. Army, enlisting voluntarily.

So, she spends her days on duty in an Army uniform, without the head scarf of the faithful she wears at home.

"Would it be nice to be able to wear it? Yeah, that's fine," she says. But she adds that she knew when she enlisted "what the uniform is."

Islam, she says, makes her a better soldier, "thoughtful, compassionate, understanding — all those things you need as a leader. That's where I pull my strength from."

It was morning and the hunger pangs of fasting had yet to set in. This sergeant on her first deployment in 20 years of service looks just like the soldiers in the room monitoring her strictly limited, 30-minute interview. She's in battle dress, combat boots, a regulation cap ready for when she steps outside.

"Me, I chose to be a soldier. This is the uniform that we wear," she said in a wide-ranging, if brief, conversation watched by several.

Here she goes about her business by day skipping meals, sometimes feeling a grumbling in her stomach at times when comrades troop off to the cafeteria. Hers is a solitary Ramadan. She starts her mornings before sunup with breakfast and prayer in her quarters at Camp America, a glorified trailer park, works out of sight of the detainees in the Detention Center Zone, then heads back after dusk for a break-fast meal and more prayers.

This Military Police platoon sergeant is Muslim and dons this attire after work, July 9, 2015. (Walter Michot/Miami Herald)

At home, she says, she'd be breaking her fast with her children, ages 13 to 25, Muslims like her. But at Guantánamo she prays alone in a time of year she sees as meant to teach the faithful the meaning of going without.

"I get the most blessings out of that," she said. "The reality is, Ramadan is to remind you of people who don't get to eat, people who don't get to participate in ... the comforts that we have.

"Ramadan puts you in that position to where you know what it feels like to be hungry, not to eat. You know what it feels like not to be able to participate at any time of day with that intimacy that we as humans need with your mate," she said. As she sees it, it's about "controlling your anger, controlling how you respond to people."

She got to Guantánamo in mid-March, and said she sees no need for Ramadan to interfere with her management routine. They call it op-temp, for operational tempo.

Unlike the captives, who were born into their faith and know no other life, she came to Islam in 1996 not long after she came to the Army through, of all things, fashion.

By then she was a mom, working in civilian life as head cashier at a grocery store in Atlanta. Now she's a self-described woman of many trades — a life coach, poet, author and beauty consultant in northern California.

Then, she says, she was working at a strip mall near a shop specializing in modest Muslim clothing. A shop worker asked her to model some. She agreed, so long as it was colorful clothing, not the drab attire that some associate with Islam.

"The prophet, peace and blessings be upon him, wore color, and so did his wife," she said after invoking her motto, "ABC, Always Be Cute."

The clothes fit, and then so did Islam. So now she belongs to a mosque in Oakland, California, a two-hour drive from her home, not unlike the distance some National Guard troops drive to drill. And the comparisons don't end there.

"My soldiers, my peers, they show me the same love, the same understanding, the same respect as if I was standing in the middle of a *masjid* in Oakland," she said, referring to her place of worship.

One evening, hours after her interview, five captives were about to pray, each man to a single cell in a maximum-security lockup, B Block. Moments before the prayers, the prisoners realized there were visitors on the block and one called out something about human rights, Barack Obama and asked to meet the commander's cultural advisor. One captive said they were hunger strikers.

"We don't have any rights," a captive announced. "And we haven't done any crime. Where is the American freedom?"

Muslims are scarce among the 2,000 or so troops and civilians who staff the prison. Some are linguists, contractors on the cellblocks, mostly men, who conduct their prayers at a mosque not far from the base McDonald's — a drive from the Detention Center Zone that is home to both A and the captives. So she prays alone, knows no other Muslim here.

Captives in communal detention conduct prayers during
Ramadan, August 6, 2012. (Walter Michot/Miami Herald)

But if you think she has any affinity for the men behind the
barbed wire, you'd be wrong.

"Not particularly, because the Quran teaches us that, you
know, you follow the laws, and if you break the laws, then it is
what it is. I don't believe in using the religion to break the laws
because the Quran is clear on that."

It was suggested to her that just one captive at Guantánamo
this Ramadan was ever convicted of a crime. The rest are, so far, in
Law of War detention, akin to a POW.

"For me I've been charged to do a job," she replied of her duties handling logistics and personnel issues for her platoon. "The other part of that, that's somebody else's responsibility. Not mine."

Tuesday, December 22, 2015

AIRMAN SUPPORTS AND DEFENDS CONSTITUTION

It was a misty Monday morning when a knot of lawyers, both U.S. troops and civilians, gathered beneath a flagpole at Camp Justice to hear a 14-year Air Force veteran swear to "support and defend the Constitution of the United States against all enemies foreign and domestic."

Tech Sergeant Michael Badilla, 32, a paralegal who started his career as a crew chief on the B-2 Stealth bomber, raised his right hand to reenlist in a time-honored tradition on a date specified by the military.

At Guantánamo, where thousands of soldiers do temporary duty at the detention center, troops have sworn the oath underwater in scuba gear, at the base kennel with a guard dog bearing witness and at the Marine-patrolled fence line opposite Cuba's minefield.

But Badilla works between the prison and court compounds — on the legal team defending the alleged mastermind of the 9/11 attacks, Khalid Sheik Mohammed — and chose the site not far from the courtroom flanked by Air Force tents typical of those used on battlefield air bases.

There was a solemnity to the occasion if not exactly a celebration at a time when attorneys are digging through grim reports about what the CIA did to the alleged plotters, admittedly reviled men, in the years before they got to Guantánamo.

"Frequently you feel like it's literally you against the world, or you and your crew against the world," Marine Brigadier General John Baker, the chief defense counsel, told the gathering before administering the sacred oath. "It's moments like this and men like this that make it so worth it."

Badilla's duties include drafting legal documents, meeting with Mohammed and lawyers, helping coordinate travel and managing case evidence. One-on-one meetings with the man accused of orchestrating the hijackings that killed nearly 3,000 people, he said, are not much different than when he helped others get legal aid before this case: "Pleasantries, business, more pleasantries."

Before, it was American airmen he was helping, and "regardless of the heinousness of the acts that were alleged, I knew that this person needed assistance and I was there to help," he said.

"There's a gravity to it," said Badilla, who aspires to get a law degree. But the job's the same. "I serve my client with the same amount of tenacity and drive and dedication and pride as the lowest private."

A sign on the road to the Detention Center Zone greets troops with one of the different Army values — Loyalty, Duty, Respect, Honor, Integrity, Personal Courage and Selfless Service. (Carol Rosenberg /Miami Herald)

There's a solidarity here among these U.S. troops. They call themselves the Defense Community, and argue that fighting to defend their clients is as much a duty as an honor. They sometimes sound defensive, in no small measure because of their frequent conflict with the prison over conditions or with the prosecution over evidence.

Badilla was assigned to Team KSM, as it is sometimes called, in 2013. The job has meant frequent travel from defense headquarters near Washington, D.C., to this remote base, long periods of separation from his wife and children, 5 and 8, too young to understand exactly what Dad does.

"They know I'm a paralegal, and that I go to Cuba and that I help people," he said.

He was asked whether he could have refused the assignment.

"Probably," he said. "But that's what I'm tasked to do. And I'm not the type of person to say no."

Attendance was optional at the dawn ceremony, which drew a couple of dozen soldiers and civilians, fellow paralegals like Badilla and four lawyers on Mohammed's defense team. Two reporters wandered up to watch, having been invited the night before in the base bar where enlisted troops can go.

"People wonder why we serve," said General Baker. "It's not for the money. It's not for the cool clothes."

Instead, he said, it's out of a sense of community and devotion to fellow service members "like Tech Sergeant Badilla."

Many of the men and women in service you meet at Guantánamo say they signed up after the September 11 attacks out of a sense of duty. The prison and war court were created because of that day. But Badilla (the son of a paralegal and grandson of a Marine) got his mother to sign for him at age 17, and formally joined on September 4, 2001. As it happened, his ID card was issued on 9/11/2001.

For the ceremony, Badilla stood below a 4-foot-by-6-foot flag he'd brought from home to fly for the occasion. His personal Stars and Stripes. He'd taken it on assignment to such far-flung places as Afghanistan, England and Minot, North Dakota, where he served until joining the defense two years ago.

For this occasion, his wife and kids were home, back in the United States, and there was work to be done. So he kept his remarks short. "Thank you very much for coming out and braving the mosquitoes and the day," he said.

And the group headed off in different directions to get ready for another day at the war court.

Chapter 10

MOST EXPENSIVE PRISON ON EARTH

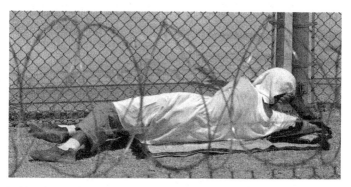

A detainee in a recreation area at Camp 6, March 31, 2009. (John Van Beekum/Miami Herald)

Wednesday, November 9, 2011

$800,000 A YEAR FOR EACH CAPTIVE

Guards at Guantánamo get combat pay, just like troops in Afghanistan, without the risk of being blown up. Some commanders get to bring their families on their war-on-terror deployment. And each captive gets $38.45 worth of food a day.

The Pentagon detention center that started out in January 2002 as a collection of crude outdoor cells guarded by Marines living in a muddy tent city is today arguably the most expensive prison on earth, costing taxpayers $800,000 annually for each of the 171 captives by Obama administration reckoning.

That's more than 30 times the cost of keeping a captive on U.S. soil.

It's still funded as an open-ended battlefield necessity, although the last prisoner arrived in March 2008. But it functions more like a gated community in an American suburb than a forward-operating base in one of Afghanistan's violent provinces.

Congress, charged with cutting $1.5 trillion from the federal budget by Christmas, provided $139 million to operate the center last year, and has made every effort to keep it open — even as a former deputy commander of the detention center calls it "expensive" and "inefficient."

"It's a slow-motion Berlin Airlift that's been going on for 10 years," says retired Army Brigadier General Greg Zanetti, a West Point graduate who in 2008 was deputy commander at the detention center.

Both Guantánamo's location and temporary nature drive up costs, Zanetti says. While there, he wrote a secret study that compared the operation to Alcatraz, noting that Attorney General Robert F. Kennedy had closed that notorious prison in 1963 because it was too expensive.

Everything comes in by barge or aircraft "from paper clips to bulldozers," Zanetti says, as well as the revolving guard force. Also, more recently, a massage chair for stressed-out prison camp staff.

Zanetti, now a Seattle-based money manager, was a financial advisor in civilian life before his New Mexico National Guard unit's call-up to Guantánamo. He has never disputed that America needed the detention center after 9/11 but argues that today it deserves a cost-benefit analysis.

"What complicates the overall command further is you have the lawyers, interrogators and guards all operating under separate budgets and command structures," he said. "It's like combining the corporate cultures and budgets of Goldman, Apple and Coke. Business schools would have a field day dissecting the structure of Guantánamo."

An examination of the expenses shows that now, with no strategy for meeting President Obama's January 22, 2009, closure order, the military is preparing for the prison's next decade. Spending is not just aimed at upgrades for the captive population, most in medium-security confinement, but also for the revolving staff of 1,850 troops, linguists, intelligence analysts, federal agents and contract laborers.

Ankle shackles are stored in a corner near the entrance of a cellblock at Camp 6, March 31, 2009. (John Van Beekum/Miami Herald)

Commanders are contracting for improvements, including $2 million of new computer equipment to grow storage space under a fast-track, noncompetitive contract with Dell recently posted on a government website. And that doesn't include the non-networked laptops the prison provides captives taking a life-skills class that includes a résumé-writing lesson, in case anyone gets to go home.

Meantime, the guard force commander is getting a new 3,000- to 3,500-square-foot headquarters for what is predicted to cost less than $750,000, below the amount that needs Congress' sign-off.

The military is also spending up to $750,000 to replace the rusting prison camp hospital with a new "infirmary hub" and "expeditionary medical shelters" around the prison camps. Equipping the new hospital will cost more, so the Navy Medical Logistics Command has put out a bid for everything from microscopes to resuscitators. Price? Unknown.

Millions go to an intelligence operation whose early Guantánamo interrogations might have fed tips to the U.S. manhunt that tracked Osama Bin Laden to his hideout in Pakistan this year. It continues to interrogate some of the captives and maintains risk assessments on each one.

A guard with four years in the Navy, with the rank of petty officer third class, gets $2,985.84 a month, including the same hazardous duty pay as he or she would pull in Kabul. A Navy commander with 15 years but no kids gets $7,840 a month, including hazardous duty pay.

But Guantánamo's a place where today an Army colonel can talk about "the battle rhythm" of the camps, have his family on the base and his children in the base's school system of, currently, 247 kids.

Prison staff have their own gym, housing and newsletter, dining rooms and first-run movie theater at Camp America, adjacent to the camps. They have their own chapel, mental health services and mini-mart that was recently selling a $99.99 scuba "body-glove" and souvenirs such as "Cuba Libre-Gitmo" fridge magnets and a full aisle of protein supplements.

Guards and other staff also cross over to the larger Navy base for recreational activities available to any sailor or contractor pulling permanent duty on the base — a golf course and deep-sea diving, beach parties and fishing trips.

They can hit the Irish pub, which was built after the al-Qaida airlifts began, take classes over the internet, which were established once the prison was opened, and can grab McDonald's drive-thru on their way to work.

And that's just for the guards.

Both captives and captors also have their own kitchen, health services, transportation and security services all fueled by a steady supply line.

In their cellblocks, cooperative captives get satellite television with sports, news and religious programming as well as Arabic soap operas. Pentagon contract workers maintain a 24,000-title book, video and magazine library and are building a new soccer field for cooperative captives. Each detainee is offered up to 4,500 calories a day — including lamb certified as halal, Islam's version of kosher.

"We are running a five-star resort and not a detention facility for terrorists," says Florida Republican Rep. Allen West, a fiscal conservative and former Army lieutenant colonel who visited in March. "For example, why do they need 24 cable TV channels?"

Soldiers and sailors consistently gripe that the internet is slow inside their private quarters, mostly trailer parks and townhouses.

Entrance to Camp America, the area of the Detention Center Zone for prison staff, March 31, 2009. (John Van Beekum/Miami Herald)

But, unlike in Afghanistan, some prison camp staff officers have brought their families, gotten suburban-style housing and put the kids in the Navy base school. Sailors say it is better than ship duty. Sure it's surrounded by water. But you get private quarters, scuba diving and can check in on weekends at guest housing complete with big-screen TVs and backyard patios with barbecue grills.

"This is great. You get the opportunity to serve your country and nobody's shooting at us. Plus, there's no mortars coming in," said Army Staff Sergeant Fred Plimpton, 55, who was a New York state trooper dispatched to Ground Zero on 9/11 and later deployed to Baghdad.

And, it's close enough to home that members of the New York Army National Guard infantry unit now patrolling the prison camps' perimeter can race back for an emergency. "Peter's wife just had a baby and we got him right home," Plimpton said in September. "Moffit's wife went into labor and we got him out of here right away. It's good to see the guys get out of here when a baby's born."

Only in an operation bursting with personnel and charter aircraft can that happen.

At Southcom, Army Colonel Scott Malcom notes that because the Pentagon is holding its prisoners "on a military base in a foreign country," it needs more security measures than on U.S. soil. He also cautions "against making a straight comparison between military detention operations and civilian correctional facilities."

For example, for federal prison guards, being a correctional officer is a career, a commuter job. They sleep at home, carry their own meals, entertain themselves on their days off. Prison staff come and go on mostly 9- to 12-month rotations, aboard charter flights, are put up in special housing, help themselves to all-you-can-eat rations at the same dining hall that cooks for the captives.

But the comparison was made when the Obama administration this summer sent a letter to Congress. The Department of Defense "spends approximately $150 million per year on detention operations at Guantánamo, currently at a rate of more than $800,000 per detainee," Attorney General Eric Holder, Defense Secretary Leon Panetta and other Cabinet members wrote to Senate Republican leader Mitch McConnell and others.

"Meanwhile, our federal prisons spend a little over $25,000 per year, per prisoner, and federal courts and prosecutors routinely handle numerous terrorist cases a year well within their operating budgets."

The Herald sought to do a line-by-line analysis of the expenses. Guantánamo prison refused to participate and instead advised the paper to file for the information under the Freedom of Information Act, a request the Southern Command refused to expedite despite the ongoing budget debate.

Instead, the Herald was able to create a snapshot of the costs.

The Pentagon confirmed that U.S. troops working at the prison camps get the same "hostile fire" and "imminent danger" pay as their battlefield counterparts in Afghanistan.

In September, a massage chair was the centerpiece of an office for a special Navy mental health unit that was set up to minister to stressed-out prison staff. It was such a success that the unit ordered up another and two biorhythm machines.

It's two months later, and the Navy Bureau of Medicine and Surgery still hasn't been able to figure out how much it spent on purchasing and delivering even the first massage chair.

The prison spokeswoman, Navy Commander Tamsen Reese, said by email October 27 that the prison "executed $2.4M in FY11 for detainee rations." Feeding the 1,850 prison staff who eat from the same kitchen is not included, she said.

That's $38.45 a captive a day for food delivered to each prisoner in fiscal year 2011.

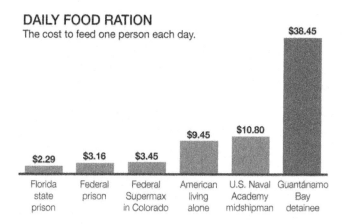

DAILY FOOD RATION
The cost to feed one person each day.

Florida state prison	Federal prison	Federal Supermax in Colorado	American living alone	U.S. Naval Academy midshipman	Guantánamo Bay detainee
$2.29	$3.16	$3.45	$9.45	$10.80	$38.45

Sources: Florida Department of Corrections, Federal Bureau of Prisons, 2010 Bureau of Labor Statistics Consumer Expenditure Survey, Joint Task Force Guantánamo and Naval Academy. (Marco Ruiz/Miami Herald)

That is more than four times as much as the average American spends on food a day and nearly 17 times as much as the state of Florida spends to feed its prisoners.

At Guantánamo, the military imports all its food by both cargo airplane and barge from Jacksonville. A Florida Department of Corrections spokeswoman, Jo Elly Rackleff, notes that the state grows some of the food.

Tuesday, February 28, 2012

PENTAGON BUILDS A $744,000 SOCCER FIELD

The military unveiled a new $744,000 soccer field, a dusty enclosure with two-toned gravel and barbed-wire-topped fences — designed as a quality of life improvement for cooperative captives.

The goalposts were missing, but the military had erected two guard towers, lights and surveillance cameras at the site outside a penitentiary-style building called Camp 6, where the Pentagon is holding about 120 of the 171 captives.

News photography was forbidden for security reasons, said Commander Reese, the prison spokeswoman whose staff released photos of the 28,000-square-foot field later in the day.

The $744,000 "Super-Rec" soccer field for cooperative captives, July 8, 2015. (Walter Michot/Miami Herald)

The showcase soccer field is half the size of an American field and being built by Burns and Roe Services Corp., said Pentagon spokesman Lieutenant Colonel Todd Breasseale. When open in April it becomes the third recreation yard at Guantánamo's main prison camp complex. When it was suggested that the price tag was excessive, Reese replied that the base's remote location at times doubles construction costs.

Monday, December 29, 2014

CONGRESS FUNDS NEW $65 MILLION SCHOOL

Guantánamo, the base with "The Most Expensive Prison on Earth," is getting one of the world's priciest schools — a $65 million building with classroom space for, at most, 275 kindergarten through high school students.

Do the math: That's nearly a quarter-million dollars per school child. In Florida's Miami-Dade County a new school costs perhaps $30,000 per student.

Congress recently allocated the funds for the new W.T. Sampson School to put the children of American sailors stationed at Guantánamo under one roof. It will meet Americans with Disabilities Act standards, have a proper public address system, computer and science labs, art and music rooms, a playground, cafeteria and gym — just like any new school anywhere in America.

But the investment also illustrates the Pentagon's intent to keep this base open even if President Obama manages to move out the last war-on-terror captives, and close the prison run by 2,000 or more temporary troops and contractors.

And it offers a lesson on the cost of doing business out here on Cuba's southeastern tip, where under the U.S. trade embargo all business is conducted independent of the local economy.

Guantánamo Bay functions like a small town of 6,000 residents.

Sailors and civilians on long-term contracts run the airport, seaport, public works division and a small community hospital. They bring their families and belongings, get suburban-style homes, scuba dive in the Caribbean — and send their children to two U.S. government schools that are nearer to the base McDonald's and bowling alley than the Detention Center Zone.

This year, there are 243 students — 164 at the elementary school and the rest at a separate building for middle and high school students whose mascot is a pirate.

In Florida, it typically costs $20,000 to $30,000 per student to build a school, according to Jaime Torrens, chief facilities officer for Miami-Dade County Public Schools. But South Florida has a "competitive environment where labor is readily available, materials are readily available."

Guantánamo's costs are so much higher "because all materials must be barged to the island, and the construction contractor's crews must live on site for the duration of construction," said Cindy Gibson, spokeswoman for the unit that runs the Department of Defense schools.

Ronald McDonald on the 20th anniversary of the establishment of the first and so far only McDonald's on Cuban soil, April 24, 2006. (Carol Rosenberg/Miami Herald)

She estimated that building costs are "70 percent higher than the average construction costs experienced in the United States."

The money for the new Sampson School is tucked inside the massive $585 billion national defense spending act that, among other things, funds the war on the Islamic State and requires that new construction projects at Guantánamo have an "enduring military value" independent of the detention operations.

It also funds the renovation or new construction of six other Department of Defense schools in Belgium, Japan and North Carolina. The next most expensive, at a cost of $173,441 per pupil, is another pre-K-12 school being built on the outskirts of Brussels for the children of Americans assigned to the U.S. Army or NATO at a cost of $173,441 per pupil.

The Sampson School is being built for a maximum 275-member student body at one location, something smaller but similar to the exclusive 1,200-student Miami Country Day School, whose head of school John Davies' first reaction to the pricetag was "Wow, $65 million?"

For $65 million, he said, "we could probably do our entire new master plan for the campus, a center for the arts, parking garage, new gym, new cafeteria and pretty substantial classroom building."

But Davies studied the building proposal and found "a pretty adequate but not over-the-top construction program." He searched the specifications and justification and "it doesn't strike me as one of those $600 toilets or $1,000 hammer kinds of things that we get every once and a while from the GAO" — the Government Accountability Office that sometimes uncovers embarrassing examples of profligate U.S. government spending.

"Obviously we're thinking we'll be in Guantánamo for a long time," he said.

Students will go to school in trailers and other available space while their current building is demolished and replaced by the new one. Once the high school students move in, workers will demolish their 1975 building behind the base pub, O'Kelly's, not far from the scrubby nine-hole golf course.

The Sampson school system, established in 1931, is named for a 19th century U.S. Navy rear admiral who was responsible for the blockade of Cuba in the Spanish-American War. It has a storied history of closings that no occasional hurricane or snow day can match.

Sampson students were sent home — evacuated back to the United States — during World War II and for three months in 1962 during the Cuban Missile Crisis. The schools also closed in the mid-'90s when families were sent away as the base coped with a huge influx of tens of thousands of Cuban and Haitian migrants, housed in tent cities, taxing the base water desalination system and other resources.

The new school's plan includes the latest in physics, chemistry and video-broadcast labs, a music suite, LED lighting and a wireless network. It will also have space for 50 faculty and administration members, two or more floors and a stucco finish, according to the proposal to Congress.

It's not possible to ask the kids what they think about it because Department of Defense policy shields schoolchildren from speaking with reporters on base. Besides, today's students are mostly from military families that move every few years, meaning they'll likely be gone by the time the new school opens.

It is projected to be finished in April 2018. By then, Obama's successor will be in office, the Pentagon will have completed a $35 million underwater fiber-optic cable between the base and South Florida and, unless Congress lifts the U.S. embargo on trade with Cuba, the blockade will be in its 57th year.

Thursday, December 31, 2015

PENTAGON RELEASES DECADE-OLD DOCUMENT

In 2005, a desk officer at the Department of Defense dutifully assembled facts and figures, the cost of doing business at the place the Miami Herald would later dub "The Most Expensive Prison on Earth."

To defend the waters around Guantánamo Bay from fears of an al-Qaida attack in 2004, the prison spent $1.9 million on a temporary U.S. Coast Guard unit. Camp Delta contractor costs totaled $22.5 million for that year, when the Pentagon held about 660 war-on-terror prisoners in Cuba. The prison spent $2.4 million on detainee food alone, plus another $3 million to run the dining hall that prepared the captives' meals and fed prison staff.

But the Air Force officer who gathered the figures was forbidden to release them, by order of a superior.

Now, a reply to a decade-old filing under the Freedom of Information Act found that secrecy was wrong.

"I am sorry that this response was not provided in a more timely manner," Michael Rhodes, director of administration and management at the Pentagon, wrote on December 14, 2015, as he released three pages of documents the Herald sought in a February 3, 2005, Freedom of Information Act filing.

With the advantage of hindsight, the figures contained in the three-page release may not be surprising. The Obama administration, after all, estimated that with 107 captives on New Year's Eve Guantánamo's per-prisoner cost was $3.7 million a year.

But back in 2004, the Pentagon under President Bush was preparing for the war crimes tribunals of Osama Bin Laden's driver who was since convicted, repatriated and exonerated. And nobody but the Herald was particularly interested in examining costs. In fact, Democrats in Congress would only tally up the expense in 2013 — at least $5 billion since it opened — after President Obama had called the detention center a waste of resources.

Moreover, back in 2004 the men who would become Guantánamo's most infamous captives, the alleged 9/11 conspirators, were still at CIA black sites and the building boom at the detention center had yet to begin in earnest.

The costs of military commissions, according to the fact sheet compiled by then-Air Force Major Michael Shavers, was $9.1 million a year for "personnel, travel, offices, etc." By contrast to last year's costs — $78 million, excluding military costs for 153 uniformed personnel — it was a war court on the cheap.

But that was before the U.S. Supreme Court shut down the format that Bush created, declaring it an unconstitutional usurpation of power by the executive branch. Bush got Congress' blessing to reopen the court and then built a $12 million compound whose centerpiece is a maximum-security, snoop-proof court complex.

While some costs rose, others apparently did not. The document says the prison spent $107,782 on "detainee stock item purchases" in 2004. Since then, the prison has stopped purchasing books for the detainees and is shopping for a supplier of up to $1 million in detainee basic-issue supplies through 2020.

Food costs, however, may not have changed. In 2004, according to the document, the Joint Task Force "spent $2.4 million for food for detainees," a period when the prison held "approximately 660" detainees and had a staff of "approximately 2,000 folks," according to a December 3, 2004, email from detention center spokesman Army Lieutenant Colonel Leon Sumpter.

A cell at Camp 6 with a display of the different supplies a cooperative captive gets, February 9, 2016. (Walter Michot/Miami Herald)

Flash forward to October 27, 2011, when then-prison spokeswoman Commander Tamsen Reese gave an identical figure — $2.4 million — for "detainee rations" at a time when the prison was holding 174 captives.

In 2005, the Camp 6 penitentiary-style building that was meant to make guarding the captives more efficient had yet to be built. But, according to Shavers' fact sheet, the military was putting the final touches on $48.1 million in capital expenditures that included guard housing, tribunal facilities, the $17 million state-of-the-art 100-cell Camp 5 and the $13.5 million prison headquarters, now known as the "Red Roof Inn."

In addition, the Army had chipped in another $7.6 million for "approximately 200 minor construction projects" that the prison would need. No details were provided.

Behind the scenes, Shavers, working as the public affairs officer at the Pentagon, was advocating for transparency — a term the detention center had yet to adopt as part of its motto. Then, the expression was "Honor Bound to Defend Freedom," and the Air Force major wrote to a lieutenant colonel that he considered the figures sought "to be a legitimate media query submitted in a timely manner."

Shavers was compiling the fact sheet in response to a series of questions the Herald designed to try to reveal costs at a complex, temporary operation that drew resources from across government. "I haven't forgotten about your cost query," Shavers wrote by email on December 29, 2004. Later, by telephone, he said he was under orders not to deliver the information.

But the document Rhodes released showed a good-faith effort to assemble some costs — even if it took a Freedom of Information Act filing followed by an appeal and 3,966 days to release the data.

The Air Force officer could not land a price tag for the air bridge that in 2004 continued to bring captives from Afghanistan beyond a fraction: $2.5 million for "transportation of things."

Intelligence figures were harder to find. The Criminal Investigation Task Force, a Department of Defense entity created after the 9/11 attacks to help build criminal cases, spent about $3 million at Guantánamo. But Shavers was unable to get figures on how much the CIA and FBI spent at the prison in 2004.

Instead, his suppressed fact sheet showed him referring the reporter to those agencies.

The question would prove prescient. When the Senate Intelligence Committee on the CIA's Rendition, Detention and Interrogation Report came out last year, it noted that the spy agency had two black sites at Guantánamo from September 2003 to April 2004. The agency shut down the operation before the U.S. Supreme Court would grant Guantánamo's captives access to attorneys.

Monday, February 22, 2016

18 TROOPS FOR EACH DETAINEE

With the Obama administration poised to present its prison closure plan to Congress, one question it may answer is how many guards it really takes to secure the declining number of detainees.

Today, the Pentagon has 2,000 troops and civilians stationed at Guantánamo to staff the prison and court alone, by one measure working out to $4.4 million a year for each of the 91 detainees.

That's not because the huge staff is on standby for the possibility that the prison population might grow. Obama administration policy prohibits bringing new captives to Guantánamo.

Rather, the warden said in a recent interview that he staffs for the worst-case scenario at the outpost on Cuba's southeastern tip: a sudden disruption that requires each and every captive to be confined alone inside a cell, rather than the current climate of most captives living communally, cooperating with their guards.

"I don't have the state police. I don't have the county sheriff," Colonel David Heath said. "I don't have anybody else to call to help me keep things under control here. And it would be several weeks before we could get a unit mobilized and in here."

Army Colonel David Heath, the chief of the guard force, briefs reporters, February 9, 2019. (Walter Michot/Miami Herald)

In its 2016 policy bill, Congress set a deadline for the White House to present a "comprehensive detention strategy" for how to handle current and future war-on-terror captives.

Obama administration officials have said they're designing an endgame for Guantánamo that involves sending some cleared detainees to other countries and the rest to military detention somewhere in the United States — something that Congress currently forbids.

Meantime, on a recent media visit, the last 91 prisoners were scattered across at least six different lockups at the sprawling Detention Center Zone that has been built in fits and starts since Camp X-Ray opened four months after the September 11 attacks.

All but at most three captives that day were deemed compliant, cooperating with camp guards, mostly living in groups that signaled little strife behind the razor wire.

But the far-flung nature of today's prison, different sites built to solve different problems across a decade of construction, some discarded, some repurposed, also accounts for the need for 1,700 troops — about 18 soldiers for every captive.

Some stand guard on cellblocks where it takes the same number of guards to stand watch whether there is one detainee or 10 inside, says Heath. Others do escort duty, moving captives between prison buildings to legal meetings, Red Cross visits, calls from home, the hospital and parole board sessions, each with a different location, each requiring its own security.

Add to that the war court, a 15-minute drive from the prison, which requires more security. The prison also has a temporary maritime unit, borrowed from the Coast Guard to protect the shoreline, and Air Force engineers who maintain temporary tent cities and trailer parks.

Heath has said consolidation of some prison functions in fewer buildings could cut some troop needs, suggesting cost savings could be realized.

"I'm not saying that it's going to stay at the number it is forever," Heath said of the current 2,000 staff level. "I consider myself a steward of the taxpayer. And I'm not spending any dollar that I don't think needs to be spent down here."

You would expect that fewer prisoners would mean fewer chores for the U.S. forces. But Heath says the troops are kept busy.

A scattering of moviegoers attend the Saturday night feature at the outdoor cinema, March 29, 2009. (John Van Beekum/Miami Herald)

"My battalion commanders have different training activities planned to keep these guys gainfully employed," said Heath of the place where the military has provided more and more distractions for off-duty troops, including an outdoor cinema and Jet Skis.

The New Orleans band Spice and the Po Boys came through recently to celebrate Mardi Gras with a show at the base Tiki Bar.

Still, with all the troops and so few detainees, Heath said, "discipline is not a problem here. We have incidents just like every place does, but there is no greater instance of any kind of misbehavior here than I've seen in my 26 years in the Army."

Make no mistake, he said, "This is not spring break down here. They are not sitting on the beach."

Chapter 11

PLATINUM PRISONERS

The path former CIA prisoners walk from the war court to a holding cell at Camp Justice, June 19, 2014. (Carol Rosenberg /Miami Herald)

Thursday, February 7, 2008

FORMER CIA CAPTIVES IN OFF-LIMITS CAMP

Call them the platinum prisoners.

Somewhere on this isolated outpost, strictly off-limits from the Pentagon's media tour, is a secret prison housing 15 alleged senior al-Qaida captives called high-value detainees. It is Camp 7, and run by a special unit code-named Task Force Platinum.

Khalid Sheik Mohammed, called KSM, is there. He's the alleged al-Qaida kingpin whom the CIA confirms it covertly waterboarded somewhere overseas to break his will, using a technique that simulates drowning and is widely condemned as torture.

Six months after he got to Guantánamo, transcripts show, KSM confessed to plotting a virtual, global campaign of terror — everything from the September 11 assaults on New York and the Pentagon to the never-realized assassinations of American presidents.

Also there is Majid Khan, a 27-year-old suburban Baltimore high school graduate who was allegedly tasked by KSM to research one unrealized plot. Khan told a military panel that he was so desperate in his earliest months here that he gnawed at the artery in his arm, wanting to die.

Who runs this camp? Who built it? How does it function? Who comes and goes and gets to talk with the detainees? When and how will they see lawyers? Some of these questions will be front and center at the military commissions in the case of Salim Hamdan of Yemen — Osama Bin Laden's driver, who the Pentagon says is a war criminal.

His charge sheets allege he conspired with the top leadership of al-Qaida's campaign of terror from the 9/11 attacks to the suicide bombings of the USS Cole off Aden, Yemen, in October 2000.

Hamdan's lawyers are in a struggle with the prosecution over access to the captives of Camp 7, who arrived at Guantánamo in September 2006 after years of secret CIA interrogation.

And they want the judge, Navy Captain Keith Allred, to resolve the dispute.

The lawyers want to ask seven of the men (who may someday face the war court themselves) what they know about the wiry $200-a-month driver who has claimed for years that he was a working stiff, not a terrorist.

"Maybe you sit down with Khalid Sheik Mohammed and he says, 'I had nothing to do with 9/11. I was waterboarded. I was a driver in Pakistan and nothing to do with it,'" says Navy Lieutenant Commander Brian Mizer, Hamdan's lead military lawyer.

"But some of these guys may be proud of what they've done and will tell us what they know: Who is Hamdan, how does he fit into the al-Qaida puzzle."

The military has so far denied the request, citing national security. If they talk to outsiders, the argument goes, al-Qaida's inner circle could spill U.S. intelligence secrets, including how the CIA held and interrogated them, and tip off other terrorists.

Hamdan's team argues that a core of the alleged al-Qaida brain trust is just a jeep ride away from the war court.

Only once Mizer has questioned them — likely shackled and chained to the floor, as in any other captive-lawyer meeting — can the defense decide whether any might serve as a character witness at a trial before U.S. military officers.

No reporter has seen Camp 7 on the weekly tours for U.S. and foreign media that showcase a U.S. program of "safe and humane detention" while the Pentagon decides whether to try them at "full, fair and open" trials.

"Quite frankly, for security reasons and policies that come down from the Secretary of Defense, we can't divulge the location of where it is," said Army Lieutenant Colonel Ed Bush, a prison camps spokesman on a media tour.

Monday, February 27, 2012

PLEA REVEALS NEW TRIAL STRATEGY

When a suburban Baltimore high school graduate steps out of the shadows of CIA detention this week to admit to serving the senior leadership of al-Qaida, the Obama administration will be unveiling its latest strategy toward an endgame.

Majid Khan has agreed to be a government witness at future military commissions, sources say, in exchange for the guilty plea and the possibility of return to his native Pakistan in four years.

It's part of an evolving effort to quell criticism that confessions were extracted through torture by offering live testimony from willing captive witnesses.

"It's like organized crime," said retired Air Force Colonel Morris, a Bush-era Pentagon war crimes prosecutor. "Sometimes you pick the lesser of the two evils and bargain with who you can."

Federal prosecutors describe Khan, who turns 32 Tuesday, as a one-time willing foot soldier for radical Islam. He allegedly recorded a martyr's message and donned a fake bomb vest in 2003 in a test to see whether he was willing to kill then-Pakistani President Pervez Musharraf. He allegedly delivered $50,000 from Pakistan to Thailand, money used to fund an al-Qaida affiliate's August 2003 suicide attack on a Marriott hotel in Jakarta, Indonesia. Eleven people died, and more than 80 others were wounded.

The attack's alleged architect, Riduan bin Ismouddin, an Indonesian man known as Hambali, and two reputed Malaysian deputies were, like Khan, subjected to years of secret CIA interrogations. They've never been charged but are still at Guantánamo and, according to a Malaysian newspaper, in the queue for military trials.

Less clear is how Khan would help at a 9/11 trial. His charge sheet alleges he joined al-Qaida after the September 11 terror attacks.

The Majid Khan plea also illustrates a new merging of military and federal prosecutorial techniques that was absent at the start of the war court, said veteran New York defense lawyer Joshua Dratel whose client, David Hicks, pleaded guilty in 2007. He was the first war criminal convicted at Guantánamo.

"They didn't have a clue how to make a deal," Dratel said.

Then it was driven by politics. Hicks was released to his native Australia ostensibly to help then-Prime Minister John Howard silence critics of Australia's war-on-terror alliance with the Bush administration as he was seeking re-election. Howard lost anyway and military prosecutors got no live testimony from Hicks, a potentially useful English-speaking insider who, like Khan, could straddle both cultures in explaining how al-Qaida worked to a military jury.

Now, says Dratel, the prosecutors are trying to institute a more "traditional criminal law approach to these cases: Get cooperators, move up the ladder and look for ways to neutralize defense arguments by creating different independent avenues of presenting the same evidence."

Or, put another way, "the deal bank is open," said Dratel.

Pentagon officials won't discuss the strategy, except to say that at the Obama war court evidence gleaned through torture is both inadmissible and illegal. "We are approaching the public prosecution function as military and federal prosecutors do, seeking evidence through every available and lawful process," said Army Brigadier General Mark Martins, the chief war court prosecutor.

Khan has always been a bit of an anomaly among the CIA's so-called "ghost prisoners" who were subjected to "enhanced interrogation techniques." His parents live in suburban Baltimore, where they moved the family in the '90s and became legal residents. Khan graduated from Owings Mills High School in 1999 and went back to Pakistan after the 9/11 attacks over the objections of his parents, who hid his passport.

Pakistani security forces arrested him in 2003. FBI agents searched the family's Baltimore house and trailed them for a time. The family heard no news of their son until September 2006 when President Bush announced that "a terrorist named Majid Khan" was in custody and had confessed under interrogation to delivering "$50,000 to individuals working for a suspected terrorist leader named Hambali, the leader of al-Qaida's Southeast Asian affiliate."

A year later, defense attorneys filed a brief in federal court declaring him a torture victim of the CIA's enhanced interrogation program. "Khan admitted anything his interrogators demanded of him," his lawyers wrote, "regardless of the truth, in order to end his suffering."

According to transcripts, Khan told a military board in April 2007 that he emerged from CIA custody so despairing of his isolation that he tried to kill himself by chewing through an artery in his arm.

Two Sudanese men who served as al-Qaida recruits have deals to finish their sentences in Obama's second term, should he receive one.

But the case of Khan is following a far different script that sources say is taking a page from the federal court system: His sentencing hearing will come much later — after four years of testimony in other war court trials. Then his lawyers can argue for leniency and invoke CIA treatment they call torture.

Much of the Khan case is being played out in secret. The timeline of the deal itself was under seal at the Pentagon's war court website. Military sources say Khan has been moved to a new maximum-security lockup that was set up out of public view. Where is it? That's a secret. How much did it cost? No comment. When was it built? Ditto.

A Pentagon spokesman would say only that Khan is secure, and unlike during the three years he spent with the CIA, his attorneys and Red Cross delegates will be allowed to see him. "We treat all detainees with the same level of dignity and respect that is due any human being," Lieutenant Colonel Todd Breasseale said.

Khan is pleading guilty after nearly a decade in detention.

During that time he was interrogated without charge, kept in isolation, and, according to his 2007 federal lawsuit, subjected to "a sophisticated, refined program of torture operating with impunity outside the boundaries of any domestic or international law" at the CIA's secret overseas prisons.

His lawyers will be allowed to bring this up at sentencing, according to sources familiar with the Khan deal. But first, says retired Navy Lieutenant Commander Charlie Swift, a veteran of the war court, expect other defense lawyers to try to use Khan's CIA treatment whenever he's brought as a government witness, to challenge the credibility of his testimony.

"The way you avoid the door to the dark sites is you don't use the material," said Swift, who challenged George W. Bush's military commissions at the U.S. Supreme Court, and won. "But in the end they can't avoid it. They wouldn't know he was a potential witness unless they tortured him."

Thursday, October 16, 2014

COED RUCKUS AT CAMP 7

The military now has female soldiers escorting former CIA captives around Guantánamo's prison for high-value detainees, an apparent personnel change that defense lawyers say is causing an uproar over religious insensitivity.

When one captive refused to be touched by a female soldier, the military called in a special unit to move him using the detention center's tackle-and-shackle technique, a Forced Cell Extraction. Since that incident, at least four of the 9/11 defendants have boycotted legal meetings over the issue, attorneys say.

The prison would not confirm the tension at Guantánamo's most secretive Camp 7 detention facility. But Navy Captain Tom Gresback, a spokesman, said the U.S. military has a policy of being gender neutral in its relations with detainees.

The prison has "no intention in modifying its assignment of job responsibilities to members of the guard force based on gender," Gresback said.

Prisoners are generally moved from place to place in shackles, often at the wrists and ankles, with a guard on each side clasping the captive by the arm or shoulder. Among those refusing meetings over the issue is Khalid Sheik Mohammed, the accused mastermind of the September 11 terror attacks.

"This is viewed as an attack on Islam because for years the guard force accommodated their religious objections to unwanted touching by someone of the opposite sex," said Marine Major Derek Poteet, KSM's military attorney. "It's not about objection to women in the military or women's roles. It's just about unwanted touching."

The coed escort issue apparently came to a head October 8 after captive Abd al Hadi al Iraqi, in his 50s, held a "peaceful legal meeting" with his U.S. military defense team, said his lawyer Marine Lieutenant Colonel Thomas Jasper.

Afterward, Hadi "was forcibly extracted from his cell" at the meeting place and returned to his prison building. At issue, Jasper said, was "the use of a female guard to escort Hadi between locations," an apparent change of prison camp policy.

Defense attorney Cheryl Bormann, who represents accused 9/11 plotter Walid Bin Attash, said the recent addition of female guards as escorts appears to breach détente at the detention center.

Sometime after the CIA brought the 9/11 defendants to Guantánamo in 2006, Bormann says she was told, some female soldiers were briefly assigned to Camp 7 escort duty. The captives protested and the prison replaced them with men, she said.

"Now all of a sudden there are women who are touching these men who find it religiously offensive."

Bormann, who consistently wears a black *abaya* in her client's company, said she has "never, ever" touched him — and he has likewise never touched her. "It isn't that it offends his personal integrity," she said. "It is because his religion teaches him that it is forbidden."

Female U.S. troops are still excluded from detainee groin searches and monitoring their showers, the detention center's cultural advisor said. "These are male-female issues; it has nothing to do with culture or religion," he said.

He's a Pentagon employee, a Muslim man called Zaki, and he has no access to Camp 7, where the former CIA prisoners are kept. But he said Guantánamo's detainees cannot dictate whether male or female guards can "hold the shoulder and move them along."

They can, however, refuse to go to appointments over the issue, and have done so, he said.

Detention center staff emphasize that troops respect their captives' religion, Islam.

The detention center has an arrow indicating the direction of Mecca painted inside each cell. The guard force says it observes quiet time during the five-times-daily prayer. Medical staff adjust the tube-feeding hours for hunger strikers to after dark during the holy month of Ramadan.

Zaki got to Guantánamo before the September 11 defendants and says captives have in the past raised religious objections in order to "create some issue to draw attention to Guantánamo."

"When you are in detention you have no option, no choice of who handles you," he said. "You have to live with the circumstances that you're in."

Book editor's note: A war court judge forbade female guards from touching the alleged 9/11 plotters between January 7, 2015 and October 28, 2016 while he considered the issue. He ultimately ruled for the military's gender neutrality over the detainees' cultural and religious claims.

Thursday, February 12, 2015

LAWYER DESCRIBES CIA RECTAL ABUSE

A defense lawyer for an alleged 9/11 plotter says his Saudi client had been rectally abused while in CIA custody – and that he continues to bleed now, at least eight years later.

Attorney Walter Ruiz made the disclosure in open court in a bid to get a military judge to intervene in the medical care of Mustafa al Hawsawi, 46, accused of helping the September 11 hijackers with travel and money.

Hawsawi, who was captured in March 2003 with alleged 9/11 mastermind KSM, was subjected to unauthorized "enhanced interrogation techniques" at a secret CIA prison, according to the recently released so-called Senate Torture Report. He got to Guantánamo in September 2006.

The five-foot five-inch man has sat on a pillow over years of pretrial hearings in the death penalty trial of five men accused of conspiring in the terror attacks that killed nearly 3,000 people on September 11, 2001. Thursday was the first time that Ruiz was permitted to explain it under a loosening of censorship at the court that lets lawyers talk about the released, redacted 524-page portion of the 6,200-page Senate report.

"It started somewhere between 2003 and 2006 by members and agents of our government who violated our laws and tortured. It is our responsibility now to provide the adequate medical care," said Ruiz.

He also added that, although these are death penalty proceedings, the court is obliged to ensure adequate healthcare.

Guantánamo's prison spokesmen say captives get the same level of care as U.S. service members.

Ruiz specifically cited a reference to an investigation of allegations that CIA agents conducted medically unnecessary rectal exams with excessive force on two detainees, one of them Hawsawi, who afterward suffered an anal fissure, rectal prolapse and hemorrhoids.

"Some would call that sodomy," Ruiz said, adding that "those acts caused long-standing, chronic and medical conditions that have yet to be resolved."

Ruiz said that guards sometimes find blood in Hawsawi's clothes. With permission of his client, Ruiz wants access to Hawsawi's secret medical records and to consult with prison legal and medical staff, including a visiting gastrointestinal expert.

Prosecutors urged the Army judge not to intervene in Hawsawi's healthcare, saying it is the province of professional U.S. military medical and prison officials.

"No doctor should be treating with a lawyer looking over his shoulder," said Ed Ryan, a federal attorney on chief prosecutor Martins' team.

Ruiz's remarks were the first direct mention in court of the Senate report that was released December 9, 2014. This week's hearings were stalled on the discovery that an ex-CIA black site interpreter was assigned to translate for another ex-CIA prisoner, alleged 9/11 accomplice Ramzi Bin al Shibh.

Despite the delays in court, eight relatives of September 11 victims still said it was a worthwhile trip.

"I'm personally against the death penalty, which is a hard thing in this particular case," said Adele Welty, who lost her son Tim on 9/11. He was a New York City firefighter.

She added that the trial is about "whether or not we allow barbarians to model our behavior. If we allow that, they win."

Hawsawi's lawyers also want the judge to intervene in the Saudi's conditions of confinement at Camp 7 to bring them in line with the Geneva Conventions – something prosecutor Clay Trivett opposed, saying that it would be a slippery slope that could see the court litigating ice cream requests, and that it was illegal.

"In fact, he is statutorily barred from asserting the Geneva Conventions by the Military Commission Act of 2009," Trivett said.

Thursday, February 18, 2016

COURT SEES 'ZERO DARK THIRTY' TORTURE SCENES

Defense lawyers in the September 11 case screened grisly scenes of torture from the Hollywood movie *Zero Dark Thirty* at the war court in their bid to argue that the CIA gave filmmakers more access to evidence than lawyers in the death penalty case.

The clips shown by attorneys for alleged 9/11 conspirator Ammar al Baluchi included a bruised and battered character named "Ammar" being put in a coffin-sized box, being doused with ice water in a mock waterboarding scene and being strung up by his arms during rounds of CIA interrogation.

"This is a movie, not a documentary," protested prosecutor Jeffrey Groharing. Colonel Pohl, the trial judge, overruled the objection.

In the courtroom at the time was Baluchi, whose attorney Jay Connell said was subjected to some of the techniques, including being told to stand on a mat and threatened with a beating if he stepped off. That actually happened to Baluchi, Connell said, but it was not publicly known when the filmmakers included it.

The stark images of torture punctuated a day of largely technical presentations by prosecutors on how they wanted to proceed with providing the captives' lawyers with evidence about the alleged September 11 plotters' years in the CIA black sites.

Lawyers for all of the accused terrorists call the details of their clients' torture critical to challenging the legitimacy of statements that their clients gave to law enforcement authorities at Guantánamo, after the black sites. They also want them to argue that the United States has lost the moral authority to execute them if they are convicted.

Undated Ammar al Baluchi in an International Red Cross photo obtained by the Miami Herald.

Prosecutors argue that some information needs protection as national security secrets and that some is not relevant. They say that, under the rules that govern the war court, they and the judge decide what the defense lawyers get.

In their *Zero Dark Thirty* motion, filed in 2013, Baluchi's attorneys argue that the U.S. government gave screenwriter Mark Boal and director Kathryn Bigelow more information for the movie than the lawyers have themselves seen of Baluchi's years in CIA custody.

They are seeking information about the CIA's briefings of Bigelow and Boal beyond a series of partially redacted emails released to Judicial Watch under the Freedom of Information Act. But Groharing told Pohl that he had examined the redacted emails and, while they contained classified information, none of the information withheld under FOIA met the defenders' requests.

Pohl looked baffled by the suggestion that the information furnished to the filmmakers was unavailable to the defense attorneys. "Did Bigelow and Boal have a clearance?" he asked.

"No," Groharing replied.

The screening itself was a departure from the dry legal arguments in years of pretrial hearings of the five men who allegedly conspired to direct, train and fund the hijackers who killed nearly 3,000 people on September 11, 2001.

After court, Connell said that the film contained uncanny representations of Baluchi's real-life CIA experiences. Connell said Baluchi had seen the clips before but "was visibly upset" during the screening. "Mr. al Baluchi sat in court today and watched film clips about his own torture," he said.

Chapter 12

REPORTING FROM REDACTISTAN

This testimony was given in open court in the 9/11 case on October 30, 2015. When the Pentagon released a transcript a month later only the words "Thank you" survived after a classification review. (Miami Herald)

Friday, January 13, 2006

REPORTER'S NOTEBOOK: CAMP X-RAY A MEMORY

With the 500 or so suspected terrorists now held at a prison camp called Delta, the military wants to underscore the message that the iconic Camp X-Ray is now history.

So it was with all the aplomb of a package-tour guide that a military escort led a dozen visiting Canadian and U.S. reporters through the weed-choked warren of the now abandoned lockup for suspected terrorists.

Carol Rosenberg

"We are going to come over into the adjoining cellblocks and grab you guys some souvenir locks," said Army Major Jeffrey Weir, weaving between vacant chain-linked cells inside X-Ray. A few correspondents pocketed some rusty broken padlocks, strewn on the ground around the abandoned cellblocks, which first received prisoners on January 11, 2002.

Old photo, new story: Most of the world knows accused teen terrorist Omar Khadr as a fresh-faced adolescent school boy. In stark contrast, the Toronto-born youth who was captured at age 15 in a gunfight in Afghanistan shuffled into his military commission hearing as a 19-year-old, six-foot-tall young man with a black beard.

But the boyish picture is all the public gets to see. The military refuses to permit photographers in the commissions, citing Geneva Conventions protections that prevent the military from parading war prisoners before the cameras.

An al Jazeera correspondent noted the ban was inconsistent with the U.S. release of photos of a bedraggled Saddam Hussein shortly after U.S. troops snatched him from his snake hole in Iraq in December 2003.

A Pentagon spokesman shrugged off the inconsistency.

Thursday, June 5, 2008

KSM CENSORS HIS FIRST SKETCH

Alleged 9/11 mastermind Khalid Sheik Mohammed was granted, and wielded, the right to censor the sketch of him that emerged from his first court appearance since he disappeared into CIA custody in 2003.

Pool sketch artist Janet Hamlin said that a court security officer brought her drawing to KSM inside the courtroom for approval during a lunchtime recess at his arraignment.

From a window into the spectator's gallery, Hamlin could see the Pakistani-born, U.S.-educated captive lean back in his court chair, hold up her sketch and point disapprovingly at a portion. "He said, 'Look at my FBI photo. Fix the nose. Then bring it back to me,' " she said, quoting the instructions to her as related through a U.S. officer.

The image was released after lunch, with the new nose job.

A Pentagon spokesman said the court artist whittled down the width of the nose, and the security officer authorized its release. "He wanted his nose to look like the FBI photo. We honored his wishes," said Navy Commander Jeffrey Gordon. "I think it shows the remarkable lengths we go to that we take their desires into consideration."

Gordon said the court security officer handed the sketch to KSM's attorneys, who in turn handed it to the defendant. Earlier, the military judge presiding at the first court appearance of the five alleged 9/11 conspirators ruled that the 43-year-old "mastermind" was competent to serve as his own defense attorney.

Hamlin has been drawing detainees at the Guantánamo court for years. This was the first known instance of a detainee getting to review an image.

"I did give him quite the beak," Hamlin conceded, as she headed back to the top security courtroom to fix the nose. In her hand was a copy of the widely circulated photo of KSM after his capture in Pakistan, showing him in a rumpled T-shirt, in need of a shave and with tousled hair.

Saturday, May 1, 2010

COURT CLOSES FOR CLASSIFIED 'YOUTUBE VIDEO'

Officers cleared the public from a war court hearing on whether Canadian captive Omar Khadr was tortured in U.S. custody to screen a 2003-era interrogation video just days after a prosecutor pledged "no secret evidence."

Paradoxically, the videotape screened in secret was released by Canada's Supreme Court two years ago. It shows the Toronto-born teen weeping in a Guantánamo interrogation booth, excerpts of which are widely available on the internet.

But court security officers said the video was still technically classified.

The development occurred on the fourth day of hearings in which Khadr's lawyers want a military judge to exclude the teen's various confessions to military and FBI interrogators from his upcoming trial. They argue that because of his youth, and treatment, he did not voluntarily cooperate with his captors, a new standard for evidence at Obama-era military commissions.

An NCIS agent, Jocelyn Dillard, testified that Khadr cooperated while she and an FBI agent interrogated him at the Guantánamo prison hospital in 2003, once while he was receiving IV antibiotics because his year-old war wounds were festering.

Prosecutors declined to seek the death penalty in the case because of his age. Khadr, 23, is Guantánamo's youngest and last Western captive among the 183 now held here, and The Washington Post reported that Obama administration officials were open to a plea agreement.

The session opened on Wednesday with a pledge from case prosecutor Jeffrey Groharing, "There is no secret evidence in this case."

Defense attorneys, not the Pentagon's prosecutors, asked to air the video at the war court. But the government agencies control interrogation videos, which are invariably classified.

The judge opened the rare Saturday military commission session at 7:30 a.m. and by 9 a.m. had the courtroom cleared for the video screening. Only a dozen observers were in the gallery — lawyers, three reporters, a sketch artist and a Canadian government observer.

All were escorted out of the hilltop courthouse, and technicians cut a closed-circuit feed from the court to the media center in a crude abandoned airport hangar below. During the blackout, journalists watched on Youtube.com chunks of the same video being screened in secret.

Sunday, January 6, 2013

A PLACE OF SOMETIMES PUZZLING SECRECY

When victims of al-Qaida attacks want to talk to reporters at Guantánamo, retired Navy Captain Karen Loftus squires the "victim family members" to Camp Justice's press shed and introduces herself as their escort.

When the New York Post put a spotlight on Loftus' unique role as victim and witness advocate in the coming 9/11 death penalty trial, the native New Yorker posed for a photo at the Brooklyn Bridge.

So it came as a puzzlement in December when the Pentagon blacked out her name on a military judge's order compelling her to testify this month in a pretrial hearing of a Guantánamo death penalty case. The job description in the order made it clear that Loftus would be the witness — even with her name covered up.

So why the secrecy in postings on the Pentagon's military commissions website, the portal for tribunal documents whose motto is "fairness, transparency, justice"?

"I'm following the office policy because I'm a witness," said Loftus, who works from the Pentagon's war crimes prosecutor's office near Washington.

Yes, the woman in charge of arranging travel for victims and witnesses is herself being treated as an anonymous witness in the case of Abd al Rahim al Nashiri, the alleged architect of the October 2000 bombing of the USS Cole. The al-Qaida attack killed 17 U.S. sailors.

Meantime, the episode serves as the latest illustration of the peculiar pick-and-choose transparency that exists in the war court that the Bush and Obama administrations built after the 9/11 attacks.

The Pentagon's death penalty trials are months, if not years, away, and the court is systematically constructing a patchwork of secrecy to surround the trials that, by order of Congress, are being held outside the United States at Guantánamo Bay.

The CIA delivered Nashiri to Guantánamo for trial in 2006, according to declassified documents, after agents waterboarded him, threatened his mother, and held a revving drill and cocked gun to his head. But where he was held or anything about the CIA interrogation techniques, which President Obama banned upon taking office cannot be revealed in open court by order of the judge. The same is true about what the CIA did to the five accused conspirators in the 9/11 attacks.

A U.S. government censor sits in the Guantánamo court, his finger on the button of a white-noise machine that can muffle sound if he suspects someone is about to utter a state secret. Spectators hear courtroom conversation on a judicially sanctioned 40-second delay.

It is in this court that Loftus is being called to testify about her job the week of February 4. She runs a Pentagon lottery for family members of victims who want to watch the Guantánamo proceedings. She also operates a portal for victims on the Pentagon website and arranges their travel. She travels with the victims to Guantánamo, where she has been seen comforting some in court and dining with them at the base pub.

In court, she can instruct a guard to pull a curtain around the victims inside the spectators' gallery to shield them from the searching eyes of other observers. She helps them decide if, or when, they talk to reporters.

Defense lawyers for Nashiri say they need their own staff member authorized to approach Pentagon-approved victims. Over the prosecution's objections, defense lawyers got the trial judge's order for Loftus to testify in court along with a non-government expert on victim-witness relations, Tammy Krause, whose name, perplexingly, is *not* blacked out in a separate judge's order.

As for Loftus' identity, it's being "protected from disclosure to the public" because it meets the definition of "general discovery materials," says Lieutenant Colonel Todd Breasseale, a Pentagon spokesman. She's entitled to anonymity until her "actual testimony," said Breasseale, who would not elaborate on why a government-salaried worker gets anonymity but the civilian defense witness does not.

Zachary Katznelson, a sometime Guantánamo court observer as senior attorney with the American Civil Liberties Union's National Security Project, called the redaction of Loftus' name an example of "confusing and inconsistent application of opaque rules."

If her name had never been made public, and the judge likewise had Krause's name blacked out prior to testimony, that would make sense, he said.

But, "her name is already in the record by name and it wasn't bleeped out in our 40-second delay and it's already in the transcript," said Katznelson.

Katznelson is a lawyer who has filed unlawful detention suits for some of Guantánamo's captives, and throughout the interview was careful never once to speak Loftus' name, just in case.

That's because lawyers, as well as journalists, must navigate a minefield of rules that can suddenly and inexplicably pop up.

In 2010, the Pentagon banned four reporters from covering the war court — for life — for publishing the name of former Army Sergeant Joshua Claus, a military interrogator who was to testify anonymously in a war court hearing.

He previously had been interviewed and identified by name in a Toronto Star article. Some of the reporters hired a lawyer, and the Pentagon relented. Now reporters have to sign 12 pages of ground rules to get access to the Guantánamo court compound. But rule C.3. makes it clear that the Pentagon can't punish reporters for publishing Loftus' name.

The judge, however, can let even people who are identified in the court record by name testify incognito.

That's what happened at a 9/11 hearing in October when Colonel Pohl, chief of the war court, agreed to let a deputy prison camps lawyer testify anonymously — even though her name, rank and duties are publicly available in uncensored documents at the court.

Why? One prosecutor said she was entitled to anonymity as part of the security force. The chief prosecutor argued that, in the absence of a protective order, she should get protection.

And the protective order, which lays out what can be kept secret, is sometimes a secret, too.

On December 20, Judge Pohl signed a protective order covering "Unclassified Discovery Material" in the September 11 case — outlining the obligations of lawyers and court workers on what they must keep secret in the run-up to the trial. The Pentagon waited a week, until two days after Christmas, to notify the public of the existence of "Protective Order #2."

Ever since Barack Obama was elected on a pledge to increase "transparency" in government, then had his lawyers reform the military commissions, the term has become nearly a mantra at Guantánamo. The prison camps already had adopted the motto of "safe, humane, legal, transparent" detention.

Then the Department of Defense spent nearly $500,000 to construct a war court website decorated with "fairness, transparency, justice" on each and every page. It's where the Pentagon posts war court documents — after the intelligence agencies get up to 15 days to scrub them.

Whole prosecution filings are secret, notably legal motions in both the 9/11 and Nashiri death penalty cases that seek a secret finding from the judge that even the defense lawyers have not seen.

Defense attorney Rick Kammen of Indianapolis sported a kangaroo lapel pin at a hearing of the war court, June 14, 2013. (Carol Rosenberg/Miami Herald)

During a recent talk, the chief prosecutor, Army Brigadier General Mark Martins, said that "openness is an absolutely critical" value at the Guantánamo court. "It provides sun, disinfectant, allows people to feel comfortable that corruption is not happening in their processes," he told Miami law students in November.

"But this is also about finding the truth, seeking accountability and also about protecting the public interest, which isn't always in the advertising of every piece of information," Martins said. "In the areas of national security, in the areas of privacy information, not all of that should be trotted out in front of everybody. That's the basic rationale."

So, with the blessing of the judge, the names of foreign nations where the CIA held captives are redacted — blacked out — when motions about Nashiri's overseas capture and treatment are made public. Declassified investigative reports illustrate abuse. But the prosecutor, Martins, has pledged that no involuntary confessions would be used against a war court accused.

In the case of Loftus, defense lawyers want to have someone from their side trained to approach victims.

If there's a conviction, victims typically advise the military jury on whether they want the criminal executed. If there's a proposal for a plea agreement, victims may want to hear something from the accused, and defense lawyers can serve as go-between.

As the government's witness/victim advocate, Loftus is "not a neutral person," said attorney Rick Kammen, Nashiri's civilian death penalty defense lawyer. "There may be a whole host of survivors or victims who for varying reasons aren't as engaged or may be engaged differently. We need to reach out."

Asked why the government covered up Loftus' name in his motion to call her as a witness, he replied: "I can't possibly imagine."

Neither can Nashiri's Pentagon defender, Navy Lieutenant Commander Stephen Reyes, who has taken to referring to the nations that might have information about his client's treatment as "Redactistan." Each and every time a foreign country appears in their filings, the name is redacted, blacked out as a national security secret.

"This whole 'Redactistan, Redactigate' issue does show disparate treatment," says Reyes, who never once in a lengthy interview spoke Loftus' name. Just in case.

JUDGE MAKES SECRET RULING ON SECRET MOTION

During a secret hearing at Guantánamo, the military judge in the 9/11 death penalty case ruled against a secret government request to withhold information from defense lawyers for accused September 11 mastermind Khalid Sheik Mohammed and his four alleged co-conspirators, according to a partially redacted transcript.

The hearing, held August 19 at the U.S. Navy base in Cuba, was the first closed pretrial hearing of the September 11 capital case. The subject matter was so secret that the judge cleared the court of the public and the five men who, if convicted, could be executed for conspiring to carry out the worst attack on U.S. soil, including 2,976 counts of murder.

And, while the 31-page transcript of the 29-minute hearing is so riddled with redactions that it is unclear what the Pentagon prosecution team was trying to shield from the defense attorneys, it shows the judge denying the request.

"I'm ruling it is discoverable," Judge Pohl said in response to a secret prosecution motion that argues something "is not discoverable."

At issue in the hearing was a pretrial motion labeled Appellate Exhibit 52 by the prosecution that sought a secret ruling from the judge. It was called a "government consolidated notice regarding ex parte, in camera filing and motion for finding" on the Pentagon's war court website whose motto is "fairness, transparency, justice."

A government protective order in the case blocks from public view the details of the CIA's secret prison network where the five alleged plotters were held for years and, they and their lawyers say, were tortured. A censor in the court can cut off the audio to the public if he or the judge fears national security secrets will be spilled.

But the judge ruled that in this instance the risk was so great that he closed the August 19 hearing entirely. On Tuesday, the Pentagon released the partial transcript after U.S. intelligence agencies redacted secret information from it.

Prosecutor Joanna Baltes, a Justice Department classification expert, tried to pin Pohl down on what he would allow the defense lawyers to see.

"I'm not ruling on whether they █████████," the judge says in the public portion of the transcript. "I'm not ruling on whether █████████. I'm not ruling on whether █████████. I'm simply saying the information is discoverable and I will address the form at a later date."

Discovery, in a legal setting, is evidence that the prosecution is obliged to show the accused before a trial.

At the Pentagon, chief prosecutor Martins declined to answer a question on whether the ruling constituted a setback, or whether his office was considering challenging the judge's ruling at a special military commissions appeals panel.

In his place, a Pentagon spokesman refused to elaborate on what went on in the secret session.

"All rulings are of some consequence to the path forward," said Lieutenant Colonel Todd Breasseale, adding that the Pentagon prosecutor "remains committed to seeking accountability under law and will continue to do so."

Retired Air Force Colonel Morris Davis, who was chief prosecutor when the 9/11 accused were brought to Guantánamo in 2006, questioned what needed to be kept secret in the case a decade after Mohammed's capture. Declassified CIA documents have already disclosed that agents waterboarded him 183 times.

"Whatever need there was for secrecy you'd think a decade would have cured," he said. After reading the partially redacted transcript, he said there was "so much blacked out" that it was hard to discern the significance of the lost prosecution motion.

Disclosure of the ruling itself is "beneficial," Davis said, because it challenges "the perception that the government can do whatever the hell it wants. To the extent that the judge said, '*au contraire*,' there's some value in it."

In this case, because of the national security court being run by the Obama administration, some discovery will be shown to the accused September 11 plotters' attorneys, who have security clearances, but not the men being put on trial.

Human Rights Watch counterterrorism counsel Andrea Prasow, who has followed the proceedings from the start, called the substance disclosed Tuesday "breathtaking."

"The overclassification is of course troubling," she said. "But what I find more concerning is that the government believed all along that the defense had no right to the information.

"The defendants are on trial for their lives, and while they sit in their cells, forbidden from entering the courtroom, the prosecution tries to hide evidence from their lawyers. If you want to know what is wrong with the military commissions, read this transcript."

Saturday, January 4, 2014

TRANSPARENT DETENTION? NOT ANYMORE

After a tumultuous year at the war-on-terror detention center in Guantánamo Bay, Cuba — where the U.S. military's motto is "safe, humane, legal, transparent" — operations are cloaked in secrecy.

The prison approaches the start of its 13th year with a new reclusive regime that no longer discloses what was once routinely released information.

The daily tally of hunger-striking detainees — the protest that engulfed more than 100 prisoners at its peak this summer — stopped in December.

Guards and other prison camp troops are under orders to withhold their names when talking to reporters.

On the witness stand in the war court recently a lawyer in the uniform of an Air Force officer gave sworn testimony under a curious, unexplained fake name — "Major Krueger."

Guantánamo is remote, and what is happening there in this new era has mostly gone unnoticed. However, one person is rattled: New Yorker Rita Lasar, an octogenarian peace activist whose brother died in the 9/11 attacks that spawned America's offshore detention center.

"I pay attention to this very much," says Lasar who has visited Guantánamo to watch a week of war court proceedings. Her brother, Abraham Zelmanowitz, was a 9/11 hero. He died staying at the side of a paraplegic office mate on the 27th floor of the North Tower of the World Trade Center.

Lasar wanted the 9/11 trial in New York not only for proximity but because, as she saw it: "Guantánamo was set up for one reason only, to keep everything secret.

"Just because my brother died, that doesn't mean my country has to be changed completely. I'm 82 years old. I lived through McCarthy for God's sake. This is worse than McCarthy."

The government controls access to everything pertaining to Guantánamo. Journalists have to get the military's permission to go there, navigate censorship of their pictures, wait 40 seconds to hear what happens in court and then wait weeks to see court filings.

Until recently, soldiers and sailors serving there could decide for themselves whether to give a reporter their names. Many didn't, saying they feared retribution by al-Qaida. Some did, eager to talk about their work to counter claims of torture or talk about the hardship of service.

General John F. Kelly decided in December that only a few senior officers could disclose their names to reporters. Kelly is commander of the U.S. Southern Command, which supervises the prison.

Southcom spokesman Army Colonel Greg Julian said Kelly imposed the new rules on contact with reporters for "force protection" purposes, invoking a military catchall that generally suggests a heightened state of alert triggered by intelligence.

No specific threat prompted the move, said Julian, and the new policy is not written down anywhere.

The current crackdown on information can range from the mildly curious to the outright comedic.

At times it seems to signify a gratuitous use of power by troops on rotation with the sudden authority to yield a censor's scissors. At times, it suggests a government bureaucracy whose default policy is knee-jerk secrecy.

• In November, the Obama administration finally got its long-promised parole-board hearings underway at Guantánamo, with a session run by a Pentagon team whose motto is "Principled. Credible. Sustainable." No reporters or other observers were allowed to watch.

More than a month later, the unit has yet to make public the part of the transcript where a prisoner pleads for his freedom. The process, which is called a Periodic Review Board, is partly meant to reassure the public that the administration is making sound decisions on whether to let detainees leave Guantánamo.

Why the delay? An official blamed bureaucracy, an "interagency process" that lets six different government officers, including the Directorate of National Intelligence, weigh in on what should be kept secret.

• An Army staff sergeant serving as a censor seized several days' worth of video from a French television reporter who traveled to the base in December under the sponsorship of the Secretary of Defense's public affairs operation — and deleted imagery of children sitting on Santa's lap at the base commissary.

A few days later, the public affairs team published a similar photo — Santa and smiling kids — on the cover of the prison staff newsletter, The Wire.

The reporter for Canal+, France's version of HBO, had gotten permission to interview Santa but not to include children in the image.

Navy Commander John Filostrat, the prison spokesman, has refused to take questions on the inner workings of the 19,000-book prison camp library, a place that other public affairs officers routinely discussed.

• Another example of pick-and-choose transparency occurred at the war court during a hearing creating the conditions for the trial of the five alleged September 11 plotters.

A military staff attorney assigned to the prison camp for ex-CIA captives testified as Air Force Major Krueger, a pseudonym.

Two Navy Reserve lawyers who did that job earlier — George Massucco, a federal prosecutor in Puerto Rico, and Jennifer Strazza, a civilian employee of the National Security Agency — were afforded no such anonymity. Why "Krueger?" The explanation may be contained in a so-far sealed court filing.

Using a pseudonym "puts a patina of normality on a thing that could be designed purposefully to be misleading," said David Nevin, the Pentagon-paid civilian lawyer for alleged 9/11 plot mastermind Khalid Sheik Mohammed.

"When you use a fake name, a casual observer looks at the thing and sees something that looks completely normal," said Nevin, an Idaho-based criminal defense attorney. "You use 'Mr. X' or 'Mr. Y' or 'Mr. Z,' someone knows on its face that it's a code."

Defense lawyers actually were provided the officer's name in case they wanted to do a typical witness background check. It's the public who can't know who he is. The government explained why in a war court filing that's currently under seal.

The new era seems to have started last year when Kelly became disenchanted with news coverage of the long-running hunger strike that captured not only headlines but the attention of the commander in chief.

In an August speech to Guantánamo troops, Kelly cast media reports of what goes on there as the product of an "agenda-driven chattering class" and "self-serving and misguided pundits" who ought to be "ashamed of themselves for reporting in the way they do."

The hunger strike began in February. Detainee lawyers said the captives were protesting conditions at the camp. Kelly told Congress they were frustrated at their indefinite detention.

The military began issuing daily figures in March and by May, President Obama was so moved by the mass protest that he renewed his efforts to close the prison.

The figures became a staple of daily news reports, which showed participation soar, and then drop once the military allowed protesting prisoners to leave their single cells to pray and eat together — as long as they nourished themselves enough to no longer require nasogastric feedings.

Commanders disclosed hunger-strike figures daily to show they had nothing to hide and that the protest wasn't as broad as detainees claimed. But the military couldn't control the narrative.

Defense lawyers criticized the count as too low. Medics bemoaned portrayals of what they did as inhumane; especially after the rapper Mos Def did a video dramatization of a Guantánamo force-feeding that went viral.

Kelly, meanwhile, had differed publicly with the president's description of what was going on in his prison. Obama called it force-feeding; the general called it "hunger-strike lite." Ultimately, the hunger strike largely disappeared when the daily tally stopped.

At the last report on December 2, 2014, the count stood at 15. It peaked at 106 in June and went as low as 11 in November.

"The release of this information serves no operational purpose and detracts from the more important issues, which are the welfare of detainees and the safety and security of our troops," Filostrat said in a statement.

Left unexplained is whether or how nine months of daily disclosure may have harmed the troops' "safety and security."

"It has become a self-perpetuating story," Southcom's Julian said. Apparently unaware that the prison had disclosed hunger strike and force-feeding figures from the prison's earliest days, he said, "these statistics were never reported before the recent mass protest."

For years, in fact, the prison spokesman doled out any given day's figure on request to demonstrate the double-barreled message that hunger striking was considered a peaceful act of protest and that the prison had nothing to hide.

The new policy creates confusion. At the prison, Filostrat was presented an image from a recent CBS *60 Minutes* report that showed a prison camp guard's face. The commander suggested that the image would survive the new censorship regime.

"The guard in your screen shot is not identified and was not interviewed," said Filostrat, who has oversight of the soldiers who serve as censors.

At Southcom, Julian's interpretation was opposite. "Only the senior leaders and spokesman can be quoted by name and their images portrayed," he said. "Others can be interviewed and faceless, or unidentifiable images can be portrayed and they can be identified by rank and position."

Chapter 13

CLOSING GITMO

U.S. Navy Chief Petty Officer Bill Mesta replaces the official commander in chief photo at base headquarters on Inauguration Day, January 20, 2009. (Brennan Linsley/Photo Pool)

Sunday, January 25, 2009

PLAN FOR DETAINEES: DIVIDE AND CONQUER

Khalid Sheik Mohammed, alleged 9/11 mastermind, could be coming to a lockup in America. Not today, not tomorrow, but soon. President Barack Obama's order to empty the U.S. prison camps in Cuba is designed to avoid a Guantánamo North on American soil by scattering the 245 detainees between federal trials and shipping some overseas by this time next year.

The order doesn't rule out new military commissions at domestic bases.

To achieve the president's goal, the Cabinet-level task force weighing the options must determine whether intelligence should be declassified for criminal trials on U.S. soil.

The order encourages trial in federal courts as an alternative to the suspended war crimes tribunals. The plan could spread the detainees around, rather than consolidate them in one place.

Under one widely considered scenario, the Justice Department would assign some of the war crimes cases to federal prosecutors in New York and near Washington and move those men first to the United States.

Prime candidates are Mohammed, who already is under indictment in New York, since 1996, for an ill-fated plot to bomb U.S. airliners in Manila, and Ahmed Ghailani, also indicted there in the 1998 East Africa embassy bombings. Both men are at Guantánamo, where they have been charged with war crimes.

The president's order, signed January 22, 2009, "does not eliminate or extinguish the military commissions. It just stays all proceedings," a senior administration lawyer told reporters, leaving open the possibility that a modified war crimes court could be set up at a military base.

Of the 245 detainees now at Guantánamo, 21 are accused of war crimes. But it is not clear how many could be charged in the federal court system, a process that could move them out in stages and spread them around the nation. Some analysts have pointed to New York and Virginia as possible locations for federal trials. But administration officials say it is too early to know who might face trial, or where.

"All the relevant agencies will first have to conduct a thorough review to determine the best available option for addressing each individual," Justice Department spokesman Dean Boyd said.

If found guilty, federal convicts could join other terrorists at the Supermax prison in Florence, Colorado. "Unabomber" Theodore Kaczynski and 1993 World Trade Center bombing mastermind Ramzi Yousef are there.

People being charged could be transferred to federal lockups. José Padilla, now in Florence, was held on terrorism charges for two years in a federal lockup in downtown Miami after President Bush ordered his 2006 transfer from the Charleston, South Carolina, Navy brig to stand trial.

But Republican leaders conjured up frightening images of a wholesale transfer of all 245 to one site. Or of unwise releases that could put America at risk — stoked by a fresh report that a Saudi man, sent home from Guantánamo in 2007, had emerged as a leader of an al-Qaida cell with suspected links to a deadly bombing at the U.S. Embassy in Yemen.

"Most families neither want nor need hundreds of terrorists seeking to kill Americans in their communities," said Republican Representative Eric Cantor of Virginia.

"Kansas is no place for enemy combatants or terrorists," said Senator Sam Brownback, who has campaigned fiercely against moving Guantánamo detainees to Fort Leavenworth in his state, where the U.S. military holds criminal soldiers and which has a Death Row.

Other ideas floated at times include using the brig at Camp Pendleton, California, or building a new maximum-security prison, perhaps at Fort Huachuca in Arizona.

If so, someone would have to decide whether to move Guantánamo's Army-Navy guard force or turn to the Federal Bureau of Prisons.

Meantime, the president's order does not rule out new and improved military commissions or creating a special security court for those who couldn't be convicted in federal court.

Former Clinton administration U.S. Attorney Mary Jo White, whose New York office prosecuted and won the al-Qaida terrorism cases of the 1990s, favors tribunals.

"Masked by the fact that we won them all," she said, "was that they were excruciatingly difficult to do." Prosecutors have an obligation to provide discovery (all evidence favorable to the accused and not so much so) to defense attorneys, who in turn share it with their client and could make it public.

Release of every intelligence morsel must be screened through a separate national security filter, addressing whether disclosure could endanger national security. Intelligence agencies don't want to divulge their sources, saying they could jeopardize ongoing terrorism investigations.

And that was true long before the capture of Mohammed and at least two other Guantánamo detainees, whom the CIA water-

boarded and subjected to other harsh interrogations at an undis-
closed location.

At issue is whether evidence taken through the technique
known as water torture would "shock the conscience" of a federal
judge, a legal concept that can cause evidence and sometimes
whole cases to be thrown out.

Once at Guantánamo, FBI agents with so-called "clean teams"
interrogated the same men and reportedly got confessions without
duress. But there is another legal principle called the fruit of the
poison tree, meaning that evidence taken after abuse is tainted.

So, for Mohammed to face a criminal trial, prosecutors must
decide for which crimes, at which court.

One model may be the 2007 terrorism conspiracy conviction
in Miami of Padilla, whom President Bush originally designated as
an "enemy combatant" in June 2002. Interrogators subjected him
to sleep deprivation and other rough techniques to learn what he
knew of an alleged dirty-bomb plot.

So, federal prosecutors built a case against him on evidence
obtained before his capture, and before 9/11.

"There's no right answer, in my point of view. You're never
going to satisfy any of the critics," ex-prosecutor White said.
"We've sort of damaged our credibility to do anything except go to
the federal civilian courts." So the filter for federal prosecutions is
an examination of "the evidence," White said. "Is it usable and
admissible?"

That is especially so for those captured by U.S. forces in Afghanistan. "Would you be able to find the soldier who arrested
them on the field?" said a Justice Department official, comment-
ing on background because no one has yet been put in charge of
the Guantánamo review process there. "Did they actually get the
shell cases on the ground and get them back to the FBI crime lab?"

Wherever the court may be, there is also the question of how
to prevent alleged terrorists — who have declared their rejection of
any American law — from using their trials as al-Qaida recruiting
tools, or political platforms. In another 9/11 case, Zacarias Mous-
saoui at times served as his own attorney, offered an incoherent
defense, then was stunned when a civilian jury spared him the
death sentence. After, he wrote to Judge Leonie Brinkema, requesting a do-over. The motion was denied.

Confessed al-Qaida kingpin Mohammed and some of his alleged co-conspirators used their Guantánamo hearings to celebrate Osama Bin Laden, jihad and martyrdom.

The 1990s trials of Ramzi Yousef and others for the 1993 World Trade Center bombing were a balancing act, said White, of what intelligence bits could be divulged, even before Yousef won the right to defend himself.

"One of the most riveting experiences of my career — and frightening, quite frankly — was watching how good he was," she recalled. "He was really, really good."

Saturday, May 9, 2009

CLOSURE ORDER STIRS DAYS OF UNCERTAINTY

Captives watch in confusion as workers weld fences around new soccer fields, part of the Pentagon's plan to improve prison camp conditions. Around the base, U.S. troops arrive on regular rotations and wonder what comes next.

Everyone at Guantánamo knows that President Obama ordered the prison camps emptied by January 22, 2010. But aside from the president's Executive Order posted at the prison camps, signs of the coming shutdown are hard to find.

These are days of uncertainty at Guantánamo.

"Some detainees are saying, 'You are still doing construction. Are we leaving or not?' " says Zaki, a Muslim cultural advisor who doesn't want his last name published for fear of retribution.

The guards have no answers: "We just say, 'It's coming.' " The renovations will continue, he says, "until the last detainee."

Even as they do, Washington politicians churn with opposition to bringing the men to U.S. soil.

When the detainees do leave, so will the guards and interrogators, commanders and contractors at Joint Task Force Guantánamo, 2,000-plus men and women now on temporary assignment among the 7,000 troops and civilians living here.

President Obama's January 22, 2009, Executive Order on a bulletin board for detainees, April 2, 2009 at Camp 4. (John Van Beekum/Miami Herald)

The Navy will still need sailors and other workers at the airstrip, port, and base hospital for the Marines on the fence line and other U.S. forces who come and go.

But there will be trailer parks to dismantle and cells to sweep, shackles to send stateside and brainstorming about what to do with a sprawling razor-wire-ringed detention facility.

A federal judge has ordered that the prison camps themselves be kept intact as potential evidence in unlawful detention suits being heard in federal court.

Guantánamo Bay, the Navy's oldest overseas base, has long weathered a succession of challenges — from the Bay of Pigs through the 1994-95 rafter surge to the prison camps that have become the defining image of America's lone military outpost on communist soil.

The uncertainty of the moment is waiting for the Obama administration to decide what to do with the remaining prisoners who were swept up in the war on terror, many held with no charges for more than seven years.

Attorney General Eric Holder, whom President Obama has tasked with determining what to do with the captives, recently appealed to European allies to accept some. For now, prosecutors are studying each detainee file, deciding which cases to bring to trial. The Holder team is also struggling with how to constitutionally hold others who can't be tried but are too dangerous to release.

Navy Commander Jeffrey Johnston, the base public works officer, compares what is coming to "a big auto plant closing in a town."

With one key difference: There will be no idle workers. The Pentagon controls the flow of mostly foreign contractors, which today number about 2,000 Filipinos and Jamaicans. Those with no work must go home.

Even before the arrival of the al-Qaida suspects, the Coast Guard and Navy used the airstrip and seaport to search for drugs and rafters in the Caribbean. Marines stood guard on watchtowers and patrolled the U.S. side of a Cuban minefield.

Under a 1996 law, the United States cannot give the base back or renegotiate the century-old lease (the United States pays $4,085 annually) until there's a democratic Cuba.

On the eastern end of the 45-square-mile base are the prison camps, hundreds of cells spread across a site called Radio Range. On the west, the Department of Homeland Security has staked out space to shelter 10,000 people in tents should the United States decide to provide a haven during a Caribbean humanitarian crisis.

"Everyone is trying to figure out how fast it'll empty," said Navy Chief Petty Officer Bill Mesta, the base public affairs officer.

But, he says, Guantánamo's "core mission" as a Navy seaport and airstrip will remain: "We're going to continue on. We're the only base in the Caribbean. We're the only base in the Fourth Fleet. We're not going anywhere."

Adding to the uncertainty is this: House Democrats this past week sliced $50 million from a Pentagon budget request, put there provisionally to retrofit or build a new prison somewhere else. The Senate has yet to say whether it will also block the funding.

But there's a mounting clamor among both Democrats and Republicans in Congress for the Obama White House to articulate an evacuation and relocation plan.

Meantime, people posted on the base for long periods often compare Guantánamo with 1950s small-town America, complete with a school system whose graduating class this year has a record 19 seniors.

Longtime residents have learned to tolerate the temporary troops on 6- to 12-month rotations the way Floridians welcome snowbirds. More people means more flights from the United States, more chances to socialize, better supplies.

It also means slower service and longer lines everywhere, from the barber who gives a $6.75 haircut to the lone supermarket, where a pound of salami sells for $2.85.

The McDonald's was here before the prison camps. So were the outdoor cinema and bowling alley. But the war on terror brought more downtime distractions, more first-run movies, mini-golf, Starbucks and Taco Bell.

A detainee walks up to others eating in a common area of Camp 4, March 31, 2009. (John Van Beekum/Miami Herald)

The hospital got a CT scan. The Navy added fresh fruit and meat cargo flights to the twice-monthly shipments of food by barge from Jacksonville.

Now old-timers wonder how soon it will be before shops and celebrity visits disappear along with the detainees.

Before the detention center, flights and visitors were rare. It was so sleepy that the base commander, a Navy captain, met a Cuban general without fanfare each month over coffee and pastries.

Now, the control tower is staffed around the clock to handle a steady stream of visitors: journalists for package tours, Red Cross delegates to inspect conditions, technicians to fine-tune equipment, Miss Universe and others to entertain the troops.

Members of Congress come through on day trips to praise the prison. Civil liberties lawyers fly in to see captive clients and then condemn their detention.

These days, residents wonder, how many guest quarters will Guantánamo really need? How many maids? Will there be a new assignment before services shut down?

It has gotten more crowded at the schools for sailors' kids, and there's suburban-style tract housing, barbecues on the beach, bake sales and holiday parades in this community surrounded by Cuban minefields where national security is part of the fabric of life.

On a recent Friday, members of the Coast Guard stripped a drug boat as they searched for tons of hidden cocaine while sailors' wives drove toddlers to story time at the public library.

A pair of Navy cops set up a checkpoint for speeders near a mini-mart and ticketed two drivers for exceeding the 10-mile-per-hour limit approaching it.

Filipino contract workers served sailors and soldiers in the cafeteria, while Jamaican maids changed sheets at officers' guest quarters.

Navy engineers, Seabees, were building a bridge over the Guantánamo River for Marines who patrol the fence that separates the base from the rest of Cuba.

And Desiree Rivers, a Navy petty officer who works as a career counselor, reenlisted on a bluff overlooking the bay. Her husband, a Marine on temporary duty, wore his dress blues and later produced a saber to slice the celebratory cake.

But absent a new assignment, longtimers imagine a return to the quiet days of downsizing and anonymity that ended when the

first 20 detainees arrived on January 11, 2002 — to give Guantánamo the at-times unwanted international spotlight.

"It's the kind of place that will be easily forgotten, and easily
ignored," says Johnston. "Until it's desperately needed again."

Over time, many came to see Guantánamo as something sinis-
ter, especially after the Pentagon distributed early images from
Camp X-Ray showing captives in orange jumpsuits in shackles on
their knees.

The interrogation hut portion of Camp X-Ray, under a U.S. federal court
preservation order, sits empty and overrun by nature, August 8, 2012.
(Walter Michot/Miami Herald)

"Camp X-Ray is like Kryptonite," says Johnston.

Even if a judge eventually allows the Pentagon to dismantle
the camps, he says, and "put an orphanage there, everything that
happened at that site will cripple it."

The Pentagon is still offering tours of the camps. Florida National Guard Lieutenant Cody Starken read aloud during a slide
show for two visiting photographers recently, reciting talking
points fine-tuned through the years. The military spends $3.1 mil-
lion a year — nearly $8,500 a day — to feed 240 or so detainees at
"the most transparent facility in the world," he said.

Even with the camps' closure on the horizon, the choreogra-
phy of bitter acrimony continues.

Detainees use their pro-bono lawyers to accuse the guards of continuing abusive behavior, of provoking the prisoners through gratuitous cell shakedowns, or roughly moving hunger strikers to tube-feedings. The Pentagon flatly denies the allegations.

Any notion that guards are getting in their last licks is "absolutely, unequivocally false," says Rear Admiral Dave Thomas, who is leaving to command a Carrier Strike Group before the camps close. "There could not possibly be a more scrutinized performance than my guard and the medical folks go through."

He swats aside discussion of what the Pentagon might do with the sprawling infrastructure — cells, trailer parks, snoop-proof command headquarters, wooden cottages — built for millions of dollars through war-on-terror funding.

Make it a training center for future detainee operations? Turn it over to the Navy's new Fourth Fleet? Level it? See what the Marines would make of it?

"We still have detainees here. That's the focus," says Thomas, who calls the ongoing expansion of prison camp recreation yards and diversions part of "getting it right. Until the last detainee's gone, my focus is on the safe, humane and transparent custody."

Sunday, August 2, 2009

EMPTYING THE CAMPS, ONE DEAL AT A TIME

On May 20, the premier of Bermuda was paying his respects at the White House when he offered a lifeline to the Obama administration's struggle to find countries for some of Guantánamo's most stigmatized detainees.

"I wonder if Bermuda can help," Ewart Brown offered.

Three weeks later, four former prisoners were smiling, posing for photographs on a Bermuda beach. The freeze-frame moment capped rare collaboration between a U.S. ally, attorneys and an American administration determined to close the Pentagon prison in Cuba by January 22, 2010.

Bermuda's hospitality illustrates how much the Obama administration is relying on outsiders to make good on the president's mandate to empty the prison. And it shows how the attorneys who fought the Bush administration tooth and nail on its detention policies are now emerging as key partners in the effort to craft safe solutions for some of the men.

A case in point came from the federal courts.

Long before Judge Ellen Segal Huvelle ordered the U.S. government to free a young Afghan named Mohammed Jawad, his military lawyers arranged with UNICEF and the Afghan Human Rights Commission to get him education and support, once back home with his mother.

Defense lawyers argued Jawad was 12, not 17, at his capture. They wanted to show a federal task force that "we had everything in place to ensure a smooth transition to civilian life," said Air Force Reserve Major David Frakt.

Frakt, a college professor doing reserve duty, put the post-release program together with a Marine lawyer who traveled to Afghanistan and a Navy reservist lawyer, a lieutenant commander.

A total of 13 detainees have left Guantánamo since Obama took office. Six were resettled in Bermuda, Britain and France, not their native countries; five went to their homelands in Chad, Iraq and Saudi Arabia; and a Yemeni went home dead, an apparent suicide victim. The 13th went to New York for trial as an al-Qaida conspirator.

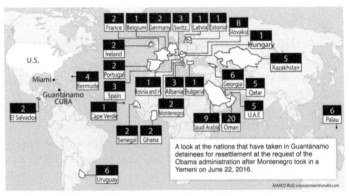

A look at the nations that have taken in Guantánamo detainees for resettlement at the request of the Obama administration after Montenegro took in a Yemeni on June 22, 2016.

MARCO RUIZ mruiz@miamiherald.com

About 230 remain. Lawyers estimated that 50 of them need sanctuary in third countries, for fear of torture if returned home. Also, the federal courts are reviewing detainee cases, and ordering that more be let go.

About 100 Guantánamo captives today are Yemeni. But the United States and Yemen can't agree on how to rehabilitate those the U.S. alleges answered Osama Bin Laden's call to jihad in their teens and 20s.

It all falls on the State Department to negotiate each repatriation or transfer. Ambassador Daniel Fried, who had been responsible for European affairs, heads the effort as Special Envoy for Guantánamo Closure.

"The Bermuda thing was unusual and is almost certain not to be repeated," said an administration official. "This is not easy stuff. We have to be methodical and we have to act with dispatch."

The official has knowledge about the State Department role but gave an interview on condition that he not be named.

Said White House spokesman Benjamin LaBolt: "The administration is engaged in a dialogue with our allies around the world and the need to close Guantánamo in order to strengthen our security and take a propaganda rallying cry off the table of our adversaries."

So, for the moment, the June 11 transfer to Bermuda was the last success: Four Muslim Uighurs from China, picked up in Afghanistan and held for years at Guantánamo, moved to the British colonial paradise known for its pink sand beaches.

Since then, Congress has prohibited the use of federal funds for transfers and now requires detailed notice two weeks before a move.

Bermuda provided the plane that flew the Uighurs to freedom, sparking a brief row with Britain over whether it had been properly informed.

Other transfer deals that simmered during the Bush years came to fruition once Obama announced plans to close the camps.

Consider Lakhdar Boumediene, an Algerian made famous because his is the first name on a landmark U.S. Supreme Court decision.

Now 42, Boumediene lives in the south of France, an idea that jelled over a March 10, 2009, lunch at the French Embassy in Washington.

Attorney Rob Kirsch drank Perrier. Two diplomats drank wine. A tuxedoed waiter served veal while Kirsch told his client's story: Captured in Sarajevo. Taken to Guantánamo by way of the

U.S. base at Incirlik, Turkey. Accused and cleared of an unrealized plot to attack the U.S. Embassy in Bosnia and Herzegovina. Fought and won the right for all Guantánamo captives to have their cases heard by civilian courts in Boumediene v. Bush.

An empty guard tower at a mostly unused area of the prison camps, November 5, 2014. (Walter Michot/Miami Herald)

"In my five years on the case, it was the best working meal I ever had," Kirsch said. On April 1, he got a call from a French diplomat who said that President Nicolas Sarkozy had agreed to take in Boumediene. Two days later, in Strasbourg, Sarkozy announced after a bilateral meeting with Obama that France would resettle a Guantánamo detainee.

"I was delivering an extremely low-risk, high-profile prisoner and I thought that would be attractive to President Sarkozy," Kirsch said.

On its own, Boumediene's legal team lobbied France's equivalent of a CIA director, Bernard Bajolet. Bajolet was French ambassador to Sarajevo in 2002, and condemned it when Boumediene was hustled off to Guantánamo.

The French and Algerian governments cooperated to get Boumediene's wife and daughters travel papers to leave Algeria, something that would usually require a husband or father accompanying them. They were in France to greet him May 15.

Kirsch and the captive worked together between Boston and the prison's Camp Iguana to write a formal request to French Foreign Minister Bernard Kouchner.

It was all exchanged by computer and shuttled between Boston and Boumediene's barbed-wire-encircled wooden hut by prison camp staff, so Boumediene was able to leave Guantánamo with travel papers from France — using a photo downloaded from Wikipedia.

"It showed what would happen if they cooperate with the lawyers," Kirsch said of the State Department, "how easily they could get the place emptied."

Earlier this month, an administration official said, a lawyer from the New York Center for Constitutional Rights met special envoy Fried's staffers at the State Department. The law group joined European and U.S. human rights groups championing the detainees' cause during the Bush administration.

"We could only do so much without the U.S. government working with us," says CCR attorney Gitanjali Gutierrez. "They're a partner at the table now, and I think it's a good thing."

Lawyers from the London-based human rights group Reprieve took two trips to N'Djamena, Chad, in 2007 and 2008, to interest the government there in the case of Mohammed Gharani. His lawyers say he was 14 at capture, and grew his first beard behind the razor wire in Cuba.

Born in Saudi Arabia to guest worker parents, he went to Pakistan as a citizen of Chad to study the Quran. The kingdom didn't want him back even after Guantánamo cleared him of terror suspicions.

So Reprieve lawyers traveled to Africa to make their case, according to attorney Zachary Katznelson. "The pitch was, 'This is a national of yours. He's never been charged with a crime. He's been abused ... racially abused, psychologically abused, physically abused, cut off from his family. He's the only Chadian national there and he needs your help.' "

Chad eventually contacted the State Department and asked for his return, says Katznelson.

But he didn't go quietly. The young man made headlines when a prison-approved family phone call to an uncle turned into a recorded chat with an al Jazeera reporter. It was the only broadcast interview with a detainee in the prison's history, and broke a Guantánamo policy prohibiting captives from talking to journalists.

The tactic made some lawyers wince. But Guantánamo attorneys have long argued their clients' cases in the media, especially when the Bush administration blocked them from the courts.

A father-and-son team from Boston, Michael Mone and Michael Mone Jr., worked with Irish-American contacts and Amnesty International and lobbied parliament members and media in Ireland to get their client's dossier before the Foreign Office in 2007.

The son traveled to Dublin in June 2008 and told government representatives from the foreign and justice departments that Uzbek Oybek Jabbarov, 31, wanted to leave Guantánamo to become a sheep herder in Ireland.

"We knew Ireland would be a good place for Oybek. We worked very hard to lay the groundwork with the Irish government. They have a strong commitment to human rights. We knew he'd be treated fairly," Mone Jr. said.

"Plus, he speaks English. There's no language barrier."

Irish diplomats interviewed detainees at Guantánamo and announced last week that it had agreed to take two men, reported to be from Uzbekistan. Now it's up to the State Department's Fried to seal the deal.

"He's The Closer," Mone said. "And God love him."

Sunday, September 27, 2009

UZBEKS ARRIVE IN IRELAND

Two Uzbeks freed from Guantánamo Bay arrived in Ireland, and Amnesty International appealed to other European nations to deliver on pledges to give new home to U.S. terror detainees.

Irish Justice Minister Dermot Ahern asked media to give privacy to the two Uzbeks, one of whom has been identified as 31-year-old Oybek Jabbarov. Both men were taken captive by U.S. forces in Afghanistan in 2001, and held at the U.S. prison in Cuba since 2002.

"The resettlement of the two individuals is a humanitarian gesture. They should be allowed time and space to rebuild their lives," Ahern said. "Ireland is a welcoming country and we are pleased to play our part with President Obama in assisting the closing of this center."

Ireland, like many European Union nations, long condemned the U.S. policy of detaining terror suspects for years without trial at the U.S. military enclave in Cuba. But the Europeans have been slow to follow through on pledges to help close the prison by giving new homes to approximately 60 captives who would face imprisonment, torture or execution if deported to their homelands.

The Justice Department said the Ireland transfer raised to 17 the number of inmates resettled overseas since Obama's January announcement pledging to shut the Guantánamo detention center within 12 months. U.S. officials now say the deadline is unlikely to be met.

Ireland said the two Uzbeks would get state-provided housing and permanent residency rights rather than be treated as refugees. This legal status will allow them to work in Ireland and travel within the 27-nation European Union.

Sunday, January 23, 2011

HOW CONGRESS THWARTED OBAMA'S PLEDGE

Two years after the newly minted Obama administration moved to undo what had become one of the most controversial legacies of the George W. Bush presidency by ordering the closure of the prison camps at Guantánamo Bay, a trove of State Department documents is providing new information about why that effort failed.

Key among the factors, the cables suggest: Congress' refusal to allow any of the captives to be brought to the United States.

In cable after cable made public by WikiLeaks, American diplomats make it clear that the unwillingness of the United States to resettle a single detainee in this country (even from among 17 ethnic Muslim Uighurs considered enemies of China's Communist government) made other countries reluctant to take in detainees.

Europe balked and said the United States should go first. Yemen at one point proposed that the United States move the detainees from Cuba to America's Supermax prison in the Colorado Rockies. Saudi Arabia's king suggested that the military plant microchips in Guantánamo captives before setting them free.

A January 2009 cable from Paris is a case in point: France's chief diplomat on security matters insisted, the cable said, that as a precondition of France's resettling Guantánamo captives the United States wants to let go, "the U.S. must agree to resettle some of these same LOW-RISK DETAINEES in the U.S." In the end, France took two.

Closing the Guantánamo detention center had been a key promise of the Obama presidential campaign, and the new president moved quickly to fulfill it. Just two days after taking the oath of office, on January 22, 2009, Obama signed an order instructing the military to close Guantánamo within a year. European countries were effusive in their praise.

But two years after that order, the prospects for closure are dim. Prosecutors are poised to ramp up the military trials that Obama once condemned, and the new Republican chairman of the House Armed Services Committee, Rep. Buck McKeon of California, said recently that the United States should grow the population to perhaps 800 from the current 173.

Many factors worked to thwart Obama's plans to close the camps — from a tangled bureaucracy to fears that released detainees would become terrorists. But Congress' prohibition on resettling any of the detainees in the United States hamstrung the administration's global search for countries willing to take the captives in.

The U.S. refusal to take in the captives "comes up all the time," acknowledged a senior Obama administration official.

"Were we willing to take a couple of detainees ourselves, it would've made the job of moving detainees out of Guantánamo significantly easier," said the official, who agreed to speak only anonymously because of the delicacy of the diplomacy.

Still, the Obama administration has managed to arrange to find new homes for 38 Guantánamo detainees in 16 countries, including Bermuda, Bulgaria, Palau and Portugal.

Why?

Some countries found the individual stories of men at Guantánamo with no place to go "compelling," the official said. "Some wanted to help the United States in general. Some wanted to help Obama in particular."

Placing Guantánamo detainees was even more difficult during the Bush administration, the WikiLeaks cables show.

Sweden in 2007 turned down a request that Stockholm provide safe haven for two Uzbek detainees who feared going home.

A cable quotes Sweden's counterterrorism ambassador, Cecilia Ruthström-Ruin, as declaring that "it is natural to wonder why," if as freemen the ex-captives need monitoring, the United States doesn't undertake to handle it.

In spite of those questions, the Bush administration transferred more than 500 detainees, nearly all to their home countries, and when Obama took office there were just 245 detainees at Guantánamo.

Resettling those who are cleared for release, however, has been difficult, and Congress, concerned by U.S. intelligence estimates that one-fourth of the captives freed over nine years are suspected of having joined anti-American insurgencies, has placed ever stricter limits on their transfers to other countries.

Under the latest Defense appropriations bill that Obama signed into law two weeks ago, the administration not only can't use Pentagon funds to bring detainees to the United States for trial, but must certify that countries meet a set of security conditions before the U.S. can send detainees to them.

In a signing statement, Obama objected to those restrictions, but he did not say he'd ignore them.

Not even Yemen, whose citizens make up the largest group by nationality of Guantánamo detainees, has been helpful.

In March 2009, according to one of the cables, Yemeni President Ali Abdullah Saleh told Obama's counterterrorism advisor John Brennan that he would not agree to Yemenis going from Guantánamo to a rehabilitation program in neighboring Saudi Arabia.

Instead, he suggested that the United States send his citizens to the federal Supermax prison in Florence, Colorado. Saleh was seeking $11 million to build Yemen's own rehab center in the port city where al-Qaida suicide bombers in 2000 blew up the U.S. destroyer Cole, killing 17 American sailors.

"We will offer the land in Aden, and you and the Saudis will provide the funding," he was quoted as saying in a March 2009 cable.

A September 2009 cable from Strasbourg, France, made clear what the Obama administration was up against in setting its hopes on European resettlement for long-held Guantánamo captives with ties there.

The Council of Europe's Human Rights Commissioner, Thomas Hammarberg, told members that "the U.S. could not expect European countries to accept detainees from Guantánamo if the U.S. were not willing to accept some on U.S. soil."

The stigma of Guantánamo also was a problem, even for those eventually cleared of terror ties. In February 2009, an Estonian diplomat told an American envoy in Brussels that the United States needed to begin educating its own citizens "that while some detainees are very dangerous, many of them do not pose a serious threat."

She provided a suggestion for changing public opinion.

"We need better pictures," she said, urging the United States to replace the image of the iconic Guantánamo detainees on their knees in orange jumpsuits.

Christopher Boucek, an expert on Islamic extremist rehabilitation programs in the Arab World at the Carnegie Endowment for International Peace, says the cables illustrate the disconnect between international contempt for Guantánamo and Congress' "zero willingness" to accept that some detainees might be released into the United States.

"We let rapists and pedophiles out of custody every day, and there's an acceptance that there is a risk they will reoffend," says Boucek.

Boucek noted that neither Bush's administration nor Obama's have "made a good argument that every time you let somebody out of a custodial situation there's a risk."

Saturday, September 29, 2012

'CHILD SOLDIER' RETURNED TO CANADA

The United States sent Guantánamo's youngest captive home to a prison in his native Canada, ending the decade-long U.S. detention of the Muslim militant who grew from a teenager into adulthood at the Pentagon's prison camps in Cuba.

In 2002, at age 15, Omar Khadr hurled a grenade in war-torn Afghanistan that killed an American soldier. He was captured and kept by U.S. forces ever since. Now 26, he's home and could serve up to six more years in prison. Or authorities could release him sooner. Canada considers him a juvenile offender who can apply for parole a year from now.

"He thinks he's in a dream. He's pinching himself," said Toronto attorney John Norris, who spoke to Khadr soon after arrival. "He never believed this day would come; he's been betrayed so many times before."

Khadr departed the U.S. Navy base in Cuba before dawn, a secret transfer 10 days after a Canadian diplomat paid him a visit on his 26th birthday. The U.S. military plane carrying him landed at a Royal Canadian air base in Ontario, before he was sent to Millhaven maximum-security prison for what his lawyer described as an assessment of the most suitable place to serve out his sentence.

The case of the Toronto-born Khadr — Guantánamo's last Western captive — stirred debate in international law and human rights circles.

Because he was captured at such a young age, some called him a child soldier who was dropped off in a war zone by his father and deserving of rehabilitation, not interrogation. Others called him the respected son of an al-Qaida family, nicknamed Canada's

"First Family of Terror" in news reports, and opposed his repatriation.

Psychiatrist Michael Welner, testifying at the Guantánamo war court for the prosecution, called Khadr a continuing danger who spent his time in U.S. military detention "marinating in a community of hardened and belligerent radical Islamists."

Khadr's lawyers offered up tales of abusive treatment in U.S. custody. He was captured in a firefight after U.S. forces shot him through the chest, then questioned in Afghanistan while emerging from surgical anesthesia, they argued. He was used as a "human mop" at Guantánamo after he urinated on himself and the floor in an interrogation, during a two-year period when his lawyers were forbidden from seeing him.

U.S. troops captured Khadr, near death, in a July 27, 2002, firefight at a suspected al-Qaida compound near Khost in Afghanistan. U.S. airstrikes had leveled the compound and as Special Forces assaulted, Khadr admitted in a 2010 guilty plea, he threw a grenade from the rubble that mortally wounded a U.S. Army sergeant.

Medics saved Khadr's life and turned him over to what became a decade of on-again, off-again interrogation.

The Khadr transfer could break a logjam in efforts to get other captives to plead guilty. Canada had been slow in agreeing to take him, and defense lawyers characterized the U.S. administration's inability to return him as an obstacle to negotiations with other alleged al-Qaida foot soldiers.

In his plea agreement, Khadr also admitted to planting land mines in Afghanistan meant to shred allied forces. Once captured, and interrogated, he directed U.S. troops back to the location to safely disarm them.

Testimony at pretrial hearings showed U.S. interrogators saw their teenaged captive as a human intelligence treasure trove because, as a child, he spent time with Osama Bin Laden's family in Afghanistan. His father, who was killed in Pakistan in 2003, was profiled in Canada as an al-Qaida functionary who moved his family to South Asia in the years before the 9/11 attacks.

Since his conviction, he was confined to a maximum-security wing at Guantánamo, a mostly solitary existence that his lawyers tried to ameliorate with a Canadian college preparatory curriculum — literature, physics and videos of *Little Mosque on the Prairie,* a TV sitcom set in Saskatchewan.

He also read Shakespeare with his Pentagon lawyer, Army Lieutenant Colonel Jon Jackson, who played Juliet to Khadr's Romeo.

Amnesty International USA used the occasion of the transfer to urge President Obama to close the detention center.

"Khadr's tragic story underscores why Guantánamo should close — not tomorrow, but today," Executive Director Suzanne Nossel said in a statement. "Given the Obama administration's glacial pace towards closing the U.S.-controlled detention center, little and late though it is, today's news represents progress."

Sunday, January 12, 2014

FIRST COMMANDER SAYS IT'S TIME TO CLOSE

Retired Marine Major General Michael Lehnert, the officer who opened the prison camps at Guantánamo in January 2002 and handed it off in April 2002, has been outspoken lately about the need to close it.

Here are some comments from an interview as the detention center starts its 13th year.

On the first 20 detainees not turning out to be the 'worst of the worst': "I think we did a poor job in the beginning in determining who we needed to go to Guantánamo. Our ability to sort at the other end was not very good, particularly in the early days. We relied pretty heavily on the Afghans to tell us who they were. A good chunk of them probably were of no value and should never have been there in the first place. Some of these people that were in there shouldn't have been sent to Guantánamo. Others were just in the wrong place in the wrong time or had been caught lying about something else, and they figured they were lying about a great deal more. Some of them were fighters, probably a low level. Some of them were never fighters at all. They were the flotsam and jetsam of the war."

On closing the prison camps: "It's time we moved the conversation to who we claim to be and what we say that the U.S. Constitution and our body of laws on human rights stand for. If we treat those who have done us harm as they would treat us, ulti-mately the terrorists won because they have changed who we say we are as Americans and made us live in fear. It is time to get back to the rule of law, both domestic and international, and close Guantánamo."

On when he realized they'd gotten some of the wrong people: "By the third month, particularly once we got the ICRC in there, we were getting pretty good indications that some of these people shouldn't be in that prison."

On distinguishing between al-Qaida and Taliban at Camp X-Ray: "The Afghans definitely stuck out in a sense that there was clearly a hierarchy from the older Taliban."

Army Colonel Terry Carrico briefs, from right, Secretary of Defense Donald Rumsfeld; Air Force General Richard Myers, chairman of the Joint Chiefs of Staff; California Senator Dianne Feinstein; Hawaii Senator Daniel Inouye; Marine Brigadier General Michael Lehnert; and others at Camp X-Ray, January 27, 2002. (Helene C. Stikkel/Department of Defense)

On how Guantánamo detention changes American values: "The objective of any terrorist — be they Irish, Afghan or al-Qaida, doesn't matter — is to change their adversary, their way of doing things, to change their behavior to make them afraid. They made us afraid."

On Marine General John F. Kelly's decision to pour more guards into the prison even as the detainee population downsizes: "I wouldn't question that decision. Locking up a human being is a soul-numbing experience; I think that we need to be very careful that these young people, the guards themselves, don't become changed for the worst by just having to lock up other human beings and see what's going on."

On the need to absorb Guantánamo detainees in the federal prison system: "I'm not a fan of having military commissions. I think our federal courts have actually had a pretty good track record of handling terrorism cases since 9/11. Many lawyers would disagree with me, and I'm not a lawyer, but I think we're going to be on shaky ground as we conclude military operations in Afghanistan and still have military commissions doing this work."

On recidivism: "It's going to happen. Is that reason enough for us to turn our backs on what we say we are as American people, and on that wonderful document the Constitution to say it matters for us but doesn't matter for other members of humanity?" Besides, "We've got biometrics on these guys. If they go back to the fight, sooner or later we'll catch up with them."

On whether he foresaw it lasting a dozen years: "I knew it was going to take longer than the administration did." During the Haitian-Cuban migration crisis at Guantánamo of the '90s, "our most difficult challenge was returning third-country nationals to their country of origin. And they were accused of nothing more than getting in a leaky boat with their boyfriends or girlfriends."

On any regrets: "I have many regrets, but calling them 'the worst of the worst' is not one of them. One decision that I regret deeply is, you know, some of the guards, many of them, asked to have their names taped over. Ultimately I acquiesced. Because we taped those names over, that became a procedure in other prisons elsewhere, Abu Ghraib being the most notorious. I think it sets up a mindset in the minds of a guard that you're now anonymous." Also that we didn't follow the Geneva Conventions more closely and give them battlefield hearings "to sort these people out early."

On many of the prisoners he got at Guantánamo, years before the CIA would send the high-value detainees: "I would describe them as losers; they were people who failed in life in other things. I talked to many of them. Failed marriages, failed businesses, failed relationships with their families, and they tended to blame it on America, Israel, Jews. These were people who were in there because they had not done particularly well at home. They were losers. Apart from those who were probably higher in the hierarchy, many were individuals searching for themselves."

On his legacy as first Guantánamo prison commander: "I don't worry about it. At one point in my career I was chief of staff for the Joint Task Force Panama. So I'm the engineer who gave away the Panama Canal. I'm less interested in my own personal legacy than trying to do the right thing at the right time."

On the first 20: "I'm not trying to make the case that after I left we didn't move some very bad people into Guantánamo. We did. But I don't think if we lined up my first 20 with the true 'worst of the worst,' that most of them would have had a great deal of standing."

Tuesday, November 18, 2014

GUANTÁNAMO GRINDS ON

The detainee in the cage outside the prison hospital psych ward never broke stride on a treadmill as a knot of reporters went past.

Thunk, thunk, thunk went his feet as he kept the beat behind green sniper netting that obscured all but his silhouette. A soldier stood watch.

No one would explain who the man was, in keeping with military policy that prohibits discussion of individual patients at the war-on-terror prison.

But he was still there an hour later — *thunk, thunk, thunk* — running at the same pace as the military hustled the media out, past an idling white van with a cell inside for a detainee.

It's the first Tuesday in November, just another day as Guantánamo grinds on toward the detention center's 14th year as "The Most Expensive Prison on Earth" with no end in sight. President Obama ordered it emptied in 2009, on his second day in office, and people are dubious that it will be done before his last day.

It will close "a year from now, six months from now, 10 years from now. I don't know," says Zaki, a Pentagon employee who has served as the prison's Muslim cultural advisor since 2005.

"My focus is to ensure that I have operationally effective and safe facilities for a mission with an indeterminate end date," says Rear Admiral Kyle Cozad, the 14th commander of the prison operation.

One captive was let out this month, the seventh detainee to leave this year, to a rehabilitation center in his native Kuwait after nearly 13 years in U.S. custody. Six more men await the outcome of Uruguayan elections to see if President Jose Mujica's successor will make good on a February offer to resettle them. Another six to eight are in the pipeline for transfers to Afghanistan and Europe, according to administration officials, with security assurances.

In all around 780 foreign men have been held at Guantánamo since the prison opened on January 11, 2002. Nine died in the prison. Those who got out were repatriated or resettled by far-flung American allies such as Palau in the South Pacific and Slovakia in central Europe.

Meantime, Guantánamo grinds on, churning through temporary forces doing mostly nine-month tours managing a largely "compliant" prisoner population — as well as the so-called 10 per-centers, who constantly give the guards problems and pass their days mostly in lockdown.

The admiral has a four-year plan to build new barracks for the troops and a new kitchen to feed both guards and guarded. Also, if Congress funds it, a $69 million new lockup will be built for Guantánamo's most prized detainees — the 15 former CIA captives, seven awaiting trial, and none approved for transfer, even with security assurances.

And the warden, who arrived this summer, doesn't see the last detainee leaving before this commander in chief leaves office. "I think that's an unrealistic hope," said Colonel David Heath. "I'll run it the best I can until either I'm told to close it or I leave." His tour ends in the summer of 2016.

But there are signs that life has eased for both captives and captors since the military cracked down on disobedience during the bitter hunger strike in the summer of 2013 and locked nearly every prisoner alone in his cell for long stretches at a time.

Now, according to the guard commanders, more than half of Guantánamo's captives follow the rules — they don't spit on the guards, they aren't on hunger strike — and are allowed time with other captives in communal areas for up to 22 hours a day. Rule breakers get two to eight hours a day in outdoor communal recreation yards, according to Heath.

Heath says he has tinkered with the program, in particular offering troublemakers the eight hours in the recreation yard to try to encourage good behavior, without success. "We have a handful who continue to be actively in the fight," says his boss, Cozad.

The cultural advisor seems to have run out of ideas for incentives. "If we give them 10 CDs, they want 20. If we give them two apples, they want four," says Zaki. What they really want "is to be out of here one day."

Heath has spent much of his career in military policing and doesn't come off as particularly distressed by a phenomenon that obsessed some of his predecessors — the detainees who throw a brew of their blood, feces and other bodily fluids at passing guards.

Earlier in his career, Heath says, he ran a lockup at Fort Lewis, Washington, where U.S. soldiers did the same thing. His troops here call it "splashing." But from what Heath has seen, "they're squirting."

A captive attempts this about once a day, he says, mostly in the disciplinary cellblock for about a dozen of the most uncooperative men.

And, says Heath, his guards don't complain to him about it. They know "it's a hazard of the job" and get special protective gear for their turn on the disciplinary block, another part of the grind at Guantánamo.

Meantime, the military is still shielding basic information it once confidently disclosed.

A Miami Herald photographer who got periods of night and day access to the detention center during Ramadan a few years ago was shooed from silently photographing detainees at prayer after 90 seconds, appealed and got 150 seconds more — a total of four minutes.

How many detainees are so malnourished that military medical staff list them for a tube-feeding? No one will provide it. The prison last disclosed the number on December 2 — 15 prisoners on a list for force-feeding. The number had flatlined at 11 from a 2013 high of 46, and was rising when the military abandoned that portion of transparency.

How many people work on the detention center staff? On April 15, the prison had precisely 2,268 troops and civilians on its rolls. Now the spokesman says it's "approximately 2,000," suggesting that it dropped by approximately 268.

Other portions of the media tour have vanished as well.

The force-feeding display no longer includes a vial of olive oil, once offered as a culturally sensitive lubricant to snake the feeding tube through a nostril. A doctor decried it as risky, to the disappointment of detainees who got a taste of home as the tube reached the back of a hunger striker's throat, according to one of their lawyers.

The prison library collection is kept in two trailers in the Detention Center Zone, August 19, 2013. (Carol Rosenberg/Miami Herald)

At a detention center clinic, a guide to calculating a captive's weight has been torn off a wall, leaving a bit of glue and paper. If he's in hard leg restraints, it used to advise, subtract 1 pound. A black box and belly chains weighs 2 1/2. A wheelchair weighs 36

1/2 pounds and the prison's often photographed restraint chair weighs 76.2 pounds, meaning a soldier has probably wheeled a captive onto a scale on his way to or from a force-feeding.

Guantánamo grinds on, with some tweaks.

Prison librarians have stopped buying new books, games and videos for the captives. Instead they process donations from lawyers and the International Red Cross. One donor submitted a LEGO-Harry Potter video game just before Halloween and some novels in Russian.

At the detainee hospital, gone are the boasts that troops get themselves tube-fed to illustrate it's no big deal. "We don't want anyone to undergo a medical procedure that's not necessary," says the prison's current chief medical officer, a woman.

Navy medics still use pseudonyms. But gone are the Shakespearean characters. This rotation of troops has replaced their real names on uniform name tapes with the names of lakes and rivers — Chattanooga, Chattahoochee, Escalante, Mattoon.

Commanders portray the hunger strike as part of everyday life nearly 18 months after Obama lamented it. "We are force-feeding detainees who are being held on a hunger strike," he said at the National Defense University. "Is that the America we want to leave our children?"

There have been no real recent suicide attempts, says Cozad, just "some vague attempts at self-harm and threats of self-harm, basically a manipulation to go to more comfortable quarters in our Behavioral Health Unit" — the psych ward where the captive was logging miles on the treadmill in the cage.

Now, a new controversy has supplanted force-feedings for attention: Complaints by lawyers that the secret prison for former CIA detainees, Camp 7, has recently begun using female guards to shackle and handle captives — something that the captives and their lawyers said has been the exclusive province of male guards, just like supervising showers and conducting groin searches.

It's no big deal, says Zaki. "As long as that touch doesn't mean anything else it's OK," he says, adding that the female guards wear gloves just like the men do.

At the prison hospital, staff say they were already familiar with resistance to female troops at the low-value lockups, where the cleared captives and hunger strikers are kept.

A Navy nurse who inserts the hunger strikers' nasogastric tubes said her prison patients sometimes protest and ask for a man to do it instead. But it's her assignment, she said, and she does it, anyway.

"I understand they have a goal — they're trying to make a statement for themselves," says the nurse, who uses the pseudonym Lieutenant Beeds. "I have my mission — to do my job as a professional."

Thursday, December 10, 2015

FREED CONVICT RETURNS TO THE FIGHT

A former Guantánamo detainee who was released to Sudan after a war court guilty plea has emerged in a key position in al-Qaida of the Arabian Peninsula, according to an expert in jihadist movements.

"He's clearly a religious leader in the group," said Aaron Zelin, senior fellow at the Washington Institute for Near East Policy who edits the Jihadology blog. He found the 2002-12 detainee Ibrahim al Qosi in the latest video release from the offshoot of Osama Bin Laden's organization, *Guardians of Shariah.*

Obama administration officials would not confirm the apparent case of recidivism, which was first reported on the Long War Journal website, run by the Foundation for Defense of Democracies.

The video included Qosi's biography and said he joined the jihad in Yemen in December 2014. It also said Qosi was close to Bin Laden "until he was imprisoned in Guantánamo in 2001." Qosi, now 55, arrived at the detention center on January 13, 2002, according to documents obtained by McClatchy Newspapers from the anti-secrecy group WikiLeaks. He pleaded guilty to foot soldier war crimes in 2010 in exchange for release in 2012.

Qosi's former attorney, Paul Reichler, told the Miami Herald that he had not been in touch with the Sudanese man since Qosi left the U.S. Navy base prison for Sudan in July 2012.

"I was told by a Sudanese lawyer a year ago that al Qosi was working as a taxi driver in Khartoum," Reichler said by email. "I have received no information about his activities since then, and I do not know what he has been doing, or where he is living."

At the time of Qosi's return to Sudan, Reichler said Qosi looked forward to being reunited with his wife and family, including two daughters, and to living "among them in peace, quiet and freedom." Qosi's wife at the time was the daughter of a former chief bodyguard to Bin Laden.

On the AQAP tape, Qosi opines in Arabic on the evolving globalization of jihad. His comments were translated for the Herald by a journalist who is fluent in Arabic.

"As the U.S. has waged war on us remotely as a solution to minimize its casualties, we have fought it remotely, as well, by individual jihad," he is heard saying. "And as the U.S. has killed our men, we have killed its people. But it is not the same. Our dead are in heaven, and theirs are in the hellfire, and the war is not over yet."

Qosi, an accountant, kept the books for a Bin Laden business in Khartoum in the early '90s, according to Pentagon documents made public by WikiLeaks. He then followed Bin Laden to Afghanistan in 1996. Because the timeline for war crimes only covers the era in Afghanistan, Qosi pleaded guilty to foot-soldier crimes — sometimes driving for Bin Laden, working at al-Qaida's Star of Jihad compound in Jalalabad, and fleeing the post-9/11 U.S. invasion to Tora Bora, armed with an AK-47 rifle.

The AQAP video biography mirrors much of that, noting "he participated in the famous battle of Tora Bora" with Bin Laden "until the withdrawal."

Qosi was also one of the first at Guantánamo to formally allege torture (the use of strobe lights, sleep deprivation, sexual humiliation, being wrapped in the Israeli flag) in an unlawful detention petition that his Air Force attorney filed in federal court in 2004. It was never heard. Instead, he withdrew the habeas corpus suit as part of his 2010 plea agreement.

The disclosure comes at a complicated time. Secretary of Defense Ash Carter is considering the release to repatriation or resettlement of as many as 17 detainees who have been cleared for transfer. Qosi got out on the war court guilty plea that saw him spend his last two years at the prison's Convict's Corridor, separated from the majority detainee population.

Friday, February 12, 2016

YEMENI CHOSE CELL OVER NEW LIFE IN EUROPE

Detainee Mohammed Bwazir's fateful decision to stay in a cell at Guantánamo rather than start anew in Europe came down to a calm 10-minute standoff when the warden of the war prison urged him to board a C-17 cargo plane carrying two other captives to new lives.

Bwazir, 35, feared going to the country that offered him sanctuary — it has not been identified — and waffled in the weeks ahead of what was to be his departure from 15 years of U.S. military detention without charge. He'd gone through out-processing and about a week's segregation with two other captives and was shackled at the ankles, wrists and waist at "the bottom of the ramp of the aircraft," said Colonel David Heath.

The Yemeni captive "made it clear that, 'I don't want to leave. I want to go back to my cell.' So that's what we did," the still surprised colonel said of the January 20 episode. "It was disappointing."

Now Bwazir is one of 91 prisoners at the sprawling detention center that President Obama wants closed. In years past others among Guantánamo's almost 800 captives have rejected certain offers of third-country sanctuary, and subsequently left voluntarily. But none have been known to make it that far — through health checks, would-be host country and International Red Cross exit interviews, all the way to the steel-gray ramp of a U.S. Air Force cargo plane, its door, before balking.

"He wasn't angry. He wasn't acting out. He was very calm," said Heath, who runs the detention center guard force. In keeping with prison policy of anonymity, his description of the strange event never named the captive. But Bwazir's lawyer, John Chandler of Atlanta, did on the day it happened. He said the Yemeni feared going to a country where he had no family, knew no one — anxiety the prison staff detected as well.

The lawyer said that Bwazir only wanted to Saudi Arabia, the United Emirates or Indonesia, where he has a mother, brothers, uncles and aunts.

The State Department's special envoy for the closure of Guantánamo said that episodes like Bwazir's would not impede his efforts to empty the detention center. In fact, Lee Wolosky said he foresaw scenarios where a captive could be forced onto a plane and sent to another country.

"We're not a travel agency. We're not here to fulfill every wish and desire of a resettlee," he said. "They do not get to pick and choose where they go."

In the months before one of the most astonishing choices in the history of the detention center, Chandler urged Bwazir to go by phone and had a sympathetic lawyer on the base counsel him. The prison's cultural advisor, who blamed "negative influence around" Bwazir, had a Navy doctor give him Arabic-language information off the internet about the would-be host country. U.S. diplomats also got him a letter of assurance from the country that family members could meet him there.

"He had concerns along the way and vacillated back and forth," said the Navy doctor who delivered the literature. He specializes in family medicine. Departing detainees can experience "anxiety of the unknown, not knowing whether they'll see family members" after what he termed "a very stable, very steady, very consistent" detention center setting where the captors make life decisions for the captives.

Experts consulted by the Herald described it more like a sense of helplessness after years of institutionalization. Bwazir would have been 20 or so at capture and spent nearly half his life in detention.

"You may feel safer in a bad situation you are in than in an unknown," said JoAnne Page, president and CEO of New York's Fortune Society, which helps U.S. prisoners' reentry into society. "It takes tremendous courage and a leap of faith to go to a country you don't know. There are still people at Gitmo he knows."

Heath described Bwazir's "angst" as two-fold: He didn't know the country, and he "didn't have any family there."

Up until the last 10 minutes at the open ramp at the rear of the plane, "he wasn't definitively saying 'no.' He wasn't definitively saying 'yes. ' "

In one early exchange, the captive asked: "So you are telling me to go?"

The colonel: "I'm saying, 'Yes, you need to go. This is the fastest way for you to get back to your family.' "

Heath also said he told him: "You don't have any family here, and you can bet they're not going to come here."

The coaxing "got him all the way to the airplane," Heath said, "and ultimately he refused."

Heath has handled 58 transfers in his 20 months at the prison, and such a thing had never happened on his watch. "All the other ones that we transferred have walked willingly on the plane. Some smiling. Some not. But I have never had anyone refuse to go."

Prison commanders since the episode have offered no new ideas on how to prepare a detainee for life after Guantánamo. The detention center has no explicit rehabilitation program.

Detainees do attend English, Spanish and art lessons as well as a "life skills" class that covers "interpersonal communication skills," résumé writing, business and personal finance and computer use.

But the experts suggested several ideas for how to ease the transition, starting with a buddy system of sorts. Have the host country send someone to the base who will assist in resettlement, ideally to accompany a captive on the military plane or at least be a familiar face when he gets there, suggested Page.

Retired Army Brigadier General Stephen Xenakis, who has worked with both detainees and soldiers, suggests that the captive learn about the sanctuary country at a transition site on the base, separated from detainees not selected to go.

"Let them start living more independently," said Xenakis, a former Army psychiatrist. "There are so many habits that get embedded in your lifestyle after you've been detained under those kind of circumstances, making that transition hard."

But prison staff have been reluctant to allow access to outsiders.

In that case, said Page, let the captive have a Skype chat with someone in the receiving party, to meet the people and see the place awaiting them.

Chandler warmed to the idea. It might have made the difference, he said, if Bwazir saw and met someone saying, "I'll be here when you get there." Still Chandler was confounded. "Every other man down there who I know says, 'Send me anywhere. Get me out of Guantánamo.' "

CLOSURE PLAN: TO BE CONTINUED ...

The Obama administration's rollout of its plan to close the detention center in Cuba by releasing some captives and moving others to a site in the United States revealed some intriguing aspects of its vision of a "Guantánamo North" now forbidden by Congress.

• It envisions war-on-terror detainees captured after the 9/11 attacks being held in a U.S. military prison for the next 20 years.

• It is silent on whether President Obama believes he has unilateral authority to ignore Congress and move the men to the United States.

Soldiers on break not far from the prison psychiatric ward, February 9, 2016. (Walter Michot/Miami Herald)

• Obama said in a White House address that he wants help from Congress to tweak the military commissions, the post-9/11 war court that would come to U.S. soil along with the detainees.

• The Obama administration looked at 13 sites, seven of which are publicly known, but doesn't rule out starting from scratch and building a prison at a military base somewhere in the United States.

• The plan envisions the U.S. military moving at most 56 of the last 91 captives now at Guantánamo to the United States, and perhaps as few as 30 as more go through parole-style reviews.

- By envisioning as few as 30 detainees, the administration is signaling it can find nations to accept up to 61 captives not-yet cleared for release and provide security assurances.

- Bringing them to the United States would let federal attorneys examine their cases for federal charges, and possibly plea deals, something that the Obama administration wanted to do before Congress outlawed bringing captives to the U.S. for trial.

- It disclosed a higher cost than was previously known to run the war court and detention center — $445 million in 2015. If it costs that much now, it works out to nearly $4.9 million a year for each detainee.

- The plan offers fuzzy and confused math on what it would cost to maintain 56 or fewer detainees in a military lockup in the United States. But one portion of the plan puts annual costs of 30 to 57 prisoners and the war court at $265 million to $305 million a year. That crunches to $10.1 million per prisoner if just 30 prisoners were moved to a military detention center at a cost of $305 million a year — or $4.6 million per prisoner in a 57-captive detention center costing $265 million a year. By all these measures, it is still "The Most Expensive Prison on Earth."

- The plan anticipates cost savings by downsizing the 2,000-strong military and civilian staff that currently runs the detention center but doesn't say whether staff would be professional, military guards or would continue with temporary mostly National Guard MPs.

Monday, May 30, 2016

MILITARY PLANS FOR PRISON AFTER OBAMA

Military leaders are thinking about whether they will need to put a wheelchair lift into their showcase communal prison three or four years from now, widen some cell doors, add ramps for geriatric captives.

Not one of the 80 prisoners is now in a wheelchair, and most are in their 30s or 40s. The oldest is 68. But briefings by senior military officials here made clear that they are starting to actively think about operating an offshore Pentagon detention center long after President Barack Obama leaves office.

"At some point if detention operations continue here, we will have to address, 'Are the doors in the cells wide enough to move wheelchairs in and out? Are there ramps to reach the medical facilities?' " said Rear Admiral Peter Clarke, the detention center commander. "And we've just started looking at that. So I can't tell you we are ready or not. But it's something we can plan for."

Obama wants the prison emptied, and a Pentagon plan proposes moving 30 to 50 captives to military detention in the United States and releasing the rest to other countries. But Congress has outlawed any transfers to U.S. soil, and some members are proposing legislation to prevent transfers altogether, to anywhere, prompting speculation that the only way Obama could do it is through an Executive Order that opponents of closure warn would be illegal.

"If I'm told to transfer them to the United States or somewhere else — and I have a legal order to do so — we will carry out that order professionally, like we do any other transfer," says Clarke, the 16th prison commander, in a rare media visit.

Clarke, in the seventh month of what is traditionally a one-year assignment, offers guarded speculation on what the prison operation will look like this time next year. "I think we'll have less detainees than we have today. I think we will have consolidated Camp 5 and 6. I'm not willing to predict whether we'll have operations here at Guantánamo Bay or somewhere else."

It is Tuesday, May 24, 2016, the only day of the month the prison permitted reporters into the Detention Center Zone, and 15 former CIA captives were still in seclusion at a clandestine site called Camp 7, which Clarke declared structurally sound. Of the remaining 65 captives, 28 were on a list approved for transfer, spread out across three different sites capable of confining 300 captives.

Two among them were in orange jumpsuits, signaling they were rule breakers the military considered violent. But the other 63 were categorized as compliant, cooperative, following the rules.

As a sign of the era of cooperation, the senior medical officer, Navy Captain Richard Quattrone says the same Navy medical unit that tube-feeds hunger strikers introduced 30-minute health and wellness classes in some prison recreation areas. They began three weeks ago, he said, and 17 captives attended one.

"We were actually surprised that we didn't have to convince them to come," said Quattrone, who specializes in family medicine. "We actually had quite a bit of buy-in right off the bat."

Topics so far included "stress-reduction techniques," which offered instructions on how to do breathing exercises; and health precautions, which emphasized the importance of hand washing to avoid respiratory infections.

Quattrone called the class offerings a "luxury" that the 125-troop team of healthcare providers at the detention center can offer when relations between captives and captors are going well. The sailors teaching the class are both men and women.

At Camp 6, where most captives are kept in cellblocks that allow them to eat, pray and watch TV together, the most frequent request from the prisoners is for replacement Tupperware, says the Army captain in charge, a special education teacher in civilian life. Each cellblock has a food pantry equipped with a microwave, and they keep melting the containers. "They'll hit 5 minutes, no matter what," says the captain, a woman forbidden to say her name.

Each cellblock got couches a few weeks ago, she says, and some have complained they're too soft; others, too hard. As a measure of their independence, the captives have dragged them to different spots in their common space. One cellblock has it back by a screen with a PlayStation bolted to a wall. The others have them in view of a large flat-screen overhead TV.

One block has covered its new sofa with what looks like a white sheet, like somebody's Brooklyn grandmother might do.

The overwhelming impression that the reporters are given is of a peaceful prison. (But they're shown the communal building, not the maximum-security Camp 5 whose commander said that over the weekend a captive threw some bodily fluids on a guard.)

The chief of the guard force, Colonel Heath, confirms there's overall compliance with the military's rules. In the nearly two years he's served as Guantánamo's version of a prison warden, he said, there were just two instances of detainees fighting each other. Both times it was over the remote control for a cellblock television.

Meantime, the overall commander defends the need to maintain a dedicated detention center staff of 1,950 to 2,200 troops and civilians. The military is on its own here, no backup at the gate, which leads to a minefield and Cuba. Clarke said he might need his full force "if we had an act of mass noncompliance, a riot, something like." Besides, he said, the 80 captives are spread out across four different facilities, making it especially labor intensive.

Heath says he's under no pressure to consolidate. "I don't want to jam all those people into one place at one time," he says. "It increases the potential for conflict and friction."

But in a succession of interviews prison leaders say they assume the mood on the cellblocks will change on the day after the last transfer.

The prison sent nine Yemenis to a rehabilitation program in Saudi Arabia in April, and although the commander says he hasn't been told to prepare another transfer, there is an air of expectation that more captives are going to get to go. Two members of the admiral's management team — his cultural advisor and senior medical officer — used the same expression, "light at the end of the tunnel," to explain why the mood is still good.

But the leaders also said they expect the mood to change, to sour. Maybe in November, a reporter inquires, if Donald Trump is elected and Obama hasn't emptied the prison?

"I have no idea," says the Muslim-American cultural advisor known to the detainees as Zaki. "We're just thinking, what can we do later on when we have a small population that's ... not seeing the light at the end of the tunnel. We just have to go back, communicate with the detainees, see their feedback and see what it is they want to keep busy with."

The Army captain in charge of the 35,000-item prison library told reporters he's setting up a working group to revisit rules of what can be accessioned and what cannot.

Zaki hasn't spoken to a detainee for months. He has a sensitive, culturally appropriate linguist pass on messages to the detainees of a death in the family related by the Red Cross. But he is asked, anyway, whether the detainees see this summer's Ramadan as their last here.

"Some of them believe that," he said. "Some of them are afraid. Some of them they just don't know. Just like everybody else we do not know what happens next. Every day is a new day.

EPILOGUE

As this book went to press, the White House had downsized the number of detainees to 79, 29 of them cleared for release through task force reviews, and the detention center reported its blended military-civilian staff ranged between 1,950 and 2,200. Even as the online prison newsletter, The Wire, shows names and faces of those troops, I am under threat of a lifetime ban if I do the same.

The death penalty trials still had no start dates. The September 11 case was in pretrial hearings, and the prosecutor was appealing the USS Cole trial judge's decision to exclude certain charges. Camp X-Ray was a weed-filled warren of rusted cages, and the location of Camp 7, where the former CIA captives have been locked up since 2006, was still classified.

The Miami Herald continues to cover each war court hearing, and the aftermath that saw convictions overturned in the cases of Salim Hamdan of Yemen, David Hicks of Australia and Noor Uthman Mohammed of Sudan. The last two were sent home on plea bargains.

Another Sudanese convict, Ibrahim al Qosi, never authorized U.S. military lawyers to appeal his 2010 plea bargain that leveraged his 2012 repatriation to Khartoum. In late 2015, he emerged as a religious leader on a videotape released by the Yemen-based al-Qaida of the Arabian Peninsula.

Meantime, people at the prison have begun giving a glimpse of planning for operations after President Barack Obama leaves office. Discussions include whether to widen cell doors and add ramps for wheelchairs. At this writing, most of the captives were in their 30s to mid-40s. None was using a wheelchair.

INDEX

CPSIA information can be obtained at www.ICGtesting.com
Printed in the USA
BVOW06s0018130716

455325BV00008B/35/P